Migrant, Roma and Post-Colonial Youth in Education
across Europe

Migrant, Roma and Post-Colonial Youth in Education across Europe

Being 'Visibly Different'

Edited by

Julia Szalai

Emeritus Professor and Senior Research Fellow, Central European University, Hungary

and

Claire Schiff

Associate Professor of Sociology, University of Bordeaux, France

First published 2014 by
PALGRAVE MACMILLAN

Palgrave Macmillan in the UK is an imprint of Macmillan Publishers Limited,
registered in England, company number 785998, of Houndmills, Basingstoke,
Hampshire RG21 6XS.

Palgrave Macmillan in the US is a division of St Martin's Press LLC,
175 Fifth Avenue, New York, NY 10010.

Palgrave Macmillan is the global academic imprint of the above companies
and has companies and representatives throughout the world.

Palgrave® and Macmillan® are registered trademarks in the United States,
the United Kingdom, Europe and other countries.

ISBN 978–1–137–30862–7

This book is printed on paper suitable for recycling and made from fully
managed and sustained forest sources. Logging, pulping and manufacturing
processes are expected to conform to the environmental regulations of the
country of origin.

A catalogue record for this book is available from the British Library.

A catalog record for this book is available from the Library of Congress.

Contents

List of Tables and Figures   vii

Acknowledgements   viii

Notes on Contributors   xi

List of Abbreviations   xiii

1 Introduction: Understanding the Salience of Ethnicity in the
   Educational Experiences of Minority Adolescents across Europe   1
   Claire Schiff

**Part I Ethnic Differentiation in Education across
Europe: Internal and External Mechanisms**

2 Apart or Together: Motivations Behind Ethnic Segregation in
   Education across Europe   17
   Vera Messing

3 Inclusive Education for Children of Immigrants: The Turkish
   Second Generation in Sweden, the Netherlands and Austria   34
   Philipp Schnell and Maurice Crul

4 Teachers' Approaches to Ethnic Minority Students through
   a Comparative Lens   51
   Claire Schiff

5 The Emerging 'Ethnic Ceiling': Implications of Grading on
   Adolescents' Educational Advancement in Comparative
   Perspective   67
   Julia Szalai

6 Education in the European Multicultural Debates and Policies   84
   Violetta Zentai

**Part II International and Intergroup Comparisons of
Ethnic Minority Students' Experiences of Otherness
in Schools**

7 Intricacies of Ethnicity: A Comparative Study of Minority
   Identity Formation during Adolescence   103
   Mária Neményi and Róza Vajda

8 Dampened Voices: A Comparative Look at Roma Adolescents' Discourses on Being 'Othered' at School   120
   Margit Feischmidt

9 Educational Strategies of Minority Youth and the Social Constructions of Ethnicity   135
   Bolette Moldenhawer

Part III   Ethnic Differences in Schooling in National Contexts

10 Racism, Ethnicity and Schooling in England   151
   Ian Law and Sarah Swann

11 Experiencing Ethnicity in a Colour-Blind System: Minority Students in France   167
   Claire Schiff

12 The Interplay of School and Family and Its Impact on the Educational Careers of Ethnic Minority Youth in Germany   184
   Gaby Straßburger

13 Ethnic Identification and the Desire to Belong in the Case of Urban Roma Youth in Romania   198
   Enikő Vincze

14 Structural and Personal Forms of Discrimination in Slovak Multiethnic Schools   213
   David Kostlán

15 Conclusions: Ethnic Distinctions and the Making of Citizenship in Education   228
   Julia Szalai

References   244

Index   259

Tables and Figures

Tables

3.1 Educational level of second-generation Turks and the
comparison group, by country (%)   38

3.2 Educational level of second-generation Turks and of the
comparison group whose parents hold low educational
credentials (%)   40

3.3 Transition rates towards the academic track at the first
selection moment in percentage and odds ratios   41

3.4 Years between the start of education and tracking for
second-generation Turks   43

7.1 Patterns of identity formation   105

Figures

3.1 Predicted probabilities of leaving school early for
second-generation Turks according to parental support, by
country   46

3.2 Predicted probabilities of achieving a post-secondary/tertiary
educational level for second-generation Turks according to
parental support, by country   47

Acknowledgements

This book grew out of a recently completed comprehensive cross-country research project entitled *Ethnic Differences in Education and Diverging Prospects for Urban Youth in an Enlarged Europe* (EDUMIGROM). The generous funding that the study enjoyed under the auspices of the Seventh Framework Programme of the European Union between 2008 and 2011 made it possible for our research collective to design and implement a rather ambitious investigation into the nature of the relationships and processes in education and in its social environment that, for the most part, have resulted in keeping ethnic minority youth in a disadvantaged position both within their immediate communities and within society at large.

By taking a cross-European approach, the study looked at a range of multiethnic communities in the nine participating countries, where second and third generations of 'visible' minorities represent a significant part of the local population. Approaching the complexity of relationships within such communities and enquiring about the often tense inter-ethnic encounters at schools and in the neighbourhoods was a challenging task requiring considerable scholarly experience, a great deal of sensitivity and also a high standard of coordination. Although we, the editors, were deeply involved in all phases of the research (Julia Szalai acted as principal researcher and Claire Schiff led the French team while also engaging in the comparative endeavours), it was actually the editorial work of presenting the project's findings in the form of a book that revealed to us the extreme richness of the materials that have been accumulated by the national teams and that provide many more opportunities for further analysis than a single book could comprise. We are truly grateful to all members of the nine research teams for their dedication and also for the great proficiency in collecting often hardly accessible data and analysing them in a way that remained meaningful in the local contexts while allowing for novel cross-country comparisons in a sophisticated and disciplined way.

In addition to those colleagues who contributed to this volume, our sincere thanks go to Gary Fry, Shona Hunter, Audrey Osler, Rodanthi Tzanelli and Fiona Williams (British team); Radim Marada, Michal Nekorjak, Martina Haltufová, Petr Fučik, Ela Klementová, Denisa Katzorová, Kateřina Sidiropulu Janků, Arnošt Svoboda, Laura Laubeová, Marketa Laubeová and Ondřej Daniel (Czech team); Tina Kallehave, Jens Peter Thomsen, Marta Padovan-Özdemir and Sune Jon Hansen (Danish team); Georges Felouzis, Barbara Fouquet-Chauprade, Evelyne Barthou, Joelle Perronton, Maitena Armagnague and Jessica Pouyau (French team); Sabine Mannitz, Meryem Ucan, Miera Frauke and Rainer Ohliger (German team); Csaba Dupcsik,

Emília Molnár, Ágnes Kende, Angéla Kóczé, Cecília Kovai, János Zolnay and Anna Szász (Hungarian team); Hajnalka Harbula and Nándor L. Magyari (Romanian team); Zuzana Kusá, Peter Drál' and Jurina Rusnáková (Slovak team); and Barbara Hobson, Marcus Carson, Jenny Kallstenius and Kristina Sonmark (Swedish team).

Scholarly efforts on their own would not have been enough to support the study. We are deeply indebted to Lilla Jakobsz (Center for Policy Studies, Central European University, Hungary: without her exceptionally effective work and personal attention to all members of our rather sizeable research collective, the project would not have run as smoothly as it did, and all of us would have faced a larger administrative burden.

Members of the Advisory Board of the research project – Nicoleta Bitu (Open Society Institute, Romania), Will Kymlicka (Queen's University, Canada), Yvonne Leeman (Windesheim University, the Netherlands), Ivo Mozny (Masaryk University, Czech Republic), Michael Stewart (University College London, UK) and Verena Stolcke (Universidad Autonoma de Barcelona, Spain) – were always ready to discuss important theoretical and methodological issues and to provide comments on the first drafts of the various contributions as these emerged in the subsequent phases of the project. We are grateful for their collegiality and also for the interest that they expressed in many forms while working with our research collective.

Given the high sensitivity of ethnic identity and also our commitment to observe the personal and collective rights of minorities while working with them, the ethical aspects of the study were granted a high priority. While it was not always easy to find the necessary compromises among the diverse ways of self-identification and representation, the EDUMIGROM collective was not left without a helping hand in these matters. Gábor Halmai (Eötvös Lóránd University, Hungary), Jasmina Lukic (Central European University, Hungary) and Fiona Williams (University of Leeds, UK), as members of our Ethical Review Board, were ready to enter deliberations about these matters, and we are grateful for all the precious advice that we received from them.

Marc Goffart, our scientific officer at the European Commission, helped the project in innumerable ways. He acted as a responsive partner in establishing a bridge between the rather distanced worlds of researchers and the bureaucratic structure of the European Commission. Far beyond this, he supported us with his honest personal interest and his conviction that research can have a say in improving the situation of ethnic minorities across Europe. We are indebted to him also for his contribution to translating the findings into viable policy recommendations and for disseminating our policy ideas in broad circles at the European level.

We owe many thanks to a number of colleagues who helped our editorial work in several ways. Borbála Varga (Central European University, Hungary) expended a great deal of time and energy in helping to produce the layout and in making sure that important data did not get lost in the successive phases of technical conversion. Henrik Jacobsen (Jacobs University, Germany) and Andreea-Raluca Leru (Center for Policy Studies, Central European University) did excellent work by compiling the index of keywords for the book. Sanjay Kumar (Central European University, Hungary) undertook with great dedication the difficult task of creating a consistent style and language throughout the book; for the majority of contributors, English is a second language.

Finally, we wish to express our gratitude to Andrew James, Maryam Rutter and Beth O'Leary, our coordinating editors at Palgrave Macmillan, whose devoted work helped us to get through the subsequent phases of developing the book through to publication. We are also grateful to the anonymous reviewer of our initial proposal whose insightful comments and suggestions gave support and orientation throughout the exciting and occasionally wearying process of editing this volume.

Julia Szalai and Claire Schiff

Contributors

Maurice Crul is a sociologist and current Chair for Education and Diversity at the Free University in Amsterdam, the Netherlands.

Margit Feischmidt is a cultural anthropologist and Senior Research Fellow at the Institute of Minority Studies, Centre for Social Sciences, Hungarian Academy of Sciences, Hungary.

David Kostlán is a sociologist and Research Fellow at the Institute of Sociology, Slovak Academy of Sciences, Slovakia.

Ian Law is a sociologist and Founding Director of the Centre for Ethnicity and Racism Studies, University of Leeds, UK.

Vera Messing is a sociologist and Senior Research Fellow at the Institute of Sociology, Centre for Social Sciences, Hungarian Academy of Sciences, and Research Fellow at the Center for Policy Studies, Central European University, Budapest, Hungary.

Bolette Moldenhawer is a cultural sociologist and Associate Professor in the Division of Education, University of Copenhagen, Denmark.

Mária Neményi is a sociologist and Emeritus Professor at the Institute of Sociology, Centre for Social Sciences, Hungarian Academy of Sciences, Hungary.

Claire Schiff is a sociologist and Associate Professor in the Department of Sociology, University of Bordeaux 2, France.

Philipp Schnell is a sociologist and Associate Research Fellow at the Institute of Sociology, University of Vienna, Austria.

Gaby Straßburger is a social pedagogue and Professor of Social Pedagogy at the Catholic University of Applied Social Sciences, Berlin, Germany.

Sarah Swann is a secondary school teacher who has been affiliated with the Centre for Ethnicity and Racism Studies, University of Leeds, UK.

Julia Szalai is a sociologist and Emeritus Professor at the Institute of Sociology, Centre for Social Sciences, Hungarian Academy of Sciences, and Senior Research Fellow at the Center for Policy Studies, Central European University, Budapest, Hungary.

Róza Vajda is a sociologist and Research Fellow at the Institute of Sociology, Centre for Social Sciences, Hungarian Academy of Sciences.

Enikő Vincze is a cultural anthropologist and Professor of Anthropology in the Faculty of European Studies, Babes-Bolyai University, Cluj, Romania.

Violetta Zentai is a cultural anthropologist and Director of the Center for Policy Studies, Central European University, Budapest, Hungary.

Abbreviations

EDUMIGROM	'Ethnic Differences in Education and Diverging Prospects for Urban Youth in an Enlarged Europe' research programme
EU	European Union
OECD	Organisation for Economic Co-operation and Development
NGO	Non-governmental organisation
PISA	Programme for International Student Assessment
TIES	'The Integration of the European Second Generation' research programme

1
Introduction: Understanding the Salience of Ethnicity in the Educational Experiences of Minority Adolescents across Europe

Claire Schiff

What does it mean to be an ethnic minority student in Europe today? The research programme *Ethnic Differences in Education and Diverging Prospects for Urban Youth in an Enlarged Europe* (EDUMIGROM), which brought together a consortium of researchers from nine countries from the 'old' and 'new' member states of the European Union (EU), has sought to shed light on this issue by examining the educational experiences of adolescents who belong to some of the most stigmatised groups in their respective societies: Roma in Hungary, Romania, Slovakia and the Czech Republic, and non-Western second- and third-generation post-colonial and immigrant minorities in France, England, Germany, Sweden and Denmark.[1] These categories of young people constitute 'visible' minority groups who, although they have been living in their respective societies in many cases for many generations, tend to suffer from discrimination and low social status. Most of the contributions to this book are based on the results of this research programme, which combined a variety of methods, ranging from the administration of a common survey questionnaire to over 5,000 students aged 14–17 in over 100 schools and close to 300 classes, to in-depth interviews, focus-group discussions and in-class observations with students, school personnel and representatives of families and the local communities. The study focused on schools in which 'visible' ethnic minorities of non-Western origin or Roma youth represented a significant portion of the student body, ranging from approximately one-third to over 90 per cent, depending on the location of the schools, the degree of segregation due to factors such as residential ethnic concentration, modes of allocation and selection of students (free choice, designated catchment areas) or the existence of specific schools serving certain minority groups – for instance, Muslim schools in Scandinavia or Roma-only 'special needs' schools in Central Europe. Because high concentrations of 'visible' minorities in schools tend to exist in neighbourhoods which are characterised by poverty, high unemployment and social exclusion, many of the sites in which we carried out our investigations are regarded as quasighettos, at least from the perspective of the more middle-class, dominant groups.

The research project aimed to understand the manner in which the educational experiences, inter-ethnic relations and identities of minority students develop in the social and urban contexts in which they most frequently live. The study is, on the one hand, a sociological approach of the ethnicised aspects of the daily working of the educational institution, and, on the other hand, a multidisciplinary attempt at revealing the manner in which various actors – students, teachers and staff, as well as parents – experience and understand ethnic differences in relatively low-prestige schools in a variety of national contexts. How are such differences played out in schools receiving students who have often been negatively selected according to factors such as ethnicity, low social status, poor academic performance or residence in disadvantaged urban areas? These are the questions to which this book hopes to furnish some answers.

Looking beyond the comparative study of minority students' school performance

Most of the recent literature on the schooling of minority students in Europe has developed in the wake of the international comparisons made possible by the Organisation for Economic Co-operation and Development (OECD) Programme for International Student Assessment (PISA) and other such large-scale studies (Marks 2005, Entorf and Lauk 2008, Dronkers and Fleischmann 2010, Dustman et al. 2012, OECD 2012). The concern of much of this research has been to understand the factors which influence the performance gap between first- or second-generation immigrant students and their non-immigrant peers, and to shed light on the phenomena which might explain the differences between countries in terms of minority educational attainment. The studies in question have examined the impact of various factors, such as the more or less differentiated structure of the school system and the timing of tracking into vocational and non-vocational training (Crul and Vermeulen 2003), the extent of social and ethnic segregation and the peer effects associated with concentrations of pupils with similar backgrounds (Entorf and Lauk 2008), as well as certain specific traits associated with students' country of origin, such as the language used at home or religious affiliation (Dronkers and Fleischmann 2010). While the present collection of essays takes stock of the new knowledge and debates, the EDUMIGROM programme differs in several ways from the usual approach of immigrant students' educational attainment.

First of all, we have included Roma students in the equation since they constitute the primary focus of the research carried out in the four participating countries of Central Europe. Although the issue of Roma education has recently become a major concern for the EU, there exist very few cross-country comparisons on the schooling of Roma students (Roma Education Fund 2010, UNDP 2012), and no comparative study on minority education in Europe that includes this category of young people. In the Central European countries, the reluctance of many of those who are considered to be Roma by the majority to be identified as such constitutes both an obstacle to sociological inquiries and an interesting phenomenon for the analysis of inter-ethnic relations and processes of minority identification (Csepeli and Simon 2004). While their Roma identity was occasionally presented by our young respondents as a source of pride in face-to-face interviews and group discussions, it is clear that in terms of their educational prospects this designation essentially functions as a stigma akin to that which has been experienced by Blacks in the US until recently.

Indeed, within the framework of our comparison of second- and third-generation immigrant youth in Western Europe and Roma in Central Europe, the differences between these two broadly defined groups is reminiscent of the opposition between 'voluntary immigrant minorities' and 'involuntary caste-like minorities' theorised by the anthropologist John Ogbu in his analysis of the education of immigrant and racial minorities in the US (Ogbu and Simons 1998). Similar to what scholars of the African-American condition have observed during the first part of the twentieth century (Myrdal 1944), we encountered explanations for Roma children's low performance that tended to pathologise families' educational style, while ignoring the issues of discrimination and economic deprivation. While the struggle against Roma segregation and early school drop-out has benefitted from substantial EU funding and mobilised numerous non-governmental organisations, there is still considerable ambivalence and resistance to school integration on the part of schools and non-Roma families. One might hypothesise that within the context of social, economic and political instability brought on by the demise of the Soviet Union, the prospect of Roma assimilation and social mobility may threaten the majority's sense of group position and aggravate prejudice (Blumer 1958). Among Roma students, the mixture of ethnic pride and self-hatred, the desire for assimilation and the reflex of self-marginalisation, as well as the value placed on non-academic forms of expression, such as dance and music, recall the condition of Black Americans before the Civil Rights Movement.

A second original aspect of the EDUMIGROM research is that it addresses the experiences, the differences and the relations between minority and majority origin pupils who actually attend the same schools, and who are therefore real-life peers. By selecting particular schools as the primary unit of analysis, and by focusing on those in which minority students are over-represented, we have voluntarily chosen to consider the effects of the more or less pronounced contexts of ethnic segregation and to compare minority students with the majority peers which they actually encounter in these schools and with whom they are collaborating, competing or simply cohabitating (in the case, for instance, of strong within-school segregation between classes). In most large-scale international or national studies such as PISA, the Integration of the European Second Generation study (TIES) or the French study Trajectoires et Origines, the position of minority pupils is compared with that of a control group representative of 'average' majority origin pupils in order to assess the relative disadvantage of pupils of immigrant origin. While such studies offer pertinent information about the attainments of minority students within a larger national or international context, they do not tell us much about concrete inter-ethnic relations in disadvantaged schools attended by very significant numbers of minority origin youth. Moreover, they reveal nothing about the profiles and experiences of the non-immigrant youth who are enrolled in such schools and who often represent a particular segment of the majority population. Indeed, these students are likely to be from underprivileged families who have not resorted to 'white flight', an issue that proved to be of major concern in all of the sites observed. On the contrary, immigrant students attending schools in which they are in the majority often form a much more socially and culturally heterogeneous group than the popular perceptions of 'ghetto schools' might lead one to believe. Indeed, the latest analysis of the PISA results concerning immigrant students notes that 'immigrant children with highly-educated mothers – as well as those with mothers with lower levels of education – are over-represented in disadvantaged schools' (OECD 2012, p.13).

The third original aspect of our study is that it combines an extensive survey of students in such schools with in-depth ethnographic observations, and individual interviews and discussions on inter-ethnic relations. While the survey study offers detailed information about the characteristics of the school population and permits comparative analyses among students according to a variety of factors, the qualitative study makes it possible to delve more deeply into their experiences and perceptions. It will be of no surprise to those familiar with sociological analysis to learn that, particularly concerning sensitive issues such as racism and discrimination, there exists a certain discrepancy between what people say and what they do. Indeed, as far as issues of ethnic identity, inter-ethnic conflict and experiences of discrimination are concerned, answers to the survey questionnaire tended to point to the limited salience of such problems when they were formulated explicitly and independently of other questions. By contrast, the in-class observations, individual interviews and group discussions revealed how such issues could become pertinent frameworks of interpretation in certain situations, and how intricately they were linked to other dimensions of students' identity, such as residence, social status, academic profile and youth subcultures or styles. At least as far as students of immigrant origin are concerned, the weak effect of ethnicity as a descriptive variable in terms of the more objective academic dimensions of schooling contrasts strongly with the importance of ethnicity in the more subjective areas of interpersonal and groups relations and as a source of self-identification.

This leads us to the last important contribution of the EDUMIGROM study, which pertains to the distinction between the more formal academic aspects of minority schooling, measured by performance on standardised tests, educational attainment and the degree of ethnic segregation, on the one hand, and the more informal, relational and context-dependent dimensions of school life, such as those which relate to students' perceptions of the self and the other, to their identities and relations with teachers and peers. From an international comparative perspective, much more is known about the objective position of minority students than about their subjective experiences of schooling. Although there is a rich body of ethnographic studies on minority students' school experiences and inter-ethnic relations, especially in the Anglo-Saxon literature, most of these are limited to specific national contexts and therefore tend to adopt an analytical framework which is strongly influenced by the particular society's paradigm for understanding majority–minority relations. In the UK, qualitative studies on ethnic relations and inequalities have predominantly adopted a race-relations approach which focuses on students' experiences of discrimination and on the manner in which teachers' practices reflect structural inequalities based on race and ethnicity (Stevens 2007). In France, the few existing qualitative studies which address the issues of minority schooling and inter-ethnic relations rarely do so in an exclusive and explicit manner. Rather, they tend to subsume ethnic distinctions under the larger category of 'underprivileged' urban youth (Payet 1995, van Zanten 2012). In Scandinavia, ethnographic investigations of minority education have seldom addressed the issue in terms of race relations or of socioeconomic or residential inequalities, but rather they have reflected the predominant view that immigrant pupils' educational experiences and disadvantages are largely influenced by their linguistic and cultural distance from the native majority (Beach and Lunneblad 2011). A comparative international approach such as the one adopted here makes it possible both to reflect on the effects of national contexts and dominant discourses on the manner in which majority and minority actors make sense of ethnic differences, and to reveal some of the constants of the minority experience and its social implications as they appear by crossing national borders (Osborne 2001).

Major differences and common issues among the case studies

The national case studies differ in a variety of ways which need to be taken into account in the analysis of minority students' diverging experiences. Some of these differences relate specifically to issues of ethnicity, such as the types of minority groups observed, or the historical models of inter-ethnic relations prevailing in each society. Others pertain to the more general aspects of schooling in the different countries, such as the structure of the secondary school system, which determines the way students are selected and distributed across schools, classes and streams, as well as the educational cultures and pedagogical styles which define how schools take into account students' social, cultural and family life.

In the French and English cases, the most 'visible' ethnic groups have historically been incorporated into the society as colonial subjects and subsequently through post-colonial migration. While groups such as North Africans in France and Black Caribbeans or South Asians in England have suffered from discrimination and inferiorisation inherent to the colonial ideology, they have also undergone a degree of cultural and linguistic assimilation. Among the most disadvantaged and segregated urban minority youth, a heightened awareness of racial and ethnic distinctions and inequalities is encouraged by a post-colonial complex and played out in collective or individual outbursts of revolt against institutional authority (Lapeyronnie 2005, Gillborn and Ladson-Billings 2010). Yet this oppositional attitude is also articulated with legitimate claims to membership in the national community enforced by common citizenship, widespread use of the national language and national models of minority integration which recognise the existence of a multiethnic and multiracial society, whether explicitly through the celebration of diversity, as in the UK, or implicitly through a republican ideology which minimises and transcends ethnic difference, as in France.

In Germany and Scandinavia, non-Western minorities have been incorporated more recently, mainly through labour migration and political asylum, and their distance from the majority population is more readily formulated in terms of linguistic, cultural or religious attributes, even though, in the case of the emerging third generation, such perceptions may be more in the nature of representations than reality. In these countries, notions of cultural incompatibility, value conflicts or incomplete acculturation are part of the repertoire of explanations for differences between groups. PISA data indicate that ethnic segregation between schools, ethnic inequalities in performance and educational achievement between majority youth and young people of immigrant descent are particularly pronounced in these countries (OECD 2012). Yet claims to equal treatment and collective revolts denouncing discrimination are much less frequent than in England and France, perhaps because members of the most 'visible' minorities are more inclined to resort to the resources of their own group in order to resist marginalisation and because their framework for judging their economic and social position in the host society is more readily informed by comparisons with their country of origin than is the case for post-colonial minorities.

Roma in the four Central European countries included in our study represent a third type of minority which resembles a variant of the 'urban outcast' or 'pariah groups' described by Loïc Wacquant (2008). Despite a period of more or less enforced acculturation under the state-socialist regime, Roma are still viewed by the majority group as culturally and racially distinct and suffer from a tainted or stigmatised identity that associates poverty and deviance with their particular group. Some Roma exhibit a certain degree of ethnic pride and develop ways of protecting their self-worth through a discourse stressing their authenticity, resilience and artistic talent. However, throughout the study it appeared that efforts at maintaining social distance and group boundaries were much more pronounced on the part of the non-Roma majority, especially in cases where involuntary school integration of formally excluded Roma pupils threatened to undermine the distance created by residential segregation. While Roma are often portrayed as intrinsically or culturally deviant when they are characterised collectively, in many of the observed schools, the relegation of Roma students into special classes is not formulated as recognition of diversity but rather as a way of dealing with what is labelled as mental retardation or behavioural problems by the institution.

Beyond the specific historical tradition which structures ethnic relations in society at large, one must also consider how the educational system itself influences the meaning and salience of ethnicity for students' identity. Indeed, many of the contrasts observed in the way minority students feel about their education in the different societies reflect fundamental differences in pupils' experiences of learning (Osborne 2001), rather than the type of ethnic relations or the specific policies concerning minority integration and provisions for multiculturalism.

In Denmark and Sweden, despite the high degree of segregation in several of the schools observed and the prevailing inequalities between non-Western minorities and the majority in terms of economic resources, employment and residential standing (Horst 2010), minority pupils did not express feelings of being stigmatised or discriminated against by teachers or society at large, and seemed relatively confident in their educational prospects. Social distance and physical separation between minority students and their majority origin peers do not translate here into a sense of being disadvantaged, but rather create a context in which the school becomes a protective microcosm where the belief in equal opportunity and the promises of the welfare state are embraced by most students. Minority students' ethnic and cultural identities are not in conflict with their identity as Danish or Swedish citizens. Rather, they seem to exist on an entirely different and complementary plane. Since the main obstacle to becoming full members of the society is conceptualised in terms of their lack of fluency in the host country language – a 'problem' which teachers and bilingual assistants are there to address – the classroom is not viewed as a place of cultural conflict. Because the Scandinavian school system favours collaboration, consensus and community cohesion, and is undifferentiated until the end of ninth grade, minority students, like their majority peers, develop a sense of integration and belonging to their school and continue to believe that their options remain open, despite the reality of ethnic segregation and the evidence pointing to their limited long-term prospects (Schindler 2007, Jonsson and Rudolphi 2011).

In Germany, in contrast, the selection of students into separate and unequal tracks at an early age coexists with the fact that the most ethnically segregated schools are also low-status vocational *Hauptschule*. This creates a situation in which ethnic and cultural differences potentially function for teachers as a synonym for lack of educational conformity, while for students they become a resource for resistance against the negative evaluation of their worth as students. The classroom can thus easily appear as an arena of cultural conflict and competition between teachers and minority students. Due perhaps to the limited chances for spontaneous acculturation to take place in a system which offers few possibilities for pre-school attendance and limited hours of presence in school, teachers see it as part of their task to acculturate students of immigrant origin. Minority students, especially those of Turkish origin in vocational schools, feel in turn the need to defend their family and community against the judgements of the dominant group, by, for instance, insisting on the moral superiority of Muslim values as compared with what they portray as the hedonistic lifestyle and weak family cohesion of native German youth.

In the secondary schools observed in Britain, ethnicity was also particularly salient as a component of youthful relations between groups of students defined not so much in terms of their families' educational style or their religion, but rather through differing urban subcultures and neighbourhood affiliations. In contrast with the French, German and Scandinavian cases, where we observed a degree of inter-ethnic solidarity and instances of common identification among students of different non-European origins (Africans and Arabs in France or Turks and Lebanese in Germany), tensions and conflicts more often opposed British Afro-Caribbean and Asian students than majority and minority students. While this could be interpreted as the downside of the differentialism encouraged by the British multicultural or multiracial model of ethnic relations, it may also reflect a more engrained tradition of strong differentiation of pupils into socially defined subgroups, both outside and inside schools (Osborne 2001). Indeed the competition between the persona of the oppositional Afro-Caribbean youths and the more academically conformist Asian students resembles a contemporary ethnicised version of the conflicts between the working-class 'lads' and the middle-class 'earoles' described by Paul Willis in *Learning to Labour* (Willis 1977). Due to a pedagogy which aims to consider the various social, cultural and emotional dimensions of students' existence, and given the importance of social as well as ethnoracial distinctions in British society at large, schools appear very permeable to tensions and conflicts which are imported from the local milieu. While ethnic segregation and inequalities of educational performance and attainment between majority and minority pupils are less pronounced in England than in the other countries observed (OECD 2012), British multiethnic secondary schools are an arena in which the salience of ethnicity in defining peer-group relations and self-identification is much more explicit.

In contrast with England, where young people's identity as students seems to be relatively secondary to their sociocultural and peer-group identities, in France, the various dimensions of young people's self-image are strongly influenced by their identity as pupils and by their position within the hierarchy of schools, streams and classes. French minority students presented themselves as such in interviews and discussions only to the extent that they clearly occupied an inferior position in the academic hierarchy, when, for instance, they were relegated into dead-end vocational streams. Although some spontaneous groupings of students with similar immigrant origins were occasionally observed, inter-ethnic friendships appeared more frequent than in the other countries and were often encouraged by a sense of solidarity with those who were in the same class-group.

In the Central European countries, ethnic relations in schools between Roma and non-Roma are characterised simultaneously by ancient and engrained racial stereotypes and mutual suspicions, and by a context of considerable political transformations and upheaval in the organisation of the national educational systems over recent years, notably with the introduction of a free school market and increased pressures for Roma integration from the EU. While this has created the opportunity for a variety of innovative schools to develop experiments in Roma integration, it has also heightened the general level of hostility towards Roma and fuelled strategies of 'white flight', thus aggravating teachers' sense of powerlessness in a context in which integration reforms have often been poorly planned and unequally implemented at the local level.

The issue of ethnic segregation, which was of central concern in all of the sites investigated, reveals an interesting paradox when one looks more generally at the variety of cases examined in this book and at the link between the objective and subjective dimensions of minority education. The salience of ethnic identification and the degree of inter-ethnic tensions seems in many cases to be aggravated by the actual proximity between minority and majority pupils. In other words, the more segregated schools, which appear as quasighettos, offer a degree of protection against stigmatisation, a relative feeling of comfort to pupils who are shielded from the negative self-awareness which direct contact and unfavourable comparisons with their more privileged majority peers might imply. The schools receiving the highest proportion of minority students were not the conflict-ridden places of anomie and youthful resentment which popular opinion often assumes them to be, even though they undoubtedly tended to have a negative impact on students' educational performance, a fact of which students are not necessarily aware or overly concerned. In Allport's intergroup contact theory, four conditions must be present in order for relations to be pacified and prejudice to diminish: equal group status within the situation, common goals, intergroup cooperation and authority support (Allport 1954). Given the competitive nature of the educational process and the fact that majority and minority students seldom enter school with the same resources, these conditions are rarely united in the situations in which minority students constitute a significant proportion of the student body. It is not surprising therefore that it is often in the relatively more integrated contexts, such as those found in England, in France or in some of the recently reformed Central European schools receiving a new population of Roma students, that ethnic tensions and peer-group conflicts appear to be most pronounced.

Structure and organisation of the book

The significance of ethnic difference in schools is produced by a complex interplay between, on the one hand, the manner in which the educational system distributes students of diverse origins throughout the educational process and attributes meaning to students' ethnoracial and cultural traits, and, on the other hand, the ways in which students react to such processes by investing or contesting ethnic categories at large, using the resources which they find within their families, their communities or their peer groups. This book is structured in such a way as to address these two dimensions of the problem, first from an international comparative perspective and second from within the particular national framework of ethnic relations in several of the countries participating in the EDUMIGROM research.

Part I, 'Ethnic differentiation in education across Europe: internal and external mechanisms', is made up of five contributions that each address a different aspect of the structural determinants of ethnic differentiation in education, using a cross-national perspective which points to some of the most significant differences between the societies observed. Vera Messing (Chapter 2) addresses the complexity of ethnic segregation in schooling by describing the various forms of minority student concentrations, ranging from the voluntary schooling of Muslim students in faith-based schools in Denmark, to the enforced relegation of Roma students into 'special' schools or classes in the Central European countries. In terms of the impact that these different forms of segregation have on students' relations and their educational experiences, she shows that the most detrimental configuration is that which combines in-school ethnic segregation between classes with a diversity-blind school policy which justifies such differential treatment by 'blaming the victim', using the labels of social deviance and mental deficiency. Philipp Schnell and Maurice Crul (Chapter 3) draw on some of the data from their TIES study on Turkish and Moroccan students' educational trajectories in various European countries, focusing here on the educational outcomes of Turkish origin students in Sweden, the Netherlands and Austria. Using the framework developed by their integration context theory, they underscore the importance of various structural elements, such as the availability of early schooling, the timing of selection into differing educational tracks, and the greater or lesser dependence of schools on parental educational support, in order to show that minority attainment is largely influenced by the more general aspects of the educational system. The next two chapters analyse the role of teachers and the manner in which they act as mediators between the national frameworks of understanding of minority–majority relations and the expectations placed on minority students in terms of their conformity or non-conformity to dominant norms of behaviour and success. Claire Schiff (Chapter 4) poses the question of who teaches in minority-dominated schools, and what this experience entails in terms of teachers' professional identities. Moreover, she compares the terminology and explanations which teachers resort to when making sense of the educational performance and needs of their pupils, which reflect how the 'problems' of minority integration are formulated in each of the national contexts. Julia Szalai (Chapter 5) considers the role of grading as a mechanism for objectifying certain inequalities created by segregation and differential treatment of minority students, and demonstrates how the emergence of an 'ethnic ceiling' of educational performance can serve in a range of cases to lower minority students' aspirations by navigating them away from the mainstream. Finally in Part I (Chapter 6), Violetta Zentai summarises the findings from the substantial literature on multicultural policies in Europe and considers the extent to which general policy regimes aiming at minority inclusion in a variety of domains, such as citizenship and labour market integration, have a direct impact on minority students' educational performance and achievement.

As a complementary counterpoint to the top-down perspective adopted in the first part, Part II, 'International and inter-group comparisons of ethnic minority students' experiences of "otherness" in schools', takes a decidedly bottom-up approach by looking at how students themselves relate to ethnicity. Mária Neményi and Róza Vajda's contribution (Chapter 7) can be viewed as a complement to Messing's chapter on segregation, in the sense that it analyses how the different voluntary or involuntary regimes of segregation, as well as their implications in terms of the association between ethnicity and poverty, combine with students' educational experience to produce processes of identification which range from the assertion of a distinct 'ghetto' consciousness to striving for assimilation and a form of cosmopolitanism which transcends ethnic distinctions. Margit Feischmidt (Chapter 8) focuses on relations between pupils and teachers as well as between pupils of different origins and the manner in which ethnicity is minimised or exploited, notably during conflicts and situations of bullying or bantering between students. She shows how limited the options are for Roma students to use their ethnic identity as a resource in inter-group relations or as a strategy for educational success. Indeed, they differ from the immigrant youth in Western Europe, who resort to a variety of strategies of distinction in peer-group relations, and for whom ethnicity can occasionally be mobilised to increase their educational achievement and their prospects for social mobility. Bolette Moldenhawer (Chapter 9) explores further some of the distinctions of the previous chapter by focusing on minority students' views of their educational options and the role they attribute to schooling in their lives. She distinguishes three types of educational strategies of 'mobilisation', 'instrumentation' and 'opposition' to schooling, which are unevenly distributed across the different countries and the different ethnic groups observed.

Following the transnational comparisons of structure and agency in the construction of ethnic differences in schooling, the five chapters in Part III, 'Ethnic differences in schooling in national contexts', explore this issue within different national frameworks. They focus moreover on specific intranational differences, made possible by the selection of different schools in each country, and consider the impact of particular local contexts on ethnic relations, a perspective which remained secondary in the previous chapters on international and intergroup differences between Roma and immigrant or post-colonial youths. The contributions on England, France, Germany, Romania and Slovakia all consider the articulation between structural constraints and young people's agency in order to identify issues of particular importance in each of the domestic contexts. Ian Law and Sarah Swann (Chapter 10) discuss the British anti-racist and multicultural policy agenda and the importance of peer-group tensions linked to more or less racialised urban youth subcultures in England. Claire Schiff (Chapter 11) analyses the combined impact of the colour-blind republican ideology and of local configurations of ethnic relations due to contrasting levels of ethnic segregation in different types of urban contexts in France. Gaby Straßburger (Chapter 12) examines how young people of migrant origin, their parents and their teachers envision the influence of the family on schooling in a German system which attributes a decisive role to families' background and resources in defining students' educational careers. Enikő Vincze (Chapter 13) investigates the ambivalences and ambiguities of Roma identity in various locations of Transylvania. She shows how these are influenced both by the complex microlevel differentiations between diverse Roma subgroups and various urban localities, and by the macrolevel reality of increasing racialisation of Roma citizenship since the end of the socialist regime. David Kostlán (Chapter 14) looks at the ways in which educational segregation of Roma students, a particularly entrenched phenomenon in Slovakia, is rationalised in teachers' discourses and the manner in which these impact Roma students' experiences of interpersonal and groups relations. To conclude, Julia Szalai (Chapter 15) reflects upon the implications of the various educational inequalities and the diverging experiences of minority students revealed throughout the book in terms of citizenship rights. She demonstrates how basic rights such as equal access to quality education and freedom of choice are unequally implemented depending on the strength of the welfare state regimes and the stability of countries' democratic traditions.

Note

1. Detailed information and reports are available on the programme's site at www.edumigrom.eu.

Part I

Ethnic Differentiation in Education across Europe: Internal and External Mechanisms

2

Apart or Together: Motivations Behind Ethnic Segregation in Education across Europe

Vera Messing

The context

There is a longstanding academic and policy debate about the possible causes underlying the performance gap between ethnic majority and minority students across Europe. The fact that ethnic minority students underperform compared with their peers from the majority has been widely demonstrated by a range of national as well as cross-country comparative studies (OECD 2006, Crul and Schneider 2008, Holsinger 2009, Dronkers 2010, Park and Sandefour 2010). A number of factors underlying this gap have been identified, of which the most important are the generally lower socioeconomic status of ethnic minority populations and the linguistic disadvantages of children from such backgrounds. However, by analysing the intersecting effects of these two factors, some important country-specific differences were revealed: when groups with similar status and identical language backgrounds were compared, the gap disappeared in several countries (France, Norway and Sweden), diminished significantly in others (for example, in Germany), but stayed significant in others (Belgium, Luxembourg and Switzerland) (Park and Sandefour 2010). These results suggest that behind the performance gap there must be other factors related to the organisation and practices of education. Besides individual characteristics such as the sequence of generations since immigration, the country of origin (Dronkers 2010), systemic factors such as comprehensiveness, selectivity and inclusiveness of the school systems (Alegre and Arnett 2007, OECD 2007a), further the level of ethnosocial segregation seem to contribute to the disadvantages of ethnic minorities in education. This chapter will discuss the role of the last factor mentioned: ethnosocial segregation.

Irrespective of the method applied and the definition of the category 'ethnic minority',[1] researchers agree on the prevalence of ethnosocial segregation in European societies. Regardless of the diversity of educational policies and the organisational setup of the national educational systems, it has been demonstrated that a significant proportion of children from ethnic minority backgrounds (especially if also of low social status) tend to be educated in segregated conditions: 'Findings indicate that, in several countries, many immigrant students attend schools with high proportions of first-generation or second-generation students' (OECD 2006). Countries with highly stratified educational systems tend to have particularly high levels of ethnic segregation at a very early age (Belgium, Switzerland and the Netherlands), while countries operating more comprehensive school systems show lower levels of ethnic segregation, because tracking (special-isation) and with it ethnosocial separation reaches students at a later age (France, the UK and the Scandinavian countries) (Alegre and Ferrer-Esteban 2010). However, the actual reasons behind segregating 'children of colour' from their 'white' peers as well as the consequences of this phenomenon vary greatly. Both the causes and the outcomes depend to a large extent on the given country's educational policy, the structure and administering of compulsory education, the traditions of inter-ethnic cohabitation in com-munities and the policies to which the local managements and the schools themselves subscribe.

The EDUMIGROM research extended the focus by including in its anal-ysis both Western and Central European countries and the experiences of the students from minority backgrounds, their families and their teach-ers to understand the complexity of reasons behind the lower educational attainment of the groups in question. By applying a multimethod approach, the research identified processes that were at play in ethnically segregated school environments and revealed forms of segregation that had been left unnoticed by earlier larger-scale surveys.

In order to make my points clear, first, the concept of ethnic segregation has to be clarified. I use this term to indicate the constellation of students with ethnic minority backgrounds being significantly over-represented in certain schools and/or classes within the educational institution, while eth-nosocial segregation refers to the situation when the school's composition is characterised by an intersection of students' ethnic minority belonging and low social status. There are no *de jure* segregated schools in European countries; ethnic segregation is always a *de facto* phenomenon and arises as a consequence of macro- and microlevel social processes discussed in the following section.

Mechanisms of institutional selection and ethnosocial segregation

Early selection

Early selection of children into different school types strongly correlates with ethnosocial segregation. The data of the PISA surveys run by the

OECD demonstrate that 31 per cent of the variation in the extent of ethnic segregation may be explained by the age when the first selection into differentiated tracks takes place in a given school system (Alegre and Ferrer-Esteban 2010). There are essential differences across European countries in this respect. In some countries, tracking takes place as early as the age of 10–11 (Germany), while in others (the Scandinavian countries), children are kept together until the end of comprehensive compulsory education (for example, in Denmark until the age of 16). Indeed, as Maurice Crul and Philipp Schnell argue by analysing the educational careers of second-generation Turkish youths living in different European countries, 'the percentage of second-generation Turks who make it into an academic track increases with the rise in the number of years of common education prior to selection' (Schnell and Crul, Chapter 3 in this volume). Further evidence from research by Diefenbach (2005) in Germany supports the statement: Germany is a country where both comprehensive and non-comprehensive schools for secondary education operate in parallel in the different federal states (*Länder*). By comparing comprehensive and non-comprehensive schools, she found that significantly more migrant students reached both the medium and higher qualifications in the comprehensive schools than in the non-comprehensive ones.

The primary school systems of the post-socialist countries that provide general public education for eight (in some cases nine) years seem to be comprehensive at first glance, but at a closer look it becomes evident that they are also stratified since many countries operate several parallel arrangements. Although, for the most part, primary education lasts for eight to nine years, in fact in many schools there is a selection at the age of 10 or 12 to eight- and six-year grammar school classes, respectively, that run in parallel with the ordinary primary school groups. This means that at these early ages the best students are creamed off, most of whom come from the upper strata of society. The rest of the students stay in the primary school until eighth (or ninth) grade and then continue into less prestigious four-year academic or vocational tracks. Early tracking is practised despite the accumulated evidence in child psychology that 10–12-year-old children – especially boys – are not mature enough to make decisions that have important implications for their long-term educational opportunities and occupational chances (Brunello and Checchi 2007, Salami 2008). Consequently, such forced early decisions about further education usually reflect parents' ambitions rather than students' actual aspirations, potential and talent.

The rigidity of the secondary school system is also a factor that influences the opportunities of underprivileged students, especially from ethnic minority backgrounds. Obviously, when early tracking is coupled with an inflexible separation of the tracks and a lack of options for transition among various school types, students with any kind of difficulty, very early on, are trapped in the lower segments of the educational system. In Germany, for example, early selection together with limited options for mobility between school types[2] leads to highly unequal chances for working-class and minority students to obtain qualifications that are valued on the labour market. In contrast with this, in the Scandinavian countries, comprehensive school systems keep students together during their compulsory school age, and streaming within the same school allows students to flexibly find the ways best suited to their capacities and preferences.

Unsubstantiated tracking into special schools

A further systemic cause leading to prevalent socioethnic segregation is that ethnic minority children are disproportionately directed into remedial schools designed for children with special educational needs. This phenomenon, though to varying degrees, exists in all European countries. In all of the Central European countries, the ethnic composition in these special/remedial schools is characterised by an over-representation of Roma children (ERRC 2004). Although, officially, students entering into special schools go through a process of thorough testing by professionals, in the final outcome there are a number of instances when ordinary students or those with slight learning difficulties who are able to study in a regular school end up in special educational units. The practice of labelling ethnic minority/Roma children as mentally disadvantaged and placing them in special schools is extremely widespread in the Czech Republic and Slovakia (in the latter, 60 per cent of Roma children study in such institutions according to a report by Amnesty International) (2010). The same phenomenon exists in Romania and Hungary to a somewhat smaller, though still significant, extent. Similar trends are at work in the western part of Europe, though to a lesser extent (Artiles 2003, Heckmann and NESSE 2008). The latter report that recently has been submitted to the European Commission emphasises this fact: 'There is an overrepresentation of migrant children in schools for children with special needs'. In addition to the stigmatising effect on ethnic minority students, the problem with such practices is that the transition from special schools into regular schools hardly ever occurs. This is all the more painful since, due to lower expectations and a reduced curriculum, these schools most typically serve as a dead-end to the educational career of their students. The paradox is that all of the involved parties are interested, to a considerable extent, in maintaining this harsh form of segregation: locally elected officials can satisfy the claims for ethnic distancing from their local middle-class electorate; teachers of regular schools are happy that they do not have to bother with 'overdemanding' children; often even minority parents may accept without reservation the board's decision about their children being directed into special schools because they consider them to be 'safe' places where their children enjoy a relaxed environment, small class sizes, and increased attention and tolerance on the part of both their teachers and their peers.

School type

Educational segregation at the institutional level is often also enhanced by selection among diverse school types with regard to ownership and maintenance. Evidence shows that pupils with different socioeconomic and ethnic backgrounds, and gender, tend to enrol into different types of school. There is a divide in the Czech Republic, Denmark, France, Germany, Hungary, Slovakia and the UK between public schools financed through taxes and government grants (therefore being free of charge for the families) and private schools funded, at least partly, by fees or donations, paid by the parents. The limited presence of minority students in private schools suggests that tuition fees may constitute serious obstacles for many ethnic minority families.

Another phenomenon that deserves attention is the role of faith schools. These most typically enhance ethnosocial segregation but in very different ways across Europe. In Germany, Denmark and the UK, faith schools are institutions permitting voluntary separation of religious ethnic minority communities. As they are set up and run by the community, children of families belonging to certain ethnoreligious groups attend such institutions. Examples are Muslim schools in Denmark, Turkish schools in Germany and schools serving the Pakistani communities in the UK. However, schools run by religious communities may also boost ethnic segregation the other way round: Catholic or Protestant schools in Central Europe represent a way for white middle-class families, even those without a strong religious identity, to flee from deteriorating public schools with an increasing presence of low-status Roma children. Further, certain faith schools may also enhance segregation yet in another way: they may serve as a last resort for the children of the most marginalised families who, for a variety of reasons, were excluded from all public schools. Most recent statistical evidence suggests that the rapid expansion of faith schools since 2010 in the Hungarian educational sector has considerably increased ethnosocial segregation (Sárközi 2012).

Free choice of schools and students

A further important aspect influencing ethnosocial segregation on a systemic level is the working of catchment areas and the right of parents to opt out of them. The way in which catchment areas are defined and applied may reduce or, contrarily, enhance the impact of residential segregation on the ethnosocial composition of the schools' student body (Szalai et al. 2010).

In most of the European countries, geographically determined school districts are in place but parents have a right to express a preference for a school located outside the district. In some countries – for example, France and Germany – catchment areas are applied in a strict manner, meaning that a child's residential address designates the public school for attendance. However, evidence indicates for both countries that upper- and middle-class families find ways to circumvent the existing restrictions of the districting systems by either registering at a secondary address outside their current district of residence or choosing an educational option (for instance, a particular language course or some other specialisation) which is not offered by the local school. Furthermore, a family can choose the private or faith school sectors that are not subjected to the constraints of catchment area regulations.

Despite the prevailing regulations on attendance by geographical districts, in the majority of the European educational systems, parents still have the right to choose freely within the public school sector, though authorities may intervene to a certain extent to prevent over- or underutilisation of the school infrastructure under their control. Research has demonstrated that parents' free choice among schools contributes to enhancing ethnosocial segregation. At the same time, even in countries where no arrangement of free choice exists, it is the highly educated, middle-class parents whose children benefit most from the system and end up in the best schools (Ball 2003, Raveaud and van Zanten 2007). Factors such as the parents' educational level, their social status and their command of the majority language influence not only their inclination to live up to their right but also the degree to which they are informed of their formal right to choose between schools.

Parents' free choice of school promotes 'white flight', a spontaneous process that significantly increases ethnosocial segregation. In Europe, 'ethnic majority, middle class flight' would be a better term – a concept taken from US vocabulary – because it is typically a middle-class phenomenon that manifests itself with greater intensity among the lower segments of the middle class. The phenomenon may be revealed in almost all European countries, though to varying degrees depending on the countries' historical arrangements for inter-ethnic cohabitation. For instance, the recently introduced right of free school choice has resulted in an increased socioeconomic and ethnic segregation of schools at both primary and secondary educational levels in Sweden (Government of Sweden 2000, Söderström and Uusitalo 2010). The situation in the Central European countries is similar. Roma parents rarely choose a school outside the socially disadvantaged and marginalised district in which they live, even when they have the formal right to do so. In fact, most of them are not even aware of having such a right, while the majority – middle- and lower-middle-class parents – extensively exploit their right and invest considerable time and effort into fleeing from their initially designated school district.

An even more important factor in terms of socioethnic segregation than parents' right to opt out is the schools' entitlement to select among applicants. That is to say that not only may parents be in a position to choose among schools, but also schools may be free to decide whom they accept among the applicant children. The analysis of the PISA data on this issue demonstrated that cross-country differences in the level of ethnosocial segregation are significantly associated with the possibility of schools selecting between children (Algere and Ferrer-Esteban 2010).

Internal segregation

Internal separation is another prevalent practice in the regular schools of the Central European countries that exacerbates the separation of children of colour within formally comprehensive and untracked primary schools. Many of the schools in these countries try to fight against the spontaneous processes of 'white flight' by separating disadvantaged ethnic minority and middle-class majority students into parallel classes. By doing so, schools want to assure middle-class majority parents that their child will not share classes with low-status minority children. Depending on the proportion of ethnic minority and socially disadvantaged students, techniques range from picking out well-performing, middle-class students and placing them into classes offering specialisation in prestigious subjects, to organising socially deprived, mostly Roma, children into one separated class. Thus the struggle against spontaneous processes of ethnosocial segregation results in further segregation within the confines of the school. School systems in which students are kept together for a relatively long time might actually be highly unequal due to complex and often implicit forms of internal differentiation, such as segregation within the school. In some countries, schools start streaming students as early as the first grade (at the age of six to seven years) according to the parents' choice of subject specialisation, which results in high-status students ending up in maths or foreign language specialisation classes, and lower-status or Roma children in classes specialised for physical training or that are run without any specialisation or that serve as preparatory classes. In Slovakia, for instance, all students who are declared to be insufficiently mature to enter school by the age of seven are tracked into 'zero' (preparatory) classes. Evidence shows that they are kept together in the same class throughout their primary school career and also that it is overwhelmingly Roma children who are enrolled in these classes. Regular primary schools frequently apply internal streaming also at the end of the lower stage (after fourth grade at the age of ten) by grouping students based on their performance but often without providing additional services for the low or high performers.

The above description introduces some of the most important – implicit or explicit, purposeful or unintentional – mechanisms which may result in high levels of ethnosocial segregation. But it still remains to be shown how ethnosocial segregation leads to lower performance or diverging opportunities and, further, what processes and mechanisms are at play in producing such outcomes.

Some impacts of segregation and/or ethnic mixing on students

In terms of the ethnic composition of the schools' student body, three trends in the organisation of education for ethnic minority students may be distinguished in European schools where minority students are the numerical majority. The first category is that of segregated institutions in which the proportion of ethnic minority students is overwhelming; the second group consists of schools which mix ethnic minority and majority students; while the third category includes schools which at first glance may seem to be ethnically heterogeneous but in which internal separation of the students is revealed upon closer inspection. These three constellations, together with the schools' approach to ethnic diversity and multicultural pedagogy, seem to be decisive in terms of students' performance, their attitudes towards education, their future chances and perspectives, and their identity development and peer relations (Szalai 2010, Szalai et al. 2010).

Segregated schools

An important form of ethnic segregation at the institutional level is the separation of ethnic minority children into distinctive school types. The case of the Czech Republic provides a good illustration of this point. It turned out during the fieldwork of the EDUMIGROM research there that Roma students are hardly ever found in regular schools. Instead the majority of them attend basic practical schools, a school type that was set up following the urge of the European Union and international organisations to stop segregating Roma children into special schools for those with learning difficulties. Despite the reorganisation of the system, basic practical schools mostly 'took over' the function of the former special schools: they follow a restricted curriculum and many are ill-famed 'Roma schools' (Marada et al. 2010). It follows that students studying in these institutions are deprived of the opportunity to obtain meaningful education that would qualify them to continue onto secondary level. Despite the imbalance in ethnic composition, teachers sharply reject the hypothesis that this type of school would serve as an institution of ethnic segregation. In a focus group discussion, they unanimously stated: 'We are still accused by journalists...that we try to get rid of Roma children and we put them into practical schools. It is nonsense! We cannot push anybody anywhere.' Still, the outcome is a striking ethnic imbalance in this school type. The research identified an important mismatch of the presumed preferences of the involved actors. While Czech parents and teachers assumed that Roma parents preferred to have their children enrolled into segregated institutions with lower expectations and restricted curriculum, Roma students attending segregated schools were clear about their preference for mixed schools – they were aware of the fact that 'majority' schools were better not only in terms of instruction and future chances in education but also concerning other services, such as food and extracurricular activities. In sharp contrast with teachers' and ethnic majority parents' narrative, Roma parents recognised the drawbacks of the segregated environment and justified their preference for a mixed school, primarily due to its role in socialisation: 'Because children would better know how to behave among non-Roma... my children are only among Cigans, it is not good. I would prefer them to grow up among whites... Roma kids need positive examples.' Also, in sharp contrast with the teachers' accounts, Roma parents gave testimonies of direct discrimination during the process of enrolment: 'When I went to basic school registering to that school, there was the headmaster and he was known for not taking Gypsies and he told me right away: "No, do not try to register here. We are full"' (Focus group discussion with Roma parents in the Czech Republic).

A Slovak teacher assistant of Roma origin explained the complex mechanism that leads to the over-representation of Roma children in special schools:

> I think that these overcrowded special schools reveal a lot... the majority of Roma children are not mentally retarded... there was no willingness to find a different solution... to put them into a special school is the easiest way and it artificially produces mentally retarded children. But parents also do not understand it, because everyone presents to them how beneficial it is for their children, how happy they are in that school where not so much is demanded from them.

Less overt mechanisms of discrimination and exclusion work in most of the investigated countries. In all the investigated school systems, ethnic minority students tend to be disproportionately directed into educational units for special needs children because of being misdiagnosed or because the culturally biased tests, which they have to go through prior to enrolment, interpret social or language disadvantages as learning difficulties. The implications for students are obvious: children might feel good about the more tolerant and less demanding nature of such schools but they also feel stigmatised and thereby incorporate the notions of 'otherness' and 'inferiority' into their identities. As for their perspectives for further education and adult life, all parties are aware that students graduating from these units have essentially no chance of further education, nor do they have the opportunity to obtain a qualification which is valued in the labour market.

An essentially different case of ethnic separation on the institutional level is that of ethnic minority or faith community schools. Muslim faith/community schools in Denmark and Germany, and the Gandhi Secondary School, a community-established Roma grammar school in Hungary, are examples of educational units in which ethnic separation is a result of the voluntary choice of the minority community. Some other schools (mainly public institutions) which in the process of ethnic segregation became – in the figurative sense – 'owned' by the minority community may be classified into this category as well. One example is that of Sweden where, due to the liberalisation of the school catchment areas and to enrolment policies enhancing 'white flight', schools in some of the urban areas populated by migrants have become overwhelmingly attended by youths from migrant backgrounds. These schools differ from the segregated schools in the Central European region in several important aspects: teachers are aware of the special needs of their students and make conscious efforts to adapt the ways of instruction to such conditions (by providing language support, upgrading the knowledge of students to the majority culture and applying practices for enhancing self-confidence), but they do this without stigmatising their students. The staff are also multicultural and a significant number of ethnic minority teachers work with minority students.

The EDUMIGROM research found that if ethnic minority teachers are part of the schools' staff, their presence might be an important factor for minority students: teachers who belong to a minority and therefore can relate to similar experiences are more likely to understand and treat such students empathically. Schools with multiethnic staff also more frequently use a genuinely multicultural curriculum, organise various extracurricular activities in culturally sensitive ways and stress the importance of maintaining good relations with ethnic minority families than the ones with a personnel exclusively from the majority background. Although students are aware of their 'otherness', they experience less stigmatisation in such multiethnic settings (at least in the school environment) and their negative experiences outside the school are countervailed by a strong notion of rights for protection. Further, parents are usually more involved in the activities of the school and are regarded as partners, or at least they do not feel ashamed of not being fluent in the language and the internal culture of the institution.

Although students in ethnically separated but voluntarily organised schools do not necessarily perform better in comparison with their peers from the majority, they develop high expectations towards further education and future life. Still, attending a school exclusively with peers of their own socioethnic community, students are unsure about where to continue studying and have concerns about whether they would be able to adapt to and perform well in mixed secondary schools. Because of the lack of opportunity to socialise with majority peers, students are especially concerned about being able to adjust to their new circumstances after graduation. As put by a teacher in Sweden, 'These young people fear meeting Swedish society and the Swedes.'

Mixed schools

Many of the schools both in the West and in Central Europe have a student population which represents a genuine ethnic mix. There are, however, great differences in terms of the proportions of ethnic minority students as well as regarding teachers' attitudes and the schools' ethos towards their ethnically diverse student populations.

In the Central European countries, the level of tolerance towards ethnic diversity in schools is much lower than in the western part of Europe. Depending on the geographical parts of the country and on the traditions of cohabitation, a ratio of 20–40 per cent of Roma children in the student body sets the threshold which triggers 'white flight'. The respective proportion of ethnic minority children is usually much greater in Western Europe. The EDUMIGROM research provided a telling example when it compared the consequences of merging two schools in two countries. In the Czech example, the merger of the two schools – one with a middle-class majority and the other with a dominantly Roma student population – resulted in a massive flight of 140 non-Roma students despite the fact that the merge was solely administrative, as students of the two pre-merger schools were still kept separately in distinct classes situated in separate buildings. In the Danish case, the change in the proportion of minority students from 10 to 40 per cent gave reason only to an insignificant number of families from the majority to decide to leave the school.

The other factor producing significant differences in terms of the consequences for youth is the approach of teachers and the school community towards ethnic diversity. A *colour-blind approach to ethnic diversity* is most prevalent in France where the principle of non-differentiation among citizens on the basis of their origin is at the heart of the French republican model of integration. Schools not only avoid making a distinction between native French and migrant background students but also neither speak about ethnicity at all nor consider the need to introduce differential services to minority students (Schiff et al. 2008). In the French setting, differences of performance among various ethnic groups are attributed exclusively to the disparities in families' social backgrounds. Similar views are expressed by many schools also sharing the colour-blind approach in other countries.

Some of the ethnically mixed schools in Central Europe typically have a similar approach towards ethnic diversity. But in contrast with France, diversity-blindness in this region is not rooted in state-level ideology but is more incidental and sporadic: its occurrence is a function of the individual school principal's attitude and conviction. Furthermore, the organisation of teaching in a diversity-blind manner is not based on the idea of equality but on the conviction that the recognition of ethnic differences would lead to their reinforcement. A Slovak headmaster stated: 'I do not distinguish Roma and non-Roma...I imprint them with one theory and one principle that there are only two kinds of people – good people and bad people.' Hence, ethnically mixed classes are the norm in diversity-blind schools of Central Europe and all students are expected to adapt to the same values and standards, to accept the same rules and get the same services. In principle, no ethnic group is discriminated against either in a positive or in a negative way. A science teacher in Hungary expressed clearly the idea behind the principle of non-differentiation: 'The emerging problems, such as disorganised or unprepared students, are independent from ethnicity and one can rather blame his/her personality.' In France, students were not willing to speak about their ethnic background and identity. In the same manner, Roma students in diversity-blind schools preferred to use other categories for talking about their families and self-identity. Still, ethnicity does not vanish from their everyday life. Even in such colour-blind schools, students tend to group together with those of the same ethnicity; they do notice ethnic differences and play them out; they are aware of the negative consequences of their ethnic belonging and share experiences of discrimination and prejudice outside the school, as this testimony from a participant observation session in a French school reveals: 'Racial insults, jokes about others' ethnic origins are an integral part of the oppositional and conflict-driven class dynamic.'

Another important difference between diversity-blind mixed schools in France and Central Europe is the employment of ethnic minority teachers. While irrespective of their ethnic composition French schools employ a large number of teachers from migrant backgrounds, there are virtually no Roma teachers in Central European schools. The frequently mentioned excuse about the lack of well-educated Roma is unjustified because even university-educated Roma pedagogues do not get jobs in public schools. The only position they can reach is that of a Roma teacher assistant – a project-based, fixed-term placement. Roma teacher assistants work under the guidance of the teachers and deal exclusively with Roma students. More frequently than engaging in academic tasks, they handle problems stemming from the disadvantaged position of the students' families (helping to mitigate truancy, mediating between the school and the families, organising extracurricular events and monitoring Roma children's behaviour). Accordingly, they are usually not considered as genuine members of the school's teaching community, nor are they respected by the non-Roma students and parents.

The other subcategory of ethnically mixed schools includes those which appreciate and encourage ethnic diversity. They seek positive approaches to ethnic differences that, especially if combined with differences in cultural and socioeconomic backgrounds, usually lead to conflict. In their approach, *diversity-conscious schools* try to enhance both equal opportunities and peaceful relations among students by developing and designing a multicultural curriculum and boosting positive self-identification of groups that are usually underprivileged in the wider society. Such schools carefully and truly integrate students of various ethnic backgrounds and make sure that the division of students into parallel classes does not result in the concentration of any one ethnic or social group.

An important sign of diversity-consciousness of such schools is that they employ ethnic minority teachers and staff whose primary task is to deal with issues and problems stemming from ethnic and social diversity. The Danish multi-ethnic schools, for example, employ bilingual teachers who help bilingual students to understand the material, and some units contract an ethnic counsellor whose duty is to mediate as well as to provide a forum in which ethnic minority parents gain easier access to school matters. Other countries understand the role of ethnic minority teachers in a wider sense and attribute a broader function to them: they may provide a positive role model and make children feel more comfortable. The following quote from an interview with a teacher gives an example of what it means to be aware of the differences stemming from ethnic diversity and how to handle them. He explains that a teacher has to recognise that some students do not dare to ask things that are evident to others: 'It's hard for all the children to read, very hard, but it is even harder for her because she doesn't know what "gummirøjsere" (older phrase for gumboots) are. It's not certain that all the Danish children know, but she most definitely won't know … Danish students can ask their parents, she can't.'

All of the schools investigated on the English sites of the EDUMIGROM research were ethnically mixed secondary or comprehensive schools with a considerable proportion of students from ethnic minority backgrounds. Despite the fact that these schools occupied various positions in the educational market and showed great variations in inter-ethnic relations, all of them were successful in administering ethnic and social diversity. Even in the school in which parents from the majority felt rather negative about ethnic minority students' presence, 'diversity was appreciated and positively valued' and its aim was 'to help students … to comprehend and celebrate the multicultural nature of the city's society' (Swann and Law 2010).

Teachers in a diversity-conscious school treat bullying or teasing based on one's ethnicity or family background very seriously. A Danish teacher recalls:

There have been a couple of times when they teased [name of the boy] with the fact that he's Jewish, but I came pretty harsh across on that or talked to them about it, saying that's absolutely not ok. It's actually racism even though it's for fun. And they understand that.

According to interviews with ethnic minority students and their parents, this is not generally the case in colour-blind Central European institutions. A good example of the few diversity-conscious schools in Hungary was one that provided education for children living in a poverty-stricken urban Roma slum area and introduced a highly prestigious German multilingual track which also attracted middle-class Hungarian families. Quite uniquely in the region, the school principal was committed to a reduction in inequalities by translating her dedication into a diversity-conscious approach. Students of various social and ethnic backgrounds were distributed among parallel classes with ethnically mixed compositions, and multiculturalism was practised during the classes as well as in extracurricular activities. However, a Roma teacher could not be employed even in this school due to resistance from ethnic majority parents.

Irrespective of the country, diversity-conscious schools are the ones in which ethnicity is considered to be an 'asset' that needs not to be hidden but viewed with pride. It follows from this way of expressing and promoting diversity that ethnic background does not become a factor of 'othering' and ethnic hierarchies.

Mixed schools with internal segregation

A frequent justification for separating ethnic minority students into distinct parallel classes within a school is that this arrangement is a necessary evil in that it prevents the school from becoming the victim of 'white flight' and from the fate of ending up as a segregated Roma school. As mentioned before, the level of tolerance towards Roma among parents from the majority is extremely low in the Central European countries; as soon as they find out that the number of Roma children in class has risen above a certain point, most of them decide to change school. A school principal in Hungary described the pressure he faced after the school had been merged with a 'Roma-only' unit: 'The most important aim was to artificially maintain the "pre-merger state" and act as if nothing had happened. That is to say that Roma children were separated from the ethnic majority, and parents of the latter were convinced that everything was the same as usual.' The EDUMIGROM research revealed a number of similar stories in the region: Roma students were tracked into parallel classes, and specialisations were set up in order to keep non-Roma parents satisfied and to prevent 'white flight'. The cross-country differences in the critical ratio of ethnic minority students that trigger 'white flight' can to some extent be explained by the general level of tolerance towards diversity: in a European comparison, Hungarian society proved to be the least tolerant towards ethnic diversity, while respondents in Sweden and the UK were the most tolerant, and Germans and Danes occupied a position in the middle of the axis.[3]

A frequent justification for selecting practices is the application of meritocratic principles in organising school and teaching. A Hungarian teacher voiced the idea behind such separation: 'Classes should be divided into good and bad students...The reason why we need this separation is the fact that a huge gap develops between good and bad students by the 8th grade.' As a consequence of such organisation of teaching, the social and ethnic composition as well as the requirements and the prestige of the parallel classes may differ strongly. In highly demanding prestigious classes a few to no ethnic minority students are present, while classes with lower academic requirements are filled with minority children. Even in Denmark, pupils may be sorted and differentiated according to their teachers' evaluations, which results in segregating practices within schools and classrooms (Moldenhawer et al. 2010). A Slovak school principal formulated the outcome of such placement practices: 'We created a sort of classy class... All the time, many teachers, including myself, noticed that we had not created a good atmosphere. So we gathered the best students into the one class and teachers do not want to teach in the B, C or D classes, because it is rubbish.'

The consequence of such an arrangement is the concentration of students with low motivation and learning or behavioural problems in classes where teaching becomes extremely challenging and motivating students becomes almost impossible. It follows that such an organisation of classes leads to detrimental outcomes: low performance, high truancy and drop-out rates, and stigmatised identities of children. These worrisome phenomena are coupled with frequent occurrences of open conflict, bullying and hostility between parallel classes, which translate into ethnic tension within the school. It is an obvious consequence that teachers working in such classes frequently lose control and often consider teaching as a punishment: they are unable to maintain discipline or make children fulfil the minimum requirements.

Segregation is even more obvious and visible in those schools in which Roma classes are isolated in distant parts of the school building. Our research identified such practices in Czech, Slovak and Hungarian schools, but it is also obvious from the news and anti-discrimination legal proceedings that the stigmatising and humiliating practice of physical separation of Roma children exists across all Central European countries. The picture is similar everywhere: 'Those classes are located in a different wing of the school and they almost never meet students from the special classes. They only observe them from the window as they very often do some gardening outside. "Standard" students shout at them and they shout back' (Kusá et al. 2010).

Despite such outcomes, many still argue for the legitimacy of internal segregation. Most of the ethnic majority parents are clearly in favour of segregation, and some teachers also are of the opinion that it is better to organise students with greatly differing ethnosocial backgrounds into separate groups. Most Roma parents and students, however, refute the legitimacy and the beneficial nature of ethnic segregation within the institution and are of the opinion that students attending segregated classes suffer disproportionately. The EDUMIGROM data support their experiences: the findings show that internal segregation deprives students not only of quality education and meaningful inter-ethnic peer relations but also of their dignity and self-esteem. The decision to keep Roma students apart seems to cause the most inter-ethnic conflict in the long run. A Slovak school principal argued strongly against the long-run sustainability of segregation: 'Those children do not know each other and if we do not know each other, we do not like each other. And if we do not like each other, we do not respect each other. And in the end we can even do something bad to each other.'

Conclusion

This chapter attempts to identify the most significant mechanisms that lead to ethnosocial segregation across Europe, and to demonstrate how various constellations of the ethnosocial composition of schools may affect studying and students' feelings towards the school, their aspirations and their peer relations.

A great number of studies on ethnic minority students' school careers have pointed out that segregated conditions deprive most students from acquiring quality education and also from opportunities to obtain a valuable qualification, and thus their prospects are worse compared with their peers who are studying in integrated settings (OECD 2005, 2006, 2007b, Crul and Schneider 2008, Heckmann and NESSE 2008). Despite all of the results showing disadvantages and damaging outcomes, ethnosocial segregation is widespread and apparently resistant to anti-segregation policies. However, the nature of segregation and its consequences may differ significantly: our research demonstrated that segregation is most harmful if it coincides with a diversity-blind approach of the school and if separation has a stigmatising nature. The least favourable environments – in terms of self-esteem and aspirations – are provided by schools in which segregation takes place within the walls of the institution; where ethnic minority and majority students are separated from each other into parallel classes and the former are often also physically isolated. Even if separation is a result of other rationales – such as specialisation and meritocratic principles, or aims to provide special attention to disadvantaged students' everyday experiences – separation along ethnic lines can be disruptive to adolescents' identity formation and may negatively influence their self-esteem and future aspirations, not to mention their peer-group relations.

Institutional and internal segregation are, however, phenomena which are deeply embedded in the essential organisation and relations of the given society and thus may not be challenged with solely administrative measures. In societies in which tolerance of multiculturalism and ethnic diversity are limited, all forms of segregation are welcomed by most of the actors. Several examples across Europe show how anti-segregation policies are resisted by most parties involved in education, be they parents, schools personnel or local authorities.

Notes

1. That is, regardless of whether the category includes first or second and further generation migrants or all of them, and whether it also comprises native communities like Roma.
2. Only 3 per cent of the seventh, eighth and ninth grade students swapped across school types and the direction of such mobility was usually downwards (Altrichter et al. 2012).

3. European Social Survey (2010). As computed from the data of the European Social Survey of 2010, the index of tolerance towards ethnic minorities was composed of the difference between how much respondents would welcome migrants with the same and with a different ethnic background than their own. (Out of the EDUMIGROM countries, Romania and Slovakia were not participating in the ESS survey.)

3

Inclusive Education for Children of Immigrants: The Turkish Second Generation in Sweden, the Netherlands and Austria

Philipp Schnell and Maurice Crul

Introduction

The educational attainment of second-generation students in Europe's knowledge-based societies is an important determinant of their subsequent life chances – their occupational and economic attainment as well as their general well-being. School qualifications and university degrees are often regarded as entry tickets to specific positions in the labour market.

Fairly stable patterns have been documented by various studies indicating that children of immigrants whose parents originate from North Africa and Turkey are predominantly found to perform below their respective majority groups (Heath et al. 2008, Alba and Silberman 2009, Crul et al. 2012, Dustmann et al. 2012, Schnell 2012). The children of Turkish immigrants are one of the largest and geographically most dispersed immigrant groups in North-Western Europe. There appears to be a relatively high level of disadvantage experienced by second-generation Turks during compulsory schooling, in combination with a greater tendency to drop out or repeat grades, lower school attainment rates, and, generally, lower levels of access to higher education. Although these patterns are evident in most European countries, recent comparative studies point to remarkable differences in the spreading of these disadvantages among second-generation groups across the various countries (Crul and Vermeulen 2006, Crul et al. 2012).

In this chapter, we continue this line of research by examining more deeply the factors that potentially contribute to cross-national differences in educational attainment among second-generation Turks. More precisely, using the framework proposed by the 'integration context theory' (Crul and Schneider 2010), we examine the actual pathways of members of the Turkish second generation by drawing on comparative data for Austria, the

Netherlands and Sweden. We will focus especially on school trajectories and outcomes because the educational pathways constitute the main driving force behind social mobility. We will concentrate on the opportunities and the hindrances that the respective school systems create for second-generation Turkish youth in the three countries. More precisely, we will look at the interaction between the prevailing institutional arrangements in school and the role that family resources play in education. In the last part of the chapter, we will summarise the findings and focus on the mechanisms that explain cross-national differences in education among young people belonging to the Turkish second generation.

Explaining differences across countries: Theoretical considerations

Over the last two to three decades, structural and sociocultural explanations have been developed to explain educational inequalities between ethnic groups in North-Western Europe. Given the often disadvantaged position of the first generation of immigrants in European labour markets, and their position predominantly in the lower social strata, there has been particular emphasis on the structural approach as a means of explaining the educationally disadvantaged position of second-generation immigrants (Heath and Brinbaum 2007, Phalet et al. 2007, Van de Werfhorst and Van Tubergen 2007, Heath et al. 2008, Crul and Holdaway 2009). Because parental social class has a considerable influence on a child's educational attainment (through the transmission of resources), structural arguments primarily attribute differences in educational attainment and achievement between immigrant and non-minority children to parental socioeconomic status. It follows that parental education is probably the best indicator to explain different outcomes (Kao and Thompson 2003).

This approach has largely been applied to explain differences in educational attainment between children of immigrants and non-immigrants within North-Western European countries. But in these single-country studies, immigrants and their children are confronted with broadly similar socioeconomic conditions, while the opportunity structure of the host country is equitable for all ethnic groups. In these national studies, variations in important institutional elements, such as the education system, are 'held constant' and are only studied in terms of their differing effects on children from a range of ethnic or social origins in the country in question. But this does not tell us the whole story. As Crul and Schneider (2010) recently argued when introducing their 'integration context theory', one also needs to study school outcomes as part of the system's idiosyncrasy which generally comes to the fore only in comparisons across national school systems. Differences in national contexts may contribute to the explanation of diverse outcomes for the children of immigrants across Europe, given the very different institutional arrangements, in particular regarding their educational systems.

The first important perspective in the integration context theory is therefore its focus on the generic institutional arrangements of an education system. The most relevant aspect by which school systems vary is their degree of differentiation (Kerckhoff 2001, Breen and Buchmann 2002, Crul and Vermeulen 2003, Van de Werfhorst and Mijs 2010), which relates to institutional settings and arrangements in secondary and tertiary education. Recent research has identified a number of differences in the major institutional arrangements among European educational systems. To begin with, a number of studies have documented the effect of early selection on educational inequalities. Most studies show convincingly that early selection and tracking negatively affect children of lower-class background (Breen and Jonsson 2005). The effect of early selection and tracking on children of immigrants is much less well documented (Crul and Vermeulen 2003, Penn and Lambert 2009), although some evidence exists which shows that inequalities are magnified for ethnic minority groups through early selection (Entorf and Lauk 2008). Besides early versus late selection, the age of entry into school, notably the attendance of pre-school, the number of school contact hours in primary school, the permeability of the school system (for instance, between vocational and non-vocational tracks) and the way in which the transition to higher education is organised are additional aspects of differentiation. A number of studies discuss the impact of not attending pre-school, or attending it only for a very short period (Crul and Doomernik 2003, Herzog-Punzenberger 2003). They reveal that pre-school attendance is especially important for children of immigrants in school systems characterised by early selection. Yet the countries that apply early selection (for example, Germany and Austria) happen also to be the countries with the lowest number of contact hours in primary school (Crul et al. 2012). At the same time the number of contact hours affects the amount of homework that needs to be done outside school and the level of support that is expected from parents (Schnell 2012). The degree of permeability defines the potential for moving between tracks. If tracks and courses are based in different institutions (for example, in work-based vs. school-based arrangements), stronger boundaries prevent movement between levels (Kerckhoff 2001, Arum et al. 2007). Inversely, high permeability enables second chances through streaming upwards, an option which the Turkish second generation is especially likely to seize (Schnell 2012). On the other hand, it also leaves room for downward streaming, a phenomenon which also affects second-generation youth more strongly than the corresponding group of native parentage. Finally, in some countries the transfer at the transition from upper-secondary school to higher education is organised almost automatically, but in others it involves a conscious choice and the successful completion of certain tests, in which case the Turkish second generation seems to continue into higher education less often.

The second important perspective in the comparative integration context theory includes the agency of individuals and groups – that is, the ways in which they actively develop options, make choices and challenge given opportunities and structural configurations (Crul and Schneider 2010, p. 1260). In different contexts, individuals' subjective and objective options for gaining access to and for claiming participation in education depend on various individual and group resources (the possession of economic, social and cultural capital). Different school characteristics at each stage of the school career interact with available family resources leading to different outcomes at important selection points in education (Schnell 2012). The spectrum is broad. At worst, the lack of resources includes the difficulty for parents to offer their children practical help with their homework in primary or secondary school, while at best a resourceful state of the home contributes to the strong drive of some parents to push their children ahead through education (Kasinitz et al. 2008, Suárez-Orozco et al. 2008).

The complex puzzle formed by different school trajectories and outcomes of second-generation Turks across the three selected countries will be analysed in the empirical section presented below by considering the factors emphasised by the integration context theory and the interactions between these factors.

Data and methodology

This study makes use of the international study on *The Integration of the European Second Generation* (TIES). This is a collaborative and comparative research project carried out between 2007 and 2008 that looks at the experiences of children of immigrants from Turkey, the former Yugoslavia, and Morocco in 15 cities and in 8 Western European countries (Crul and Heering 2008, Crul et al. 2012).

From the pool of available countries participating in the TIES study, Austria, the Netherlands and Sweden have been selected as suitable 'cases' for comparison in this chapter, based on the so-called diverse case study design (Gerring 2007). Sweden has a comprehensive education system with late selection and full-day schooling. By contrast, Austria can be described, in short, as a country with a non-comprehensive system, early selection and half-day schooling. Thus the two countries represent diverse cases in this cross-national comparison, defined by large variations in the broad outlines of their educational systems. Finally, the Netherlands has been selected as a third case for this comparison. Its educational system has a slightly delayed age of selection (age 12) but a high degree of differentiation in secondary school, making the Netherlands an interesting case of contrast.

The empirical analyses are based on a total sample of 2,455 respondents, subdivided into second-generation Turks ($N = 1,209$) and a comparison group ($N = 1,246$) where both parents were born in the given country. The term 'second generation' refers to children of immigrants who have at least one parent born outside the survey country, but who were themselves born in this country and have undergone their entire education there. At the time of the interviews, all respondents were aged between 18 and 35 years.

Educational outcomes at a glance

We start our empirical analysis by examining differences in educational outcomes in order to establish the actual size of attainment differences across Austria, the Netherlands and Sweden. Table 3.1 shows the distribution of educational levels separately for second-generation Turks and the comparison groups across the three countries. Educational levels are defined as a combination of the highest diploma obtained for those who have already left school and the current educational level of those still in school.

Moving on to the results for Austria, we find that the Turkish second generation more frequently left school only with a certificate from compulsory education (primary and/or lower-secondary education) unlike their peers in the comparison group. About one-third of the Turkish second generation obtain an apprenticeship or related certificate as their highest educational level. Moreover, they are significantly over-represented in this vocational track, with a difference of 11 per cent between them and

Table 3.1 Educational level of second-generation Turks and the comparison group, by country (%)

Educational level	Austria		The Netherlands		Sweden	
	Comparison group	Second-generation Turks	Comparison group	Second-generation Turks	Comparison group	Second-generation Turks
Primary school	1.7	3.9	2.0	8.4	0.0	0.0
Lower secondary school	10.1	21.4	8.6	21.0	3.6	9.2
Apprenticeship or vocational track	22.7	33.6	5.7	10.6	–	–
Upper-secondary academic track	30.4	22.5	21.3	31.6	34.4	56.6
Post-upper secondary/ tertiary	35.1	18.6	62.5	28.4	62.0	34.3
N	484	458	512	500	250	251

Source: TIES survey 2007–2008.

the comparison group. As far as post-secondary and tertiary education are concerned, the figures indicate that the comparison group is clearly outperforming second-generation Turks.

Somewhat similar achievement differences are observable in the Netherlands with second-generation Turks being over-represented in the lower educational categories. For example, almost 30 per cent of the Turkish second generation in the Dutch education system leave school early and directly after completing compulsory education (primary and lower secondary education). The respective proportion in the comparison group is only 10.6 per cent. Large and significant differences in educational attainment can also be found in higher education: second-generation Turks are half as likely to complete their educational career with a diploma from tertiary education as their peers in the comparison group. It is worth noting, however, that among the Turkish second generation, the proportion of those in the higher echelons of the educational system (those studying beyond upper-secondary level) is almost the same as that of the group of early school leavers (those attending school at lower secondary level at the most).

The last two columns of Table 3.1 show the results for Sweden. Since the Swedish educational system consists of a comprehensive part and a post-secondary and tertiary sector in which job specialisation for the labour market takes place, the great majority of students are situated in the upper end of the education ladder. Nevertheless, there appears to be significant group differences in educational levels. Second-generation Turks are twice as likely to leave Swedish schools after compulsory education as members of the comparison group. Moving to the top of the educational ladder, the gap between the two groups amounts to nearly 30 per cent.

How can these differences in educational outcome between the Turkish second generation and their peers of non-migrant origin be explained? The link between social origin and educational attainment has been identified as the major explanation for the disadvantaged position of the Turkish second generation in education in Europe (Heath et al. 2008, Crul and Holdaway 2009). Previous studies demonstrate that the Turkish second generation in Europe frequently comes from less-advantaged social and educational backgrounds (Penn and Lambert 2009, Dustmann et al. 2012). It is therefore possible that a substantial portion of the differences, reported above between the comparison group and second-generation Turks, can be explained by differences in parents' educational background. In order to hold these possible differences 'constant', Table 3.2 shows the educational outcomes[1] for respondents of the two groups whose parents possess, at the most, low educational credentials.

The first point to note here is that within the three countries, group differences in educational outcome are substantially reduced, indicating that a large part of the educational disadvantage of second-generation Turks is related to the differences in the educational background of the parents. For

Table 3.2 Educational level of second-generation Turks and of the comparison group whose parents hold low educational credentials (%)

Educational level	Austria		The Netherlands		Sweden	
	Comparison group	Second-generation Turks	Comparison group	Second-generation Turks	Comparison group	Second-generation Turks
Lower secondary education at the most	12.2	33.6	22.4	29.1	9.5	8.8
Upper-secondary education	63.0	51.8	37.9	44.2	52.0	62.8
Post-upper secondary/ tertiary education	24.9	14.6	39.7	26.7	38.5	28.4

Source: TIES survey 2007–2008.

instance, the large group differences in post-upper secondary education in Sweden are substantially reduced once we consider students from similarly low-educational family backgrounds. Similar patterns can be observed in Austria and the Netherlands where group differences shrink at the lower end of the educational ladder once we hold parental educational background constant.

These data also show that differences in educational levels among second-generation Turks across countries persist once parents' educational background is held constant. In other words, second-generation Turks in Sweden more often achieve higher educational levels than their counterparts in the two other countries, even if their parents are from similar educational backgrounds. We conducted additional multivariate analysis in order to explore whether the differences in the educational outcomes of second-generation Turks across countries could be explained by compositional differences and immigration-related experiences of the Turkish first generation (beyond parental educational background). We controlled for parents' occupational position, ability to speak the language of their now home country, reasons for migration, region of origin in Turkey and length of residence in the destination country because the Turkish communities in Austria, the Netherlands and Sweden differ slightly according to these factors.

Although the majority of Turkish parents migrated to the three destination countries in the late 1960s and early 1970s for work and family reasons, in Sweden in particular, the Turkish first generation includes some Turkish refugees (mostly Kurdish refugees who migrated in the early 1980s to Sweden) who possess more educationally relevant resources (Schnell 2012). Our multivariate results revealed that second-generation Turks in Sweden are still four times as likely to achieve a higher educational level than the

Turkish second generation in the Netherlands and Austria, and that differences in the educational outcome of the Turkish second generation remain highly significant across countries even after adjusting for compositional and immigration-related factors for the parental generation.

The interplay of institutional arrangements during the early period of schooling

In all countries the most important first selection is that which takes place before or during secondary education and which distinguishes those pupils who are to attend academic tracks from those destined for middle and vocational tracks. This first selection determines to a large extent the paths that young students follow in their educational career. In most countries, the timing of the selection is at the beginning of secondary school.

The first selection in Austria takes place after primary school, at the age of ten. Students are streamed into two distinct types of school: vocational (*Hauptschule*) and academically orientated (*AHS-Unterstufe*) lower-secondary education. *Hauptschule* represents the lower tier and is open to everybody after primary school. On the other hand, the academically orientated track prepares students to continue in upper-secondary schools, leading to the university entrance certificate. Table 3.3 (third column) shows

Table 3.3 Transition rates towards the academic track at the first selection moment in percentage and odds ratios

Country	Group	%	M1: Gross [B]	M2: Net [B]
Austria	Comparison group	58.5	Ref.	Ref.
	Second-generation Turks	33.8	0.30***	0.64**
			(0.04)	(0.11)
			R2: 0.13	R2: 0.29
The Netherlands	Comparison group	59.5	Ref.	Ref.
	Second-generation Turks	25.6	0.23***	0.52***
			(0.03)	(0.08)
			R2: 0.16	R2: 0.27
Sweden	Comparison group	64.5	Ref.	Ref.
	Second-generation Turks	59.6	ns	ns
			R2: 0.02	R2: 0.04

Notes: Results for models M1 and M2 are derived from binomial logistic regression on track placement. Dependent variable: 1 = academic track, 0 = other. M1 controls for age, gender and city of residence (in Austria and the Netherlands). M2 adds controls for parental educational background. Standard errors are in parentheses. Significance levels: *p < 0.05, **p < 0.01, ***p < 0.001, ns = not significant.
Source: TIES survey 2007–2008.

the percentages of those who enter the more prestigious, academic track after primary school among second-generation Turks and the comparison group. Approximately three out of ten second-generation Turks are streamed into the academic track, while the continuation rate for the comparison group is six out of ten.

In the Netherlands, students are tracked for the first time at the end of primary school, at age 12. On the basis of national examinations and the recommendation of their teacher, they are assigned to different tracks in the secondary-school system. Children with the best recommendation enter the streams preparing for tertiary education, while lower-rated students are streamed into the lower and less attractive streams of secondary education. Our results indicate that only about a quarter of the Turkish second generation make the transition into the academic tracks while the proportion for the comparison group is close to 60 per cent.

In Sweden, the first transition point is after compulsory education (*Grundskolan*), at the age of 15 (before entering upper-secondary education). As shown in Table 3.3, almost 60 per cent of the Turkish second generation moves on to the academic track and thus does not differ significantly at this stage from the comparison group in terms of their continuation rates.

Table 3.3 shows the relative chances of entering the academic track in relation to the comparison group within each country (see columns M1 and M2). These are derived from binomial logistic regression on track placement and are expressed as odds ratios. The results are reported before (M1, gross) and after (M2, net) controlling for parents' educational background. Our findings show that, even after controlling for parents' educational background, second-generation Turks in Austria and the Netherlands are significantly less likely to enter the academic track compared with the comparison group[2] while group differences in entering the academic track at the first transition point are not significant in Sweden.

To understand the different chances for second-generation Turks of entering the academic track at the first selection moments in the three countries, we consider the interplay between various institutional arrangements. More precisely, we consider how many years have passed between the moment when they entered educational facilities and the time of first selection into different tracks. This time span is significant not only because it determines exposure to the majority language but also because it offers students starting from a disadvantaged position the opportunity to acquire the skills necessary for selection into an academic track. If we take the mean age at which our respondents entered school and the formal selection age in each country (Table 3.4), we find that the percentage of second-generation Turks who make it into an academic track increases with an increase in the number of years of common education prior to selection. Although direct causal effects are hard to prove with the available data, our findings do clearly point in a certain direction.

Table 3.4 Years between the start of education and tracking for second-generation Turks

	Mean age at entering (early childhood) education institution	Age at track selection	Years of education before selection
Austria	5.2	10	4.8
The Netherlands	4.0	12	8.0
Sweden	3.1	15	11.9

Source: TIES survey 2007–2008.

The situation appears most unfavourable in Austria and the Netherlands in which the length of time between entering educational institutions for the first time and the first selection point seems to be too short to overcome difficulties in early schooling.

If we first consider Austria, the combination of institutional arrangements provides a period of an average of five years of common education prior to selection. Pre-primary education in Austria usually takes place in kindergarten. In principle, children can go to kindergarten from the age of three, while the average starting age is four. But as our TIES results for the country indicate, pre-school attendance varies considerably between second-generation Turks and the comparison group. Less than 66 per cent of Turkish second-generation students had their first educational experiences in kindergarten (compared with 84 per cent in the comparison group). The majority of the Turkish second generation started later than age four, which consequently led to a shorter overall stay in kindergarten. Compulsory schooling in Austria begins only at age six with entrance into primary school, so that a considerable number of children have been in an educational institution for only five years before the most important decision about their future school careers is made. This in and of itself is rather short, but, combined with the fact that most schools only offer half-day programmes, the amount of contact hours between teachers and children is, in fact, even more limited. The limited timeframe (late start, relatively small number of contact hours and early selection) significantly reduces the opportunity for second-generation Turkish children in Austria to enter the academic track, as shown in Table 3.3.

Their counterparts in the Netherlands are located precisely in the middle range in terms of years spent in education. The average starting age for enrolling in pre-schooling facilities is four, while primary school continues until the age of 12, at which time pupils are placed into different ability tracks for the first time. Although the average number of years prior to the first selection is longer than in Austria (eight years), very similar proportions of second-generation Turks enter the more prestigious tracks at the first selection moment (Table 3.3). One reason that contributes to the relatively limited chances for second-generation Turks to enter the academic tracks is their limited participation rate in pre-school. In the Netherlands, only about 30 per cent attend pre-school facilities before entering primary education.

Sweden provides public and full-day care for children through pre-school services. Pupils can enter pre-school as early as age one. The numbers derived from the TIES survey indicate that over 90 per cent of both groups make use of this service while the average starting age is less than three. At the age of six, all pupils enter compulsory education which lasts nine years, and students usually make their first choice about the next stage of their education when they are around 16. Early start combined with late selection amount to almost 12 years of schooling before selection into different ability tracks takes place, a phenomenon which seems to increase the chances of children of Turkish immigrants. More than half of second-generation Turks follow the academic track after passing the first transition. Most importantly, their transition rate into secondary education does not differ significantly from the comparison group, indicating the existence of equal opportunities in education for children from different ethnic and social origins.

Direct and indirect pathways to higher education

Those students who successfully enter the academic tracks at the first selection moment are predominately channelled directly into higher education in all three countries. Thus the higher rate of track placement into the vocational track early in the educational career (as in Austria) explains a large part of the absolute and relative group differences in terms of access to higher education (Table 3.1). An additional feature of institutional arrangements might contribute to explaining why second-generation Turks enter higher education in the Netherlands and Sweden more frequently than in Austria. This concerns the degree of permeability which allows for up-streaming of students who have been streamed downwards earlier in their educational career.

Such a possibility for up-streaming exists in Austria at the end of lower secondary education (at the age of 15). Students who have been streamed into the vocational track (*Hauptschule*) at the age of ten have the opportunity to move upwards towards the academically orientated tracks. But the empirical results for Austria in the TIES survey show that the proportion of upward-movers of Turkish origin at the end of *Hauptschule* is relatively small. The odds seem to be set against obtaining the marks required for the upward move and entering one or the other of the two academic tracks. The Turkish second generation is found to be less upwardly mobile at this transition point (23.2 per cent) than the comparison group (41 per cent) (Schnell 2012).

The picture is somewhat different in the Dutch school system: slightly more than a quarter of the Turkish second generation enter the track with academic orientation in lower secondary education (Table 3.3). But around 28.5 per cent finally end up in higher education, indicating that a substantial proportion of students are not following the direct academic route to higher education.[3] One characteristic of the Dutch school system is that it offers indirect routes through vocational tracks and additional qualifications, which allow students to enter higher education through an indirect route. Although it takes students two or three years more, these indirect routes provide a 'second chance' for those who have been streamed downwards earlier in their educational career (Crul et al. 2009). In particular, second-generation Turks from disadvantaged family backgrounds take advantage of this indirect or long route in order to enter higher education (Schnell et al. 2013).

The Swedish educational system does not really provide 'second chances' because the permeability between tracks at the end of each education stage is always, a given, prescribed by general rules. Students in lower- and upper-secondary education can choose tracks without any restrictions, while all upper-secondary tracks provide certificates that permit students to continue in post-secondary/tertiary education. These high levels of permeability lead to greater access rates into higher education for second-generation Turks in Sweden as compared with Austria and the Netherlands.

Interactions between family resources and institutional arrangements

This section broadens the perspective by examining interaction mechanisms between institutional arrangements and family resources in order to understand differences in outcomes for the Turkish second generation in the three investigated countries. 'Interactions' become most evident when looking at how far extra support provided by family members correlates with specific educational pathways and outcomes in the different countries. Figures 3.1 and 3.2 show predicted probabilities of leaving school early (after compulsory education) and achieving a post-secondary/tertiary educational level (high achievers) in relation to the parental support provided by Turkish parents. This support index includes information about the frequency and the amount of time parents spend helping with homework, talking with their children about school or meeting with teachers. The results in Figures 3.1 and 3.2 are derived from multivariate analysis and are displayed for parents with the same educational background (lower-secondary educational level). Figure 3.1 indicates that in Austria the chances that students will leave school early decline sharply with increasing support from their parents. In contrast, the predicted probability of being an early school-leaver in Sweden is relatively small, independent of the support provided by parents,

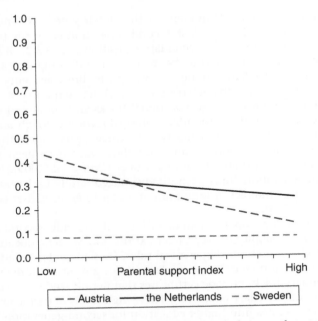

Figure 3.1 Predicted probabilities of leaving school early for second-generation Turks according to parental support, by country

Notes: The results are derived from binomial logistic regression on being an early school leaver (1, otherwise 0). Results are controlled for age, gender, parental educational background and city of residence (in Austria and the Netherlands). The parental educational level is set to 'lower-secondary education' while all other independent variables are set to the mean.
Source: TIES 2007–2008.

and it appears almost unrelated to parental involvement. The results concerning the link between the family resources of second-generation Turks in the Netherlands and the risk of leaving school early are weaker compared with Austria, but still significantly correlated with educational success.

As displayed in Figure 3.2, the predicted probability for second-generation Turks in Austria to climb the education ladder to the highest level without any parental support is below 10 per cent. The more support these children get at home, the sharper the increase in their chances of reaching the upper end of the educational ladder. In contrast, a slight 'reverse effect' in terms of the effect of parental support can be seen in Sweden. Second-generation Turks in Sweden have a slightly reduced probability of achieving the highest levels of education when they receive increased levels of parental support. The results displayed in Figure 3.2 indicate that, in the Swedish educational system, Turkish parents provide support when their child is not performing well at school. Finally, and similar to our findings in Figure 3.1, the results regarding the association between parental support and educational

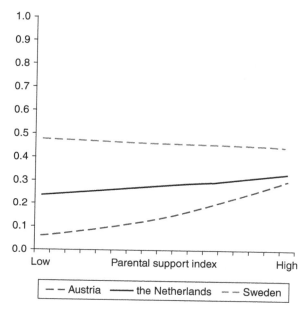

Figure 3.2 Predicted probabilities of achieving a post-secondary/tertiary educational level for second-generation Turks according to parental support, by country

Notes: The results are derived from binomial logistic regression on achieving a post-secondary/tertiary level (1, otherwise 0). The results are controlled for age, gender, parental educational background and city of residence (in Austria and the Netherlands). The parental educational level is set to 'lower-secondary education' while all other independent variables are set to the mean.

Source: TIES 2007–2008.

achievement for second-generation Turks in the Netherlands can be situated between the respective cases in Austria and Sweden.

To test if the patterns identified differ between second-generation Turks and their comparison groups within each country, we conducted additional analyses testing for differential effects among groups. We did not find any significant differential effects for second-generation Turks in Sweden. Thus the limited role played by parental involvement in determining whether children become low or high achievers applies equally to both groups and is therefore the same for the whole student population in Sweden. By contrast, in Austria and the Netherlands, our results indicate that parental involvement is of greater importance for second-generation Turks than for the comparison group. In other words, parental support is positively related to the educational success of students in the Austrian and Dutch educational systems. But second-generation Turks seem even more dependent than the comparison groups on the frequency of support provided and the involvement demonstrated by their parents.

Summary and conclusion

Second-generation Turks achieve very different educational outcomes in Austria, the Netherlands and Sweden. Our empirical investigation of absolute differences between second-generation Turks across the three countries revealed that the size of the group of high achievers (those with post-secondary education or higher) is twice as large in Sweden as it is in Austria. At the same time the highest percentage of early school leavers (those with, at the most, primary and lower-secondary education) among the Turkish second generation was found in Austria. The educational outcomes of second-generation Turks in the Netherlands can be situated between these two countries. The proportion of high achievers is only slightly smaller than in Sweden, while the proportion of students who leave the Dutch education system early is larger than in Austria. The relative comparison between second-generation Turks and the comparison groups across the three countries showed that differences in educational attainment were most pronounced at the lowest and the highest ends of the education ladders in Austria and the Netherlands. In both countries, such comparative attainment differences were higher overall than in Sweden.

Our results showed further that these cross-national differences in educational outcomes among second-generation Turks could hardly be explained by differences in the parental generation. When examining educational outcomes for second-generation Turks originating from families with similar characteristics, such as comparable levels of education, we found that the differences observed persisted across the three countries. In order to explain these remaining differences, we then considered the combination of institutional arrangements within each education system, which together form country-specific institutional constellations.

The main characteristics of the Austrian institutional constellation are the late starting age of pre-school, the early selection into different ability tracks (at the age of ten), a low degree of permeability between education tracks after the early tracking and the half-day schooling arrangement in compulsory education. The impact of this institutional constellation on the early stages of a student's education lends a good deal of importance to family resources. During this early period, parents are therefore important agents in supporting their children's learning and in making school choices. Our outcomes confirm the specific relevance of parents' educational backgrounds for the early selection process and the significance of within-family resources which are also related to the half-day schooling system that persists throughout the years of compulsory education. The responsibility for teaching is transferred to the home and studying is built on students' leisure time, which together makes parental involvement and support, in terms of learning and homework, highly influential for students. Although the relevance of family support can be seen for all students in the Austrian system, family support is of greater importance for second-generation Turks than for the comparison group.

In the Netherlands, an average pre-school starting age of four, a slightly delayed selection time (at the age of 12) and the possibility of entering higher education through indirect routes are among the main components of the national institutional constellation. Although the first selection into unequally prestigious tracks is postponed until the age of 12, we found that still only a quarter of the Turkish second generation makes it into the academic tracks in secondary education. This low transition rate among second-generation Turks can partially be explained by the lower educational background in the families of origin, which is reinforced by the low participation rates of children in pre-schooling. The lack of preparation time, of second-generation Turks, in pre-school translates into greater downward streaming, at the first transition point after primary school, compared with their peers from a non-migrant background. Nevertheless, the Dutch system can be characterised as having a high permeability between tracks in secondary education, thus allowing for upward transfers. Our results showed that a substantial number of second-generation Turks who had been streamed into the vocational track at the first selection point take advantage of these possibilities in order to enter higher education through indirect paths. This late opportunity for an upward transfer is in a rather weak association with the parents' educational background and family support.

The Swedish combination of institutional arrangements provides full-day schooling from early pre-school through primary education until the end of the integrated track in compulsory education. The prolonged and comprehensive full-day training phase makes family resources less relevant to the educational attainment process of both study groups. Since the transition takes place late in the educational career, family characteristics, such as parents' educational background or their additional educational resources, are not significant factors for managing this transition period successfully. (Such a weak association is clearly shown even at the first transition point, which takes place before entering different academic and vocational tracks in upper-secondary education.) Consequently, second-generation Turks enter academically orientated tracks in similar proportions to the comparison group, irrespective of their family background. Moreover, the high degree of permeability between tracks and the fluid linkages between upper-secondary tracks and post-secondary/tertiary education make individual-level factors less relevant to second-generation Turks who are on their way to achieving their highest educational diploma.

The empirical evidence of our study highlights the fact that cross-national differences in the educational attainment processes of second-generation Turks cannot be due to a single set of explanatory factors. Two parties are involved: on the one hand, the children of Turkish immigrants, who have their own characteristics, efforts and family background; and, on the other hand, the educational systems of the countries, with their differing institutional arrangements. It is, however, the interaction between the two that determines the direction and ultimate outcome of the educational process. Yet these two are unequal partners. The educational systems' institutional arrangements as well as the way in which such arrangements determine the relevance of family involvement and resources matter more for the outcome of this process. Education systems which provide more favourable institutional arrangements, such as 'preparing practices' through early childhood education, full-day teaching and late selection, render second-generation Turks less dependent on family factors and resources, and ultimately lead to their higher educational attainment.

Notes

1. The five categories of the dependent variable 'educational level' (as shown in Table 3.1) had to be reduced to three categories because of small case numbers and the non-existent apprenticeship track in Sweden.
2. An odds ratio of 1 would express equal opportunities.
3. The proportion is substantial because not all second-generation Turks, who started in the academic track in lower secondary education, continue until reaching the entrance point into higher education.

4

Teachers' Approaches to Ethnic Minority Students through a Comparative Lens

Claire Schiff

Within the rich body of literature on the schooling of migrant and ethnic minority pupils, studies specifically addressing the role that teachers play in the inclusion or exclusion of such pupils from the educational community are relatively scarce. Research regarding teachers' treatment and perceptions of minority pupils has mainly been carried out in the UK, and has tended to focus on appraising the more or less discriminatory or racist behaviour of teachers, and the impact that this might have on academic performance. The debate, sometimes heated, which has taken place among British researchers about the extent of teachers' participation in the stigmatisation of certain groups reveals an understanding of the 'problem' of the schooling of minority pupils which is framed in terms of 'racism and racial discrimination in school' (Stevens 2007, p. 149). From this perspective, teachers' accounts of their dealings with minority students appear to simply partake in a 'dominant educational discourse' which constructs minority pupils as particularly problematic (Archer 2008). Teachers' attitudes and discourses appear here as both expressions of their personal prejudice and reflections of an overriding dominant construction of minority students as 'deviant'. Little, if anything, is revealed by such approaches about the specific national, institutional or local dynamics that exacerbate or hinder the expression of negative racial stereotypes by teachers, or about how their training, professional trajectories, or their social and cultural backgrounds might contribute to their outlook.

It is rare that studies about teachers take an internationally comparative perspective, such as the one adopted by Osborn and Broadfoot in their research comparing primary school teachers in the UK and France (1993). The fact that the EDUMIGROM research programme was carried out in a variety of countries, as well as in diverse sites within each country, makes it possible to develop an approach to teacher–pupil relations which considers the impact of contextual factors as well as the national frame of reference in which teachers are operating. Our premise in this chapter is that teachers' views and attitudes towards minority students are influenced in large part by such factors, and that perceptions of racism and discrimination are culturally and contextually determined.

The present comparative analysis is based on the material gathered from the qualitative research carried out in several secondary schools in each of the nine countries involved in the EDUMIGROM project: Denmark, France, Germany, Hungary, Romania, Slovakia, Sweden, the Czech Republic and the UK. The material is composed of interviews with teachers and other members of school personnel from several schools in each of the countries, as well as of focus group discussions. At all of the sites at least two full days of observation were carried out with several of the classes involved, thus making it possible to compare the pedagogical style and teaching practices of a variety of teachers as well as the attitudes and behaviour of students from different classes.

In the following pages, we shall first compare the situations in the various countries involved regarding the presence and function of teachers and staff of ethnic minority origin, since this is one of the factors which distinguishes the various approaches to minority education. Second, we shall characterise the way in which teachers in the various countries approach the 'problems' of minority students and the arguments that they put forth in order to explain the positions and attitudes of minority students regarding schooling. Here we shall attempt to determine the extent to which the perceptions of such students are influenced by the more general national frameworks of majority–minority relations in society at large, or rather by the more concrete aspects of the particular local school contexts, such as the effects of recent school mergers and reforms, or by the nature of the school personnel's contacts with parents.

Who teaches minority pupils and why?

The impact that teachers who are themselves from a minority background have on pupils of immigrant or minority origin has seldom been addressed in the literature. While one might assume that their presence would be beneficial to the extent that they serve as positive role models for students, by the same token the frequent concentration of minority teachers in the least prestigious schools and classes might reinforce minority students' feeling of segregation and contribute to the tendency to consider such teachers as second rate or as auxiliary staff (Jellab 2008).

Our comparative analysis of teachers' positions in the various national school systems raises questions about who minority teachers are and, more importantly, in what capacity they have been recruited. Indeed, throughout the research we observed a great diversity of profiles among such teachers. These ranged from recent university-educated migrants who had experienced downward mobility by becoming secondary-school teachers, to cultural brokers who had been recruited solely on the basis of their linguistic and intercultural competence, to native-born second- or even third-generation members of racial minority groups who tend to be regarded either as ordinary or as 'token' teachers depending on the particular context. It is interesting to note that in the countries, such as France, Sweden and England, where minority teachers are an integral part of the school personnel, their role and position vis-à-vis minority students differ substantially, as we shall see below.

Although the proportion of minority teachers remains quite limited in all of the OECD countries (2010), there are significant variations in this respect both between countries and, more importantly, between schools within countries, with the tendency being for minority teachers to be concentrated in urban schools receiving higher than average proportions of socially disadvantaged pupils. In France and Sweden, where minority teachers make up over one-third of the staff in the schools dominated by students of immigrant origin, they figured prominently among the sample of teachers interviewed. In countries such as Germany and those of Central and Eastern Europe, only one or two staff members of minority origin were interviewed, since even in schools of high minority concentration their numbers were extremely limited. Here the adults of migrant or minority origin were mainly teaching assistants, mediators or family outreach workers rather than regular teachers.

In France, where the distribution of teachers across schools is entirely centralised, minority teachers do not perform any particular tasks or roles relating to their ethnic origins and are never recruited in this capacity. Although they tend to teach in the vocational disciplines and classes, and they are over-represented among the personnel who do not have permanent positions, this is due to the fact that many have not passed the relatively selective national examination certificate required in order to obtain a permanent teaching position in France. In everyday situations and interactions, references to their particular cultural, ethnic or racial characteristics are rarely spontaneously made either by them or by their colleagues. Moreover, it would be quite unusual for them to be heard speaking a language other than French with students or colleagues who share their mother tongue. When invited by our question to reflect on the impact of their proximity to students of immigrant backgrounds, a few minority teachers in France conceded that their ethnicity might occasionally create a degree of complicity with certain students. However, as a general rule, they were careful to avoid showing any form of differential treatment of students and were quite reticent to make any direct reference to their origins. They tended to be at least as staunch as their majority colleagues about observing a form of republican neutrality, and often avoided becoming involved in debates about issues relating to ethnic, religious or cultural diversity.

In Sweden, and to a certain extent in Denmark, the situation was very different from that observed in France. For instance, teachers of minority background spontaneously pointed to their capacity as cultural brokers, bilingual teachers and role models for students. Since the students, as compared to other countries, were more often either migrants themselves or children of migrants facing particular language barriers, these capacities of the minority teachers gained particular importance. In these countries, language barriers appeared much more pronounced than in France and England, two countries in which immigrants and minorities originate predominantly from former colonies, and where they often belong to the second or third generation. In Denmark, one of the respondents stated that: 'Sometimes the students have difficulties understanding what is going on in the class. That's why we have bilingual teachers in this school. They are part of work both concerning teaching and cooperation with parents.'

The status of bilingual and second-language teachers, who have usually undergone special training in teaching students of an immigrant background, was much more common in schools receiving a large proportion of minority students than was the case in similar schools in France, Germany or England.

If one compares the roles and statuses of teachers of minority origin in France and Denmark (two countries in which their proportions have been increasing over the past few decades), one can observe that the expectations of their majority origin colleagues and members of the administration are diametrically opposed, with regard to the functions and attitudes which they should adopt in their dealings with ethnic minority students. In her study of Turkish- and Kurdish-speaking teachers in Denmark, Moldenhawer described how these teachers encountered obstacles and resistance when they attempted to make use of their more general academic qualifications and deviated from the specific tasks assigned to them as mediators for the integration of Turkish pupils (Moldenhawer 1999). In other words, they were obliged to act as cultural brokers in order to be viewed as legitimate professionals, even though many of them aspired to act as teachers in their own right. In France, in contrast, on the relatively rare occasions when teachers of immigrant origin make use of their intercultural and linguistic skills in dealing with their minority pupils, they are regarded as operating outside the limits of their professional assignments and roles, even though such an approach might prove to be effective at a given time for solving a particular problem or facilitating communication. The following account about a particularly problematic and aggressive student told by a first-generation teacher from Algeria in charge of a class of low-performing vocational students is a telling example of such a case:

> I used to yell, I yelled because I thought that the teacher should represent authority and that you had to. Now it's totally the opposite. Now I go towards the students, I even take them in my arms sometimes. I have

learned. And then you understand that in fact often those students who are very tough, in fact they are hurting badly deep down inside. I also learned about that when I would call in the parents. As soon as I see a profile like that, I say I'm going to call in your parents. He says right away: 'No, no, Madame.' And there I understand that behind it there is mistreatment, behind they're hitting and not talking. He wants to assert himself outside so there is necessarily this behaviour. I've had situations where students denigrated me. They insulted me. And then I would understand the reason for it. So when the mother arrives, she is not allowed to speak. There was this student, he would not let his mother speak, because he considered that she didn't know how to talk. So I said to him: 'If your mother speaks Arabic, I speak Arabic. If your mother speaks Kabyle, I speak Kabyle. If she speaks French, I speak French.' He did not want to let her express herself. So I kicked him out. And there I found myself facing a mother who burst into tears. She said: 'How do you think he can respect you, respect me, when his father beats me?' I entered into another dimension. For him I am Maghreb, his mother is a victim, I am Maghreb, so I don't deserve anything else. And so I took some time, I went over things with him: 'Do you agree when your father does this?' 'No, I don't agree.' And there he started to cry. And it was a totally different person that I was seeing. After that I got a lot of respect.

Here the teacher's recourse to her cultural and linguistic skills is a spontaneous reaction to the particular case at hand, which appeared to her as a result of troubled family dynamics more than as a reflection of a particular cultural habitus.

In the British context, the teachers and staff members who were of minority origin were involved in special measures for minority pupils through participation in target projects, such as the Black Achievement Programme or the Pakistani Study Support. Here the focus was on enhancing self-esteem and on improving in-class behaviour and academic ambition among students referred to as 'Black Minority Ethnics' (BMEs). These students' difficulties were not seen as stemming from their 'foreignness' but rather from their potential inferiority complexes and their lack of recognition from wider society. As one school head pointed out, in the schools in England, other special events such as Refugee Week or Black History Month typically seek 'to help students to understand the interdependence of individuals, groups, nations and the local environment, and to both comprehend and celebrate the multicultural nature of society' (Swann and Law 2010). This trend of cultural awareness-building and promotion of minority self-esteem through a variety of ad hoc projects can be linked to the influence of multiculturalism in the British approach to ethnic minority incorporation, as well as to the prevalent view of teachers as educators whose aims and responsibilities encompass not only academic teaching but also pupils' well-being (Osborn and Broadfoot 1993). This contrasts with what was observed in the Scandinavian countries, where special measures aimed at minority pupils, such as the language study group or the parents' Ethnic Council, were concerned primarily with setting up effective ways of overcoming specific problems arising from poor mastery of the native language, or from limited knowledge among immigrant parents about the workings of the national school system. It also contrasts with the French teachers' tendency to consider that issues of cultural awareness, ethnic identity and racial diversity are exogenous to the school system's educational objectives, and that focusing on them may even be detrimental to its primary aims.

With the exceptions of Romania and Hungary, where one or two of the schools of the sample offered Romani language courses taught by teachers of Roma origin, the schools under investigation in the other countries, as well as in Germany, did not count any teachers belonging to the selected ethnic minority groups. Many of the schools in the Central and Eastern European countries employed Roma mediators and/or teaching assistants to help with specific issues, such as low attendance or poor communication between Roma parents and the schools. The general aim in these cases was to get parents and children to conform and adapt to the minimal requirements of the school system – for instance, regarding regular attendance – and to promote a process of 'normalisation', which was in most cases to be carried out through the more or less voluntary integration of Roma children into non-Roma schools. It is interesting to note that although the role of the Roma mediators and assistants is strictly limited to working with Roma students and their families, these personnel are, in fact, very different from the majority Roma population attending the school in terms of their social background, their educational credentials and their residency outside the most disadvantaged, typically Roma, neighbourhoods.

In most of the countries involved in the studies, one finds distinctions regarding the extent to which teachers have chosen to work in schools receiving a large number of minority students. In a few of the schools observed, notably in Sweden, France, Denmark, Romania and Hungary, a more or less formal process of selection or self-selection of teachers has resulted in the creation of a generally positive and constructive attitude towards minority students. Teachers in such schools have often received some form of special training that entitles them to teach ethnic minority and/or underprivileged students. The school administration often encourages innovative practices and collective work among teachers who, while they might be strongly challenged by their students' difficulties, do not feel degraded by having to teach underprivileged minority students. In such schools one finds some teachers for whom teaching disadvantaged minority students is a true vocation, even a form of social activism, and who are energised by the belief that their work is more useful than it would be if they were working with more middle-class students.

At the other end of the spectrum, one finds a few schools – notably in Germany, in all of the Central and Eastern European sites, and to a lesser extent in France – in which the large proportion of minority students is the consequence of changes, such as mergers, integration programmes or transformations in the enrolment process of students, which have been imposed by the authorities, or by modification in the recruitment process due to changes in policy or in the functioning of the educational market. Here the teachers have not been consulted, neither have they received adequate training to help them to adapt to the new situation. The considerable and often sudden increase in the proportion of minority pupils is most often equated with a worsening of the school's reputation, a process of 'white flight' and the tendency for the more experienced teachers to seek teaching appointments elsewhere. In these cases, minority students often become the most tangible symbols of the remaining teachers' dissatisfaction and sense of powerlessness. In contexts where negative stereotypes of certain minority groups are prevalent in the popular media and in political discourse, these feelings can easily be rationalised through explanations that place all of the blame for students' low academic performance and disruptive behaviour on the families and their supposed cultural or moral inadequacies.

As an illustration of the impact which rapid and unexpected changes in the local educational market can have on teachers' outlook and attitudes towards minority students, let us mention the case of a vocational school in a provincial city located in a relatively middle-class neighbourhood in France. The head of student life recounted the manner in which this new, more diverse population of students had become the incarnation of some of the older, more traditional teachers' loss of prestige and sense of downward mobility:

> This used to be a prestigious school. But when I arrived it was already declining. Historically the girls who used to come here were from good families who lived in the neighbourhood, who would come and learn a bit of accounting, a bit of secretary work to become their husbands' medical secretary. So it was a relatively privileged milieu with ratios of requests to places which were incredible. There were twenty places for hundreds of applications. So teachers who have experienced that are now faced with ratios of 0.4 to 1, with students of immigrant origin. I've got at least one teacher who is very racist, who can't help but say so some days. So we've ended up with teachers who are a bit lost. Everything is changing. One teacher is on sick leave because everything has changed too much and she couldn't take it. I heard that when some teachers who are still here used to go to other schools they would look down on their colleagues, because it was something to be a teacher here. It's not the case anymore. The recruitment has widened thanks to the tramway. Students come from the north, the sensitive urban zones, and from other disadvantaged towns.

It should be noted that the interview with the 'racist' teacher mentioned here did not reveal any anti-immigrant sentiments, nor was this teacher ever mentioned by students in their answers to questions about racism in school. Intolerance to minority students is very rarely apparent in any direct manner in teachers' discourse about students in France, given the strong taboo which exists against making any overt references to factors such as race, religion or ethnicity. Inversely, students' testimonies about teachers' racism should not necessarily be regarded as an objective measure of the actual tolerance of individual teachers to minority students, since their judgement of teachers is often influenced by the general atmosphere of the classes and schools, and the overall relationship with authority which prevails in their establishment. In a school where most student–teacher relations are relatively harmonious, as is the case here, one teacher's 'racist' remarks might go unnoticed, while in a school where relations are tense, a minor expression of disapproval or condescension on the part of a teacher might easily be viewed as 'racism' by students.

It should also be noted that among the older generation of teachers in the abovementioned school there are those who have adapted quite well to the changes in the student population and who take a certain pride and pleasure in teaching a much more diverse and disadvantaged student population. Two teachers whose classes we observed stated that their work was much more 'interesting' and 'enriching', albeit more exhausting, than 15 years ago when they felt less useful and when there was little communication with students about non-academic issues. One of them told us:

> With the students today I really enjoy myself, because I'm attached to them. I've changed my pedagogy, I've become less demanding, I've adapted to the students. I now try to think of situations that will moti-vate them, because before they used to choose this accounting section. Today they're here by default. I try to interest them, with new courses and outings. I discuss things with them, and have very good relations with them. I'll never tell a child that he's having difficulties. I'll go to him and say that he hasn't learned his lesson since he had such a bad grade in the exam. So he looks at me and says: 'Yes Madame, you're right.' So I encourage him so that he gets a better grade.

Moreover, the frame of reference of the old and new generations of teachers, for assessing the behaviour of the student population, is often diametri-cally opposite. Indeed, many of the younger, incoming teachers have had to undergo an initial period of teaching in the Parisian suburbs or in the more industrial working-class areas in the North of France, where the proportion of minority students and the general level of violence and insecurity are considerably greater. In view of their initial teaching experience in one of the Parisian 'ghettos', the overall atmosphere in even the least prestigious and ethnically mixed schools of a provincial city appears relaxed.

We see therefore that the differences observed in terms of teachers' perception and treatment of minority students are the result of a rather subtle and complex combination of factors that develops at the individual, local and national level. To encourage a more positive and pragmatic approach of teachers to such students, a variety of policy initiatives could be envisioned, ranging from specific training programmes to enhance communication with immigrant and minority parents, to improving consultation and planning of school integration and merger programmes, and to awareness-building among teachers to raise their knowledge about the specificities of the national framework within which they operate.

Framing the 'problem' and naming minority students through national taxonomies of difference

As we browsed through the interviews, we were struck by the very different ways in which teachers from the various countries referred to minority pupils. While individual teachers in the different countries sometimes held views and opinions about their minority students which differed substantially from those of their colleagues, there exists a general framework of understanding concerning the status of such students and the nature of their particular 'problems' which is very much linked to each country's citizenship model and to its particular history of immigrant and minority incorporation, as well as to traditions regarding the role of formal education and relations between schools and families.

The German teachers we met named students either through direct reference to their nationality or to their membership in a broad ethnic or religious category. They spoke about 'Turks', 'Arabs', 'Muslims', 'migrant students' or 'students from a migrant or foreign background'. Even though most of the minority students of Turkish origin interviewed in Germany belonged to the second and third generation, these labels stress the cultural, national and religious distance of these youngsters from the dominant norm represented by 'German' students and teachers. Minority students are still perceived by teachers to be foreigners or outsiders (*Ausländers*) who should be taught to adapt (not to say conform) to the dominant culture, even though many also admit to the difficulty or impossibility of the task. Many Turkish students' oppositional stance and lack of discipline, which is likely a result of their experience of relegation and of the limited opportunities of success through the school system (Tucci 2010), was interpreted as an expression of cultural norms and habits perceived to be foreign to those of the dominant culture. One teacher stated, for instance, that:

> I am not able to change the culture. As a German teacher I can only hope that they respect me and accept the things I tell them. I mean in Turkey teachers are not that highly respected. But I can't dictate the families. A Turkish colleague could do this, one who lived in Turkey before and

is familiar with the rules. But me as a German teacher, I am not able to do so.

The contradiction, between the idea that lack of respect for teachers is a cultural import and the implication that only a Turkish colleague (of whom there are in fact very few) might be successful in imposing respect for the rules of the school to students and their families, reflects the double-bind seemingly experienced by many of the encountered German teachers. This is due to their perception of an insurmountable cultural divide, while simultaneously feeling that it is their role as teachers to 'acculturate' minority students. Given the high concentration of minority students in the vocational schools (*Hauptschule*) and the relatively limited amount of time which German students spend in school compared with other school systems, such as the French or Scandinavian ones, the process of acculturation seems to be conceived less as a spontaneous phenomenon and more as a conscious part of teachers' tasks, although such a burden is obviously encountered with often ambivalent feelings. As Sabine Mannitz noted in her comparative study of students of Turkish origin living in four different European countries, German teachers' discourses on minority pupils point to the inner contradictions and incoherence of an approach which assumes the existence of 'an ethnically patterned collective lifestyle while arguing for the assimilation of ethnic minorities' (Mannitz 2004). Indeed, the interviewed German teachers expressed the feeling that while as teachers they were obliged to support the cultural habits and values of German society in the face of minority cultures often perceived as traditional and backward, they also seemed to believe that the influence of family socialisation was much stronger than that of schooling. The combination of a national tradition which emphasises the central role of the family, the local community and religious institutions, and the rather assimilationist approach of many representatives of the German school system, tend to encourage both parties – teachers and minority students alike – to act as representatives of their particular ethnic group.

The interviews with students and parents, particularly those from the less prestigious comprehensive school, reflected this portrayal of teacher–student relations in terms of a cultural, at times even a moral, conflict opposing school and family. The mothers as well as the students of Turkish origin who attended such schools expressed a feeling of being pressured by teachers to conform to the dominant cultural norms of German-ness, a process which they tended to perceive as an attack on their dignity and on the authority of parents. The sense was that they needed to protect their private family life and their ethnic pride against the encroachments of the 'German' teachers who were trying to 'force' them to assimilate.

In England, depending on the particular group under consideration, teachers use a variety of terms when speaking about their minority students.

However, the official term accepted by all is 'Black Minority Ethnics' (BME). This designation stresses first and foremost the 'racial' characteristics and the visibility of students belonging to groups who are in fact culturally and socially quite different from one another (Pakistani, Caribbean, Yemeni, Somali, etc.). The main differentiating factor between majority and minority thus appears to be colour, and this is further stressed by the fact that teachers do not hesitate to use the term 'white' when speaking about those who are not BMEs. In the interviews of British teachers working in the highly multiethnic and economically disadvantaged urban neighbourhoods serving several of the schools under investigation, it appeared that the most problematic students were not those of immigrant origin, or at least that these teachers seldom permitted themselves to voice such an opinion. Swann and Law (2010) summarise their fieldwork experience in the following way:

> In attributing causes for diverging pathways, teachers and education workers tended to focus on families [...] This was not aimed at Caribbean or Pakistani families however, but a complaint solely aimed at the white community. There was a tendency for some teachers to have particular stereotypes and misconceptions about the communities they served, but it was always the lower class white community which was discussed.

The 'politically correct' trend prevalent among British teachers, which encourages them to emphasise the positive contributions of groups who are regarded both as an integral part of multiethnic British society and as potential victims of racism, makes it very difficult for teachers to be openly critical of such students and their families. Moreover, the salience of other factors, such as youthful styles, local neighbourhood identities, social class and multiple migration flows, tends to cut across and blur ethnic and racial boundaries to such an extent that it is no longer obvious to teachers who among their students actually represents the 'other'.

Beyond the Black/White paradigm which still has some influence on teachers' more general discourses about minority pupils and on many educational policies aimed at such pupils, their daily experiences and dealings with an increasingly diverse student population reveal a more complex reality. Indeed, authors who have been critical of the limits of the race-relations perspective have noted that multiple factors other than race inform teachers' attitudes and portrayals of minority students (Foster 1992). Moreover, with the rise of 'super-diversity' there appears to have been a complication of the White-Black or British-non-British dichotomy since the 1990s, brought about by the increase in intermarriage and the diversity of hybrid youth cultures among the later generations of migrants and their children (Modood and May 2001). This creates a context in which the simple distinction between a dominant majority group and an underprivileged ethnic minority has become largely artificial.

In stark contrast with German teachers, who often portrayed minority students' difficulties in terms of cultural conflicts between families and school, and who perceived students' oppositional attitude to be a form of resistance to acculturation, the difficulties mentioned by British teachers do not appear to result from ethnic or cultural conflicts per se. Instead, their concerns stem rather from tensions between older minorities and recent arrivals, from gang violence or simply from the profound socioeconomic deprivation and dependency experienced by the poorest families in the local area (Felson et al. 1994).

In France, the most remarkable feature of teachers' talk about minority pupils is their very obvious difficulty in finding names and labels which adequately refer to what they are trying to designate. During the transcription of teachers' interviews, we noticed that almost every time French teachers were posed a question which required them to designate students according to their ethnic origins, they tended to pause, fumble for words or make use of audible quotation marks and to resort to a variety of euphemisms such as 'youth of immigrant descent', 'of foreign origin' or 'underprivileged youth'. Often they simply avoided naming in any direct manner those whom they were talking about, as if they assumed that there existed an implicit understanding shared with the interviewer about a category whose existence one should not, however, acknowledge aloud. French teachers rarely pointed to students' cultural characteristics in order to explain poor performance or the lack of motivation. They more often stressed students' socioeconomic background, the influence of anti-school peer culture and their difficult home environment. French teachers have very limited contact with parents in general and with minority parents in particular, except in certain specific instances where there is a concerted effort among colleagues to combat school attrition and failure through more regular contact with parents. In exchanges about the particular performance and behaviour of minority students it was more frequent to hear French teachers criticise what they perceived as students' tendency to overemphasise and overplay their ethnic identities than to hear them interpret students' behaviour as a consequence of ethnic or cultural differences.

In Denmark and Sweden, the term most readily used by teachers when they spoke of the selected minority was that of 'bilingual students'. Here students were defined more by their language than by their culture, race or ethnicity. Here it appears almost as if the issue of language acts as a catch-all focal point which subsumes all other dimensions of difference, making students' specificities into something which is manageable and neutralised, problematic but potentially surmountable. The fact that many students speak a foreign language at home is regarded both as an added value and as a potential source of academic difficulty. In contrast with German and French teachers' feelings that they must necessarily work 'against' the families, in the Scandinavian countries the belief seems to be that academic success is dependent on the schools' ability to work 'with' the families. This makes it necessary to find proper means of communication. One Danish teacher framed this in the following terms: 'I think the challenge for teachers with regards to getting the attention of students is much bigger than they think. We have to be more affected by their reality. We have to bring their reality over here [at the school].'

This orientation explains the central role of bilingual teachers, mediators and translators in these countries.

In their relations with minority students, German, British and French teachers feel obliged to act as 'representatives' of their society by embodying its cultural norms and values (Germany), celebrating its diversity (UK) or acting as colour-blind agents of a presumably universal culture (France). In comparison, Danish and Swedish teachers appear more pragmatic in their approach to minority students. They avoid formulating generalisations about students based on ethnicity and point more readily to practical barriers to students' understanding of the material, insisting on the vast differences between students who come from a variety of countries and social backgrounds. Within our comparative framework, this appears as somewhat of a paradox since it is in these Scandinavian countries that migration from non-European countries such as Turkey, Pakistan, Somalia, Afghanistan and Iraq is both more recent and more culturally distinct from the host society and where students experience the widest gap between the cultural norms, languages and educational styles of their parents and the norms of the host country which stress individuality and experimentation. Yet rarely do Danish and Swedish teachers mention cultural differences as the cause of these students' academic difficulties. Although issues linked to more traditional gender roles, to migrant parents' more authoritative educational style, and to their reticence to engage on equal terms with teachers are often mentioned in reference to groups such as the Somali, Afghan, Iraqi or other recent Muslim minorities, most teachers do not seem to view these as reasons for the diverging educational careers of minority and majority students. More importance is attributed to language barriers and socioeconomic problems.

In the Central and Eastern European countries, Roma students are often referred to using terms such as 'special needs', 'intellectually deficient', 'problem students' – all of which stress shortcomings that appear, rather paradoxically, as both individual limitations and as a result of collective cultural orientations. By contrast, many teachers spontaneously refer to non-Roma students as 'normal' or 'ordinary'. We detected certain differences between countries regarding the openness or the reserve with which teachers 'admitted' to regarding Roma students differently or to having 'problems' with such students.[1] While many teachers in Hungary, and to a lesser extent in the Czech Republic and Slovakia, spoke quite frankly about the problems that they encountered with Roma students, some even voicing strong moral condemnation of Roma parents, the teachers encountered in the Romanian schools appeared to be more cautious in their judgements and more intent on avoiding formulations that might be interpreted as 'racist' or anti-Roma. Such differences could be due to the extremely large proportion of drop-outs and early school leavers among Roma youth in Romania, those who remain in education representing the higher status and better-off Roma. As such, they are highly respected as 'diligent' and 'ambitious' by the school principals and teachers. It may be that where entrenched institutional discrimination and inequalities are strongest, individual expressions of disapproval and stigmatisation on the part of teachers are limited by the simple fact that most Roma students do not remain in school beyond the first few years of primary education.

The spectrum of opinions was quite wide among teachers in the four post-socialist countries as to what was the fundamental cause behind Roma students' poor academic performance. They ranged from those who believed that the Roma's lack of motivation and interest in school success was transmitted through their 'blood' or those who spoke more in terms of cultural determinism and parents' educational 'style', to those, relatively less numerous, who insisted rather on the students' difficult home environments and economic deprivation. It is interesting to note that among all of the school personnel interviewed in these four countries, only one, a Roma teaching assistant in a Czech school, formulated a rational explanation for Roma parents' lack of investment in their children's schooling which he considered to be the result of a logical adaptation to their very limited chances of eventually getting some tangible returns for their investment in the form of qualified and well-paying jobs. In effect, this view reflected the adaptation of an involuntary racialised minority to the existence of a job ceiling that severely limits any prospects for social mobility (Ogbu and Simons 1998).

The attitudes and beliefs of teachers regarding the obstacles to Roma students' success are, to a certain extent, a function of the institutional mode of integration or segregation. Over the past few decades, far-reaching and at times rather chaotic reforms, which attempt better integration of Roma students into mainstream schools and classes, have been taking place under the influence of the European Union and non-governmental institutions. The efficiency and success of such reforms vary widely depending on local and national factors, which are beyond the scope of this discussion. Yet it can be said that whether teachers express 'anti' or 'pro' Roma views depends to a certain degree on whether their school has succeeded in integrating these students in a manner that suits both the school personnel and the students themselves. Teachers' outlook on Roma students are also linked to the extent and the nature of the contacts that they have with Roma families. Understandably, those teachers who have never had any contact with parents, or only very occasionally in cases of particularly disruptive behaviour on the part of students, tend to portray Roma families as a homogeneous, defiant and unfathomable entity. Meanwhile, teachers who regularly meet with parents – either because they are encouraged to do so by their school administration or because they are personally motivated to do so – spoke more readily of the differences between families and of the need to be realistic and flexible in their teaching style and content. In one pedagogically innovative school in Hungary, where contacts between teachers and Roma parents are encouraged and organised by the administration on a regular basis, there is a concerted effort to take into account the specificities of Roma culture while maintaining high academic standards, with the development of projects to integrate Roma children in a school that also has prestigious classes and middle-class students. Teachers in this school, more often than in the other Hungarian schools, considered Roma students' difficulties in adapting to the requirements as a consequence of poverty and social deprivation rather than as an expression of deviant cultural norms. By contrast, in other Hungarian schools the integration of Roma students is seen as an unwelcome imposition on the part of the 'authorities' and has not been accompanied by the necessary pedagogical adaptations and teacher training. Here teachers felt that any effort to enhance Roma pupils' performance and attendance was doomed to fail, essentially because of what they perceived as culturally, occasionally even genetically, ingrained behaviour and values that were contrary to the dominant norms.

This link between teachers' perception of minority students as 'impossible' to manage and to educate, and their own experience of having been relegated into a low-prestige school and having to fulfil impossible requirements born of ill-conceived or poorly implemented reforms, was also quite obvious in the case of a German comprehensive school receiving a large proportion of students of Turkish origin. Many teachers had been transferred to this school against their will upon the closure of another school. Conversely, one might hypothesise that the generally more positive views of immigrant parents held by Swedish and Danish teachers might be to a large extent the result of the manner in which they are recruited and trained, and of the emphasis which is put on creating partnerships with parents in the educational system as a whole, as well as the more careful planning and implementation of mergers or other organisational interventions in these countries.

It is very difficult to ascertain whether among the Central and Eastern European countries the variation between schools in terms of teachers' more or less fatalistic, moralistic and, admittedly, racist outlook on Roma students and their families is first and foremost a consequence of teacher self-selection and recruitment or rather of a process of socialisation among teachers in a context in which Roma school integration has been unevenly planned and implemented. The head of one school in Romania which has a particularly successful outreach programme aimed at the Roma community stated: 'If I think about it better, we have passed all phases regarding integration.

It was not easy but we've overcome them, primarily through retirement of the colleagues who could not accept Roma children.'
The various examples encountered in the different countries underscore the importance of observing changes over time, of taking into consideration local contextual factors, and of examining what teaching minority students means in terms of the career development and professional identities of teachers. A more complex analysis of the causes and conditions for the expression of teachers' racism would facilitate the formulation of proposals for effective reform aimed at reducing teachers' prejudice and discrimination which go beyond the relatively limited and ineffective approaches in terms of cultural sensitivity building, anti-racist training or the unrealistic aim of eliminating racial prejudice in society at large.

Note

1. Due to the author's limited knowledge of the rapidly changing educational systems in these countries, our analysis of teachers' approaches to minority students does not delve into the differences between the post-socialist countries but only presents some of the more general trends observed.

5

The Emerging 'Ethnic Ceiling': Implications of Grading on Adolescents' Educational Advancement in Comparative Perspective

Julia Szalai

The social meanings of grading

Despite widespread criticism of the inherent 'subjectivity', 'arbitrariness' and 'cultural bias' towards middle-class values and norms of grading, and despite also its 'moral hazards' in impacting young people's careers (DiMaggio 1982, Sockett 1993, Wood 1994, Sullivan 2001, Burgess and Greaves 2009, Goldthorpe 2010, Rein 2010, Kohn 2011), the routine of ranking students' performance into preset categories in a hierarchical order remains the prime form of assessment in primary and secondary education. The manifold functions that grades serve certainly explain its persistent use. First and foremost, they send strong messages to students. By expressing teachers' evaluation in the language of scores, authoritative numeric values are attached to their individual performance and start working as labels: high scores translate into 'aptitude', 'recognition' and 'achievement', while low scores express just the opposite: 'poor ability', 'refusal' and 'lacking capabilities for progressing'. In the course of such labelling, grades often tend to turn from partial evaluation to a holistic assessment expressing the appraisal of personal qualities and 'worth'. Second, by positioning the student's performance on a ladder created by the ordering of numeric values, grades also translate into relative measures: by comparing the individuals with each other, a hierarchy of personal 'values' emerges that often becomes the frame of reference in disciplining and rewarding. Third, grades operate as a communicational channel between the school and parents: the assumed universal meaning works as the frame of reference and the grade scores serve to inform families about their child's future prospects even in cases when otherwise scarce contacts between parents and schools would hinder common deliberations and actions. Fourth, grades qualify the educational institutions: at least in part, schools are evaluated by the public according to the positioning on the invisible hierarchy that emerges from the average or dominant 'value' of the performance of their student body. In this vein, school-specific averages and the proportions of 'good' vs. 'bad' students provide information for partner educational units, especially for those secondary-level institutions which apply a complexity of exams and rulings to decide about students' acceptance. These 'objective' measures of institutional quality influence decisions about admissions: coming from a weak or a strong primary school is taken into consideration in conjunction with individual results as an additional detail for fine-tuning. In this way, while appearing to reflect 'objectivity' and 'justice', grades have significant impacts on the complex process of selection that takes place within and among the secondary schools.

Given such a range of functions and messages, grades work as a *lingua franca* across schools and in addressing the wider public: they have the potential to influence the paths of advancement while also leaving their mark on personality development. Given this power, it is understandable that grades are earnestly taken into account when teachers formulate their recommendations regarding continuation, and, in a similar way, that secondary schools consider the received information about 'personal value' as an important element when deciding about applications. These conditions have an impact also on the families who likewise cannot disregard their child's certificate: especially in cases of devaluation, poor grades start working by limiting the choices for advancement in the manner of a self-fulfilling prophecy.

However, these and similar stakes are not distributed evenly. First, grades do not carry the same degree of power everywhere. In some school systems, the right to choose freely among schools overrides the impediments of low grades: in principle, children and families can attempt to approach secondary schools where high prior performance is usually a 'card for entrance' but not a rigorously set prerequisite. Second, poor grades can be counterbalanced by outstanding performance in non-academic fields that might open the doors of the desired 'dream-school'. Third, families' dedication to education as the channel of upward social mobility might involve summoning their social capital if they benefit from helpful social contacts and patronage in accessing the best schools. Due to such countervailing potentials and forces, grades lose some of their importance: the measure of success is whether or not one is accepted by the coveted school, and grades become forgettable against this achievement.

Nevertheless, it is well known that the freedom of moving is limited: individual choices, and thus students' distribution along the hierarchy of schools, are strongly influenced by parents' social status. Differences in status involve significant departures in cultural capital which, in turn, shape students' knowledge and are ultimately acknowledged by departing grades. Country-specific studies as well as cross-country comparisons have richly demonstrated the close ties between social status and grades, as well as the intertwined effects of these on school choices (Paterson and Iannelli 2007, Holsinger 2009, Goldthorpe 2010). The univocal conclusion is clear: although the strength of the association might differ among the different countries and school systems, outstanding performance is, for the most part, a derivative of the high social position of the parental home. Nevertheless, when excellence informs continuation, selection among the departing paths appears to be an unbiased reflection of prior achievement, and in this way grading helps to hide the effect of the highly unequal forces and powers that are at play in the background.

However, as one moves down on the social scale, the associations become less clear. As recent studies in the UK and the US have demonstrated, it is not the current social status of the parents (that might be negatively affected by migration) but the families' dedication to schooling and their striving to become part of the mainstream that inspire many of the children from immigrant backgrounds to invest efforts in schooling which later pay with higher attendance in academic high schools and high rates of university entrance – often well above the respective ratios among their peers from the majority (Ferguson 2005, Modood 2005, Shah et al. 2010). At the same time, the lack of such commitment and aspirations keeps other post-migrant ethnic groups away from schooling, translates into poor grades, and brings about tracking into the lower echelons of the system or early departure from education below or just above the compulsory age.

Such a complexity of interactions between social status and minority background warrants a closer look at the role of ethnicity in shaping decisions about the paths of educational advancement and also calls for a closer examination of teachers' contribution to such deliberations by way of grading and supplemental advice. A number of important questions emerge: How do grading practices reflect ethnic diversity amidst the powerful social-class relations that forge children's options and future prospects? In more concrete terms, how do traits of ethnic 'otherness' translate into differential personal qualifications that then provide the basis for diverging pathways in education? If grades as personal 'labels' tend to diverge by ethnicity, how do such qualifications influence families' ways of thinking about the possible alternatives for continuation? Finally, how far is their freedom of choice preserved, and in what ways does the general outlook of their ethnic community inform the decisions?

The making of the 'ethnic ceiling'

The EDUMIGROM research provides a good ground for addressing the above questions. As described earlier, the study took place in relatively poor, multiethnic, working-class communities in five Western and four Central European countries. While the investigated communities as established localities with high ratios of second-generation migrant or Roma youths included a great number of households facing unemployment and enduring poverty, the proportion of better situated families occupying middle-class positions were high enough to see differences as much in parents' educational attainments as in familial occupations, well-being and social standing so that the relative importance of social and ethnic differences could be properly explored.

Young members of these communities in the concluding phase of compulsory education were approached in schools[1] by asking them about their grades[2] in the preceding semester and also about the choice they made regarding secondary-level schooling. In addition to the questionnaires filled in by all students in the selected schools in each community, a smaller group of pupils from ethnic minority backgrounds was invited to participate in in-depth interviews and focus group discussions about their plans, dreams and strategies concerning adulthood. Students' testimonies were complemented by interviews with their parents and teachers. The rich collection of qualitative materials gave us an opportunity to unwrap the sometimes sharply contrasting views and impressions about grading and its impact on the pathways of continuation.

By looking at various aspects of social background, the research pointed to the prime importance of parental cultural capital. Whether parents benefitted from weak or strong schooling has a strong and direct effect on their child's achievement. Out of those families in which at least one member holds a university degree, no less than 38 per cent of the children conclude the primary school with 'excellent' grades while the proportion falls to only 9 per cent among the offspring of uneducated parents. The association is similarly strong – though with a smaller range – at the other end of the grading scale: while 15 per cent of children of uneducated parents reach only the fragile level of 'sufficiency', such is the case of only 2.5 per cent of those coming from highly educated backgrounds, usually due to family crises and personal troubles. The strong impact of parents' education reflects the importance of the quantity and quality of knowledge that one brings from home. Even if concrete elements of this highly praised knowledge are not part of what parents themselves learned or acquired, those among them attending a university know how to search in a library, which encyclopaedia to take from the shelf, how to use a calculator and, above all, how to construct syllogisms and rational argumentation. Schools apparently build on these 'externalities' and do not consider it as their task to provide any substitute in cases where the relevant constituents of home-born knowledge and culture are missing.

However, a deeper look into the mediating role of cultural capital reveals further – largely unexpected – associations. It turns out that social status and the embodied knowledge and skills are profoundly impacted by ethnic background. Cultural capital in its full richness is valued by the school only in the case of children of highly educated parents from a majority background: the school is 'theirs', as it is reflected in the close to 50 per cent share of students in this group receiving 'excellent' grades. If parents are from an ethnic minority background, parts of their knowledge prove to be irrelevant while other parts are missing: it is as if they came from an environment with educational skills and knowledge that fail to have any use in their now home country while important other constituents are absent from their toolkit. Such unevenness in the adequacy among the constituents of cultural capital is reflected by the fact that only 21 per cent of the students from minority backgrounds attain 'excellence' while the respective ratio is still over 35 per cent among the children of parents with secondary school graduation from the majority. Devaluation continues down the cultural ladder: in a consistent way, whatever the level of cultural capital in their families, adolescents from ethnic minority backgrounds remain far below the achievement levels of their peers from the majority. At the extreme, the multiplier in difference grows huge: 8 per cent of the children from highly educated minority backgrounds conclude primary education with the high risk of class repetition due to poor results, while similar cases hardly occur (only in 1 per cent) in the respective status group of families from a majority background. These departures indicate that even if parents earned their diploma in the given country, their ethnic 'otherness' remains a source of deprivation. Religion and the perceived differences in values and routines in childrearing are often criticised by the school, and teachers feel compelled to send out signals of 'improper adaptation'. In other cases, it might be poverty and the daily difficulties of life that hinder the proper transmission of cultural capital. Yet in other cases, parents' downward occupational mobility and the implied burdensome conditions bring about obstacles to investing enough into their children's high performance (and good grades), whereby the hopes for the restitution of the family's social status by advancement of the next generation fade away within a short while.

Ethnicity seems so powerful that it overrides the general tendency for girls to hold an advantage in terms of grades. While such is the case for children from a majority background, the pattern disappears among those of ethnic minority origin. It is as if gender was 'unimportant' in the context of 'otherness': girls and boys become equally downgraded. The erasing of the gender distinctions suggests that minority children are not welcome to enter the gender-specific, distinct terrains of competition; instead they should observe the corners that are reserved for the ethnic 'others' in a rather undifferentiated way.

The picture is further refined by having a look at the institutional constellations. Given the strong tendencies of ethnic separation by schools, and also along streaming and tracking in the course of compulsory education, children from ethnic minority backgrounds find themselves in arrangements where they as 'others' are taught apart from the majority (in these communities, no less than two-thirds of ethnic minority children attend schools and classes in which peers from the majority are in the numerical minority or are actually absent). In addition to the often discriminatory enforcement of separation, such arrangements usually imply differential qualities of instruction that are frequently coupled with frustration on the part of the teachers who consider teaching ethnic minority children a matter of personal failure and devaluation. It is then no surprise that different schools with different reputations not only teach but also evaluate students according to departing standards. In schools and classes attended mainly by students from ethnic minority backgrounds, 'excellence' is rarely attained (in only 2–12 per cent of cases), while the risks of class repetition or ultimate dropping out are as high as 12–16 per cent among the students. These institutional distinctions are further exacerbated by ethnic divides on the individual level: in all school and class types, children from ethnic minority backgrounds conclude primary education with poor grades while their classmates from a majority background attain rather good assessments that, despite their school's bad reputation, assure them more or less trouble-free continuation.

By recalling the multiple functions of grading, we can learn the lesson: indeed, ethnic distinctions designate lowered positions in education as much for individual students from minority backgrounds as for the schools and classes where they dominate. In this way, minority students' low grades contribute to reinforcing social-class differences by 'othering' the value of one of its most powerful constituents: cultural capital. Early on, minority children are made aware of their inferior place in the school hierarchies of appreciation, and they are also informed that their ethnic 'otherness' matters more than do social-class and gender identities. Furthermore, their position in schools underscores and institutionalises 'otherness' by the dual stamps of individual and school-level downgrading. All in all, the associations reflect the high stakes that are implied in students' grades which influence their opportunities and set the limitations for advancement in a powerful way. Despite the fact that in the researched communities the poor and disadvantaged groups tend to be over-represented, differences in social background prove to be decisive both in terms of grades obtained and with regard to the self-projected future of the students.

However, ethnicity is an inherent part of the families' social status. As we saw above, the 'value' of the knowledge and skills of children from ethnic minority backgrounds proves to be of less worth than that of the students from a majority background, and the differences turn into departing positions and prospects. It is as if an invisible 'ethnic ceiling'[3] was emerging above which children belonging to ethnic minorities can hardly ever climb. This outcome is by nobody's design: in a certain sense, it is how the school-system translates into its own routines and processes the functioning of powerful 'ethnic ceilings' existing on the labour market and in access to prestigious occupations and lucrative positions. One may say that, in accordance with its functions to prepare for later position and status, the working of an 'ethnic ceiling' in education is part of these preparatory processes. At the same time, it also helps to maintain and regulate the prevailing inter-ethnic relations both on the personal level and in their implications for the ethnic groups' agency, influence and power in society at large. Furthermore, the 'ceiling' works as a useful means of socialisation because it seems to affect self-perception and one's views about the social order everywhere: the systematically distributed lower grades imply messages about low-esteemed status and depreciated personified value. No wonder these inputs of devaluation become part of how adolescents from ethnic minority backgrounds perceive themselves and their positions. Uncertainties in self-evaluation, low self-esteem, feelings of being discriminated against and reservations regarding one's potential for moving upward were recurrent elements in the face-to-face interviews all across our communities. The 'ceiling' likewise strongly affects future plans: resignation, turning away from education as 'useless' and lowered expectations towards the achievable adult career are frequent occurrences. If not as a limit and a threat, the 'ceiling' also informs the aspirations and self-evaluation of the most successful minority students: in their case it works as a deterrent and a source of motivation for avoidance. However, the 'ceiling' is a point of reference in their case as well: to a large extent, achievement and advancement are expressed by relating to it.

In addition to its implications for self-perception and personal development, the in-built 'ceiling' also impacts families' decisions about advancement. In fact, the social 'gains' of shaping the 'ceiling' come to the fore in this context: the set limits orient towards departing pathways and in this way reduce the competition for the precious upper echelons at the secondary level that preserve high status by maintaining exclusivity and scarcity. Furthermore, in a large part, secondary schooling prepares students for entering the world of labour at differential points. The 'ceiling' helps to orient low-performing ethnic minority adolescents to choose schools that respond to great labour market demand by preparing most of them to take up occupations with modest rewards and reputation. The unspoken public consensus finds its realisation: it is mainly those from ethnic minority backgrounds who are expected to fill such positions by which they indirectly encourage their peers from the majority to climb higher and engage in efforts targeting upward social mobility. In this way, the socialising effects and the structural impacts of the 'ethnic ceiling' meet: children and families take due consideration of the message that the lowered grades imply and they make their decisions accordingly.

Yet again the data confirm such a state of affairs. While graduation from a secondary school is widely regarded as a prerequisite for employability and as a protection against poverty in adulthood, there is a substantial ethnic gap in applying to tracks and schools that provide a high-school diploma or an equivalent certificate. When asked about their plans for continuation, the proportion of those indicating such educational paths was only somewhat less than two-thirds even among those ethnic minority students who had concluded the primary school with 'excellence', while it was close to 80 per cent among the equally well-performing peers from the majority. A deeper analysis reveals that aspiring to secondary-level graduation has become a universal norm among the majorities: regardless of children's preceding grades and the family's social standing, less or more educated parents find it compelling to at least make an attempt. At the same time, aspiring to graduation remains a direct derivative of the family's cultural capital in ethnic minority communities: in the tiny group of high-performing children of low-educated parents, it is only a third of the families who consider the option of sending the child to a school that provides graduation and thereby also opens access to higher education. The potency of the 'ethnic ceiling' is even more apparent at the lower end of the academic scale. Those with poorer grades turn to vocational training: although many of them still hope for graduation in some auxiliary form and then probably a college degree, most of them justify their choice by mentioning the advantages of an early start in gainful employment while also enjoying inclusion and equal rights that secondary schools that are overwhelmed with competition usually fail to provide. In addition to the higher proportions of ethnic minority youths in vocational training in comparison with their majority peers, the details expose sharp inequalities in placement. In short, those coming from the majority occupy the prestigious and most rewarding tracks, while children from minority backgrounds are often trained in outdated trades without access to the apprenticeship necessary to acquire expertise. The actual hazards of the working of the 'ethnic ceiling' come to light when looking at those who decide to quit school and leave education behind. Their proportion is no less than 45 per cent among the poorly performing students from ethnic minority backgrounds. True, the risk of dropping out also concerns poor working-class children from the majority. Nevertheless, the substantially lower proportion of 35 per cent of potential early leavers among those with poor results is further reduced by most of them maintaining an alternative option of a last-minute application to one of the nearby vocational schools. In this context, the 'ethnic ceiling' becomes a strong deterrent: coming from deep and lasting poverty, minority teenagers' ideas about the near future centre on adult tasks. By leaving education behind, they plan to find some work – and the further details do not matter too much. The primary goal is to help in the daily struggle of their family and their life strategy is conceived and shaped accordingly.

In sum, the 'ethnic ceiling' carries important implications well beyond the walls of the school. As we have seen, by developing the 'ceiling', schools acquire a useful tool to influence social-class relations and to fine-tune them along ethnic and cultural lines; at the same time, reference to the 'ceiling' assists them in socialising ethnic minority children towards developing behaviours and attitudes that imply the acceptance of the given state of affairs.

Although the findings justify these conclusions and show their prevalence in all of the nine, otherwise importantly differing, school systems covered by our research, it seems equally important to point to the remarkable variations in the ways in which the 'ceiling' comes into play in families' and schools' lives. The authority of the 'ceiling' also should be weighed against students' educational plans in the broader contexts of longer-term prospects and social embedding. In this latter regard, the historical arrangements and contents of inter-ethnic relations and the protective potentials of the respective welfare states make the picture highly differentiated.

The impact of the 'ethnic ceiling' in broader contexts

If one draws an invisible scale of greater or lesser degrees of power that grades from primary schools have in influencing students' future, it is the Scandinavian countries where the associations prove to be the weakest. As the interviews with minority children and their parents revealed, in Denmark and Sweden the widely shared and deeply internalised values of *equality and equity*, which shape public discourse and also people's perception of mundane relations, seem to set the framework in which ethnic minority teenagers formulate their ideas about the future and claim rights for quality education in concordance with their native peers. By taking advantage of the unrestricted freedom of choice on the educational market, and knowing that their preceding history of schooling has little implication for their admittance, they look at the range of secondary schools that might offer them a second chance. Although they report painful cases of being unfavourably distinguished and devalued by teachers and peers as 'bilinguals' who cannot hope for advancement on the social scale, such experiences apparently do not hold them back from struggling for highly praised middle-class positions. In their perception, structural discrimination in education and on the labour market creates relative hindrances but certainly does not lead to exclusion on ethnic grounds, nor does it undermine their citizenship rights with all of the rich contents that they account for among the great advantages of their now homeland. In this framework of addressing unjust inequalities, ethnic minority families claim support and affirmative interventions that make it conceivable for their children to successfully strive for high-ranking positions with public recognition, prestige and material rewards. As phrased by an Afghan boy in Stockholm: 'Parents have a lot to say about the children's future. They want you to have a job with status such as a doctor or a pilot.'

The recurring argumentation makes equality amidst diversity a firm ground for claims for inclusion: 'We are citizens as Danes are, and it is great that we have the same right for education.' Such a strong awareness of citizenship rights helps minority adolescents to engage in personal struggles for recognition: they successfully negotiate needs for extra attention and support and, though teachers often see such demands as putting an extra burden on their shoulders, schools are ready to seek some solutions, and to respond by recruiting ethnic minority teachers and employing ethnic minority personnel as mediators. However, the interviews reveal that the scope of opportunities is broader than what a school can offer: despite recent cuts in welfare spending and the rise of anti-immigrant sentiments in both countries, their welfare states are still strong enough to provide support for familial advancement. It is against this backing that the 'ethnic ceiling' is read mainly in its private and personified meanings but is not identified as blocking strategies for upward mobility. Hence, despite experiences of discrimination and the prevailing disadvantages in the attained grade scores, schooling becomes a strategy for ethnic minorities similar to how it is for the majority. As an Iranian parent in Sweden has put it, 'the clue to success is that my children have to attend a school visited by Swedes. They have to get the same education.' On the grounds of such dedication and the skilful capitalising on available resources, aspiring to become a doctor or a lawyer are popular ideas for minority adolescents in these communities, and for the most part they see it as a realistic goal to engage in occupations that are usually far above the horizon of their co-ethnic peers living in other countries.

In the post-colonial communities of France and England, the contextualisation of ideas about the future and views about the educational strategies that should be followed in order to meet one's expectations are markedly different. In both cases, people's firm visions about the *prevailing class structure* and the implications of low working-class positions shape families' aspirations to break through the invisible 'ceiling'. Such positions are often underscored by strong symbolic meanings that range from one's home address and the culturally perceived behaviours associated with given neighbourhoods, to the characteristic linguistic patterns of the peculiar 'ethnolect' that one speaks, and to the stereotypical views about 'who those people are'. In this context, residential segregation stands out as a major source of frustration for adolescents and parents from 'white' working-class backgrounds. Such sentiments recur in their accounts about the painful injustices of being confined to poor multiethnic communities and their subsequent exclusion from the mainstream to which they feel they 'should' belong. Concurrently, these deprived groups of working-class students often engage in varied forms of revolt against the unjust 'system' that, in their perception, is embodied by the school. As a result, absenteeism, truancy and class repetition are frequent occurrences that imply exclusion from school that is often followed by referral to one of the 'collector' units from where one's path rarely ever leads to continued education. These pathways of downward mobility towards marginalisation and social exclusion are also marked by ethnicity: teenagers from certain ethnic groups, such as Black Caribbean students in England and North Africans in France, who have traditionally been seriously devalued in their social environments, are over-represented among the drop-outs and early school leavers. However, widespread apprehension among these young people is of a different nature than that of their white working-class peers. These students and their parents consider outright *racism* as the primary cause of marginalisation and see themselves as victims of white cultural domination – be it phrased in socioethnic terms as in the UK, or framed as a manifestation of sharp class inequalities or as a matter of conflicting cultures, as in France.

Those minority students who see the opportunities for breaking away from poverty and attaining an acknowledged status in society also frame their ideas and claims in terms of social class. However, their perception of the prevailing class relations and their own future position seems more refined than that of the above marginalised groups. Without question, the model to follow is that of the upper segments of the urban middle class: one has to go to a good secondary school or attend a track that 'speaks for itself' and is advantageous enough to pave the road to university. All efforts have to be made to remain on the ascribed path lest one's entire life plan is compromised. A teacher in France characterised this orientation of Maghreb parents and (especially female) students:

> And also there's a lot of pressure from the families. We have the case of a girl who's dead set on getting a scientific Baccalaureate, and for the past two years things haven't been going well. And she's sick over it, really miserable. I'm thinking of another one who missed her Baccalaureate twice and who wanted to repeat for a third time and who was so unhappy and whom we had told so many times that there were other things she could do. We don't see the parents but we feel the pressure, the will to succeed.

Interviews with students and parents reinforced such a portrayal by emphasising that it is first and foremost the credentials that matter; the actual professional content of the skills that one acquires comes only next. Such a strong belief that having a degree could alter one's life also proved rather widespread among Pakistani parents in Britain who had the intention of firmly embedding themselves in British society. This was often done at the price of taking up low-prestige occupations and setting up a modest way of living. For these parents, the retrieval of the once acknowledged position of the family regardless of the prevailing 'ceiling' was seen as a primary aim. They strived for this by mobilising all possible means in order to help their children reach professional ranks by providing them with a good education:

> A good education means good GCSEs and good A-Levels, then going straight to university and then I don't mind what they want to do. I would love them to be doctors or lawyers but I can't force it on them,

whatever they want to do, but I would want them to do something professional ... because then they will have an easier life, they will have a good job. And if they have had that education ... you know that is why you want the best for your children. You don't want them to be in the same boat as you.

Another clear strategy that promises a way out of the endless reproduction of multiple ethnosocial disadvantages is demonstrated by families who are prompted by the invisible 'ethnic ceiling' to find alternative routes by accommodating within their own ethnic community. The traditions of kinship-based migration and the successful establishment of an ethnic market in significant Turkish communities in France and in important parts of the Pakistani communities living in northern cities in Britain provide entrepreneurial perspectives, decent living conditions, good reputations, and the protection and solidarity of their immediate social environments for many among the young generation. These adolescents use the same frame of reference of social-class belonging as do their more disadvantaged co-ethnic peers. However, they distance themselves from being discriminated against in the outer world by forging pathways of upward mobility within their own ethnic enclave (Zhou 2005).

Germany represents a distinct example in the macrosocial framing of longer-term perspectives and immediate educational outlook of ethnic minority youth. Our interviews and focus-group discussions clearly reflect the tense relationship between the majority and the dominantly Muslim ethnic minorities that one learns about day after day from the media and that was recently authoritatively summed up by the German chancellor, Angela Merkel, in her infamous announcement: 'Multiculturalism has utterly failed in Germany.' The tensions certainly have multiple sources. First, until very recently, Germans' self-perception as being open and tolerant towards ethnic minorities has been coupled with their tacit expectation that immigrants would return home and thus allow their 'hosts' to maintain ethnic and cultural homogeneity in their country. Second, the attempts to create a homogenous German nation-state were burdened by the post-1990 unification process that turned out to be far more arduous than expected and that, ironically, has induced hurtful rivalries for work and welfare between large groups of impoverished 'Ossies' and their Turkish, Arab and Eastern European fellow countrymen. The involved economic struggles are often viewed as conflicts of cultures, moral standards and conducts of daily life, and 'immigrant minorities' are portrayed as uninterested in progress and disloyal to their hosts. Third, ethnic differences have become heavily laden with deep and stark divides in the social structure: ethnic minority belonging has increasingly become identical with marginalised working-class positions and social exclusion in the form of sharp residential segregation. Thus the arising conflicts inseparably carry ethnic and social-class implications that are exacerbated by constant cultural clashes on religious grounds.

In this multilayered understanding of inter-ethnic relations, it is the conceptual creation of sharply differing *cultural entities* of 'us' and 'them' that guides ethnic minority families in defining their position and, especially, in orienting their children towards given pathways of education and occupation. Adolescents' ideas about the future are distinctly less clear than those of their peers in the above Western communities. The words of a Lebanese girl dreaming about becoming a doctor clearly demonstrate the sense of uncertainty: 'I shouldn't exaggerate. It might be more appropriate to get vocational training in the medical realm and then let's see. I'm unsure what's possible and what's not.'

Against such a deeply felt power of the 'ceiling' that induces uncertainties, future careers are seen in broadly perceived cultural terms. In this context, it is the recognition and respect of Islam and the traditions of a Muslim way of life that are considered to be the preconditions of young people's success. Turkish and Lebanese adolescents clearly see that they have to make a choice between two contrasting alternatives, either by accepting the strong assimilationist pressure that is mediated by the majority of their teachers, or by following the rules and patterns of their own community and establishing themselves in a closed Muslim world with modest perspectives in terms of social status that is defined as a 'parallel universe' to that of the Germans. In their daily lives, children are often torn between these two contrasting ends: the permanent exposure to criticism and clashing requirements contributes to their uncertainties and often concludes in downward mobility across schools and tracks. For those who do not give up, self-protection and the struggles to maintain open doors towards 'German-like' occupations with rewarding status and material wealth require a constant involvement in a two-sided struggle for rights and respect. A Turkish girl said:

> One does not have to adjust in every aspect. The Germans also have to understand that we have a different religion and some different opinions about how we want to live our private lives. But teachers put such a huge pressure on us that I don't know how to react. They should accept the differences. Do we criticise their way of living? No, we don't but we expect them not to do so as well.

However, it is not easy to keep a balance. One either leaves behind the community and strives for some respected position no matter what the costs may be, or abandons high aspirations and follows pathways in schooling, working and living according to the customary norms of the community. While the desire for upward mobility is part of the ideas of many minority parents and children, the risks may seem too big to make an attempt. Besides the generally known uncertainties and the hindrances generated by the working of the ethnic 'ceiling', bad experiences of some older members of the family may warn the young students against overly ambitious aspirations. A Turkish girl recalled her father's cautionary words:

> Do you want to end like your relatives? Look at them. [With all of their fine degrees] they are unemployed and have to prove to the labour agency that they are constantly applying for jobs. They are controlled all the time, always bothered by officials. – You should find a decent vocation.

Finally, the case of the four Central European countries stands out in a caste-like exclusion of Roma that allows, at best, for scattered individual attempts at integration by those who accept and internalise the assimilationist arrogance of the norm-setting mainstream but that, as a rule, keeps the minority community far removed from the opportunities and positions available for the majority. For most Roma, deep and enduring poverty transmitted from one generation to the next, scarce access to regular employment, long periods of joblessness, confined residence in ghetto-like areas in dilapidated former industrial towns or under virtually pre-modern conditions in remote villages belong to the accustomed experiences from an early age. The shared fate of being cut off from the world ruled by *gadjo* people establishes a certain degree of commonality that uniformly designates an appallingly limited scope of future paths for the new generations, despite important divisions by ethnic subgroups and also along well-remembered earlier achievements, different degrees of material possessions and personal histories of being integrated through employment during state socialism. From the majority's perspective, these conditions of utter deprivation are perceived as the Roma-specific traits of the 'culture of poverty' that Roma are morally responsible for maintaining and that provides the *ultima ratio* for their distinction and ensuing separation. In these abasing contexts of deprivation and 'justified' ethnic discrimination, Roma adolescents and their parents frame their claims for advancement in the language of *human rights and integration*. A Roma father in Romania with only five years of elementary education put it in a telling way: 'Romanians or Hungarians should not believe that they have more fingers than we have; they should not treat us as fools; that's why we need to go to school and to prove that we are their equals, we are gentlemen Gypsies.' Unlike ethnic minorities in the northern countries who, on account of their civic and political inclusion, struggle for equality in the economic and social domains, the claims of Roma target the substance of democracy: their struggle concerns the fundamental human rights of dignity, respect and personal safety. Education is seen as the battlefield of such struggles where many are harmed and defeated from the outset. An early departure from schooling (which involves Roma in a proportion exceeding all other ethnic minority groups) is a self-explanatory response to the gradual disaffection that students develop and that is deepened by the amassed experience of the community with the depreciating workings of all majority institutions, concisely expressed by a Roma teenager in Hungary: 'There is no use in graduating from high school when your origin prevents you from being hired anywhere. They always say the job has been filled.'

For Roma students, the usefulness of staying in education and continuing on the secondary level is also questioned by the pressing need to contribute to the family's difficult day-to-day struggles for survival. Under the conditions of their ongoing efforts to provide the minimally required means for mere subsistence, continued education appears to be an unaffordable luxury.

At the same time and despite the widespread occurrence of early departures from education, the majority of Roma youths and their parents are dedicated to continuing beyond the elementary level. However, the plans are shaped in awareness of the existence of a low set 'ethnic ceiling'. For the most part, adolescents dream of vocations where experience has shown that the majority tolerate the presence of Roma, as in construction work or traditional industrial occupations; or they plan to engage in certain services, such as hairdressing or shoe-making, where it is the ethnic community itself that would provide the consumers and the purchasing power. At the same time, all of the mentioned vocations imply an inferred hope to move towards becoming integrated through decent work. This is clear from the reasoning of a Czech Roma mother:

My daughter, she tells me all the time, she doesn't want to study any more, because she has no chance to work with children afterwards, so she'd rather go to the employment office, find a job and help me. But I tell her: 'No way! I did not study and... these days if one does not have a vocational certificate, one has no chance to get a good job.' Whoever it is. So I told her: 'You don't want to study? Well. It is your fault then. You are going to spoil your own life.'

At the same time, attempts to acquire a vocation above the invisible but tacitly acknowledged 'ethnic ceiling' are severely penalised by humiliation and exclusion. A Hungarian Roma mother said:

My daughter had a classmate who was also Roma and wanted to study food supply. She was accepted at the school and so a shop had to be found where she could do an internship. The reason why she has never become a shop assistant was that, wherever she tried, she was told that if she had touched the ham, no one would come to the store any more.

However, there are a few who try to break through and aspire to attain a degree in higher education. Those brave girls and boys from better-situated Roma families, who are successful students attending more esteemed schools and are striving to attain higher positions in the social hierarchy than – according to the customary patterns – most of their co-ethnic peers would, usually aspire to practice-oriented professional careers, such as nursing in a hospital or geriatric care, running a general practice as a medical doctor, working as a production analyst at a firm, primary school teaching and so on. However, their high aspirations are often subverted by the teachers who intend to 'protect' them from future disappointments by mediating the perceived refusal of the majority, as the following testimony of the mother of a Hungarian Roma student illustrates: 'my niece passed her school-leaving exam...she was a good student, her skin was dark, she was Roma. She wanted to be an economist. The teacher told her to not even dare to dream about being "Emese in the Budapest Bank" – like in the advertisement!'

In light of such harsh depreciation and the pressures to maintain Roma people at a clear distance from the majority's world, it is certainly no surprise that the proportion of young Roma attending higher education remains below 1 per cent in all four of the Central European countries, hence the lack of successful role models like those who have such a positive impact on inspiring ethnic minority youth in the West. This is yet another item on the list of painful deficits suggesting that today's Roma adolescents are apparently destined to encounter the same fate of exclusion suffered by their parents and grandparents.

Closing words

We have seen that an 'ethnic ceiling' emerging out of the overt and covert implications of grading seems to characterise the educational systems across Europe. Despite the differing power of the 'ceiling', its prime function is shared in that it implies a message about the lesser 'worth' of the inputs and achievements of young people from ethnic minority backgrounds. In this way, the 'ethnic ceiling' refines social-class relations and fine-tunes the applicability of cultural capital so that their lower grades typically orient minority students towards certain less valued segments in education than the ones occupied by their peers from the majority. While these tendencies seem to prevail everywhere, the 'ceiling' in itself does not carry enough authority to determine access to good education and valued jobs if strong countervailing forces are in place. These forces usually come from outside education: minorities' social rights, the success of their recognition struggles for equality and equity, and the provisions of the welfare states assisting minorities' efforts to overcome poverty and strive for upward social mobility may override the messages of the 'ceiling' and might suggest that minority children should ignore them. In brief, we can then say that a successful limitation of the destructive power of the 'ceiling' is a matter of the state and contents of citizenship and, as such, it measures the strength of democracy. After all, it is this latter context in which ethnic minorities' fates and futures are moulded in education as well as beyond.

Notes

1. As described earlier in this book, the EDUMIGROM research was hosted by two selected multiethnic, working-class communities in each of the nine participating countries. In these communities, preliminary fieldwork revealed the institutional arrangements of schooling for those who were in the final year of compulsory education. (Depending on the great variations among the school systems, these schools either served primary education or provided education and/or training in the first and second years at the secondary level.) When such local educational maps had been constructed, the research teams identified the schools that were attended by the majority of local ethnic minority children, who made up, at the same time, a significant part of the institutions' student body. The questionnaires were distributed among all students in all of the parallel classes (courses) of the selected schools. Our respondents were asked about a range of issues that involved details about the family (parents' education and occupation, their labour market history and, if relevant, migration history, and also the educational careers of siblings); details about liked and disliked school subjects and recently attained grade scores with respect to each; feelings of comfort and discomfort at school; peer relations and activities done together with others; experiences of discrimination at school and in the wider community; relationships with teachers; and, finally, plans for and visions about adulthood. Students' ethnic belonging was determined by their self-identification and it was their statements that then provided the basis for distinguishing the two large groups of 'minorities' and 'the majority'. Figures and proportions in this chapter emerged from processing the data of a compiled file that comprised all of the comparable variables of the national samples.
2. While grading is applied in all of the investigated countries, the actual scales and indicators show great variation. In order to assure comparability, the domestic grades were translated into the European Credit Transfer System (ECTS) that serves as the 'Esperanto' of the diverse systems of evaluation. This scoring system allowed for a comparison of students and schools with each other across borders. Furthermore, it facilitated the construction of a series of aggregate indicators.
3. In conceptualising the 'ethnic ceiling', my work was greatly inspired by John Ogbu's theory of the operating of a 'job ceiling' for Blacks in the US educational system (Ogbu 1978).

6
Education in the European Multicultural Debates and Policies

Violetta Zentai

Introduction

Long before the rise of broader multicultural debates and policies, the literature began to highlight the fact that educational systems are sites of social reproduction that offer unequal access to socially relevant knowledge to different socioethnic groups. By providing knowledge and skills to youths who differ in a number of social and cultural grounds, schooling largely determines young people's later position in the labour market and general social status. Furthermore, schools facilitate and constrain young people's paths to shaping their identities, community ties and career aspirations. Several cross-country comparative studies, such as the EDUMIGROM research programme, have revealed that ethnic, religious, linguistic minority youths often face varied forms of exclusion. The hopes and ambitions to escape from the discriminatory implications of ethnic 'otherness' and the frequently accompanying socioeconomic disadvantages greatly impact minority youths' educational careers. Educational systems and schools are differently positioned to respond to these ambitions (Crossley and Broadfoot 1992). One can argue that educational systems and their services demonstrate the quality of thinking regarding social diversity and inclusion in societies.

The literature on multiculturalism has produced a vast body of writing about the normative and theoretical underpinnings of multicultural claims and policy frames. Debates about social diversity composed by ethnic, religious, linguistic and other cultural traditions have gone through important changes in European countries during the last two decades. These changes are connected to new trends of migration, the enlargement of the European Union, and shifts in European thinking regarding inequality and social inclusion. The debates are influenced by the history of relations between mainstream societies and their respective minority and immigrant groups. In addition to these larger trends, European societies within and outside the EU have developed their own distinctive social and political practices through which they relate to their social diversity.

This chapter intends to highlight the place of education in multicultural policies in Europe, to consider some well-known and less obvious outcomes of these policies, and to reflect upon the current debates about the future of multiculturalism, social equality and fairness in the distribution of educational goods as a way to protect young people from ethnic minority backgrounds from exclusion.

Multicultural policy regimes in Europe

The very language by which social heterogeneity is addressed as a public policy issue has a dynamic history. Today we usually make a distinction between social integration, inclusion, multiculturalism and diversity management because they have different connotations and refer to different conceptual frames.

The term 'multiculturalism' is often used to portray trends in state practices since the 1960s through which Western democracies have shown increasing recognition of social diversity, either in the form of meeting land claims of indigenous peoples, or by providing language rights and regional autonomy for national minorities, and accommodation models for immigrant groups (Banting and Kymlicka 2012). Others view multicultural policies as composed by public recognition, laws, access to education and social services, the conditions for religious accommodation and distinct lifestyle (food), and access to specific media for groups with distinctive traditions, language, ethnicity, culture and faith (Vertovec and Wessendorf 2010). Another group of theorists characterise multicultural policies as a combination of welfare provisions for individual citizens and group-based recognition (Kymlicka 1995, Joppke and Lukes 1999, Koopmans et al. 2005, Parekh 2006). At the heart of all conceptualisations are the problems of regulating unity and difference in social practices, legitimising and organising the distribution of divisible and non-divisible public goods, and guiding the relations between citizens and their state where faith, language, ethnic identity and cultural traditions divide and connect people.

This chapter will use the notion of multiculturalism to address public affairs related to both migrations and national minorities, to polities of the old and new post-Cold-War democracies, and to important debates on social diversity along ethnic, racial, language, religious and cultural lines in society.

Policy regimes are understood as the complexity of the policy-making processes together with the main ideas, actors and institutions in a particular field. Along these lines we conceive of *multicultural regimes* as sets of policy paradigms or frames, designated actors, and instruments, in the field of managing social heterogeneity on different levels and in different domains of public affairs. These policies are often laced together in a patchwork of more accommodating and more restrictive measures and practices with mixed outcomes. The patchwork nature of policy regimes on broader equality matters in the European nation-states is taken on board by several authors (Bell 2003, Prügl and Thiel 2009). Therefore one should be cautious about presenting any typology in this domain to avoid overstating the degree of coherence that characterises multicultural ideas and practices in a given polity. Measures not specifically targeting migrants and national minorities, unintended consequences of past policies, and non-interventions into market, microsocial and family affairs actively and powerfully shape contextual elements of different policy regimes as much as purposeful policy efforts do. Nonetheless, the intellectual temptation is strong to explain why societies and states react differently to the challenges of social diversity and to pinpoint the consequences.

Inquiries regarding multicultural regimes are more numerous concerning the old Western democracies and scarce as far as Southern European and post-socialist countries are concerned. The most comprehensive approaches portray how from the late 1960s a number of countries, such as Australia, Canada, the US, the UK, Sweden and the Netherlands, have tried to translate the concept of multiculturalism into meaningful policy measures. There is relatively little debate about which regimes are the most and the least accommodating to migrants and national minorities. Leading scholars of multicultural affairs suggest that within Europe it is the Netherlands that has taken multiculturalism furthest in spite of a visible retreat in recent times. In addition, Sweden, Belgium and the UK are mentioned as polities which have taken serious steps towards multiculturalism. It is also reported that, ironically, several countries have never got close to the notion of multiculturalism yet nowadays they are loudly stepping back from it (Modood 2007, Triandafyllidou and Modood 2011, p. 16, Modood 2012, p. 47). In a recent comparative inquiry about multicultural regimes in Europe, Koopmans (2010) points out that, although policies developed to handle migrants' social integration initially appeared to be similar in North-Western Europe, the societies in question have moved in different directions over time. Countries with a pronounced ethnic tradition of citizenship, such as Germany, Austria and Switzerland, have set high barriers to migrants becoming full citizens and made residence rights conditional. These countries show modest recognition of cultural specificity. The Netherlands and Sweden understand integration through immigrants' easy access to full citizenship rights, secured residence and tangible respect for the immigrants' languages and cultures. France has followed a path which combines an approach to equality targeting individuals and reluctance to recognise and promote differences between cultural groups.

By referring to the Migration and Integration Policy Index (MIPEX) (Migration Policy Group 2011),[1] Koopmans offers a comprehensive picture of current multicultural regimes in 25 member states of the EU as well as in Norway, Switzerland and Canada. Each country's performance in terms of integration policy is assessed through a composite account of practices in six areas: access to nationality, long-term residence, anti-discrimination, family reunion, labour market access and political participation (Koopmans 2010, p. 4). Resonating with influential theorems of Kymlicka, Parekh and Modood, Koopmans proposes identifying a second dimension of migrant rights in addition to the legal protection of individual immigrants: they should have group-based cultural rights and they also have to develop some cultural knowledge of and respect for the host country in order to obtain full citizenship. By comparing the 2007 values of the MIPEX with the outcomes of an earlier measurement tool, Koopmans found that cross-national differences have been remarkably stable over the period 1995–2007. Sweden, Belgium and the Netherlands came out as the top three countries in both years. Austria and Switzerland offered the least equality-friendly legal provisions in both years. France and Germany scored in the middle of the pool in both years. The UK showed a clear advance from 1995 to 2007 (a result that should be read with some reserve due to imperfections in the measurements). When adding to the index the acknowledgment of cultural rights, the Netherlands came top followed by the UK in second place and Germany in an intermediate position. France and Switzerland grant relatively few cultural rights to immigrants and demand a relatively high degree of cultural conformity in public institutions. France shows a clear contrast when setting the two dimensions of citizenship because it is relatively inclusive in the individual equality dimension but reluctant to grant cultural rights on the basis of group membership (Koopmans 2010, p. 6).

In a new volume edited by Triandafyllidou and Zapata-Barrero (2012), a geographically broader overview is provided about the policy regimes on social diversity across Europe. In addition to assessing the large Western European host countries, the editors offer insights into the policies towards the minorities of Greece, Italy, Spain, Ireland and Cyprus that have also experienced major labour migration during the past two decades. These new host countries have rather restrictive naturalisation policies and see citizenship as a prize that should be deserved by integration rather than as a tool for integration. It is also pointed out that the integration policies of the new hosts are mainly shaped by the grassroots initiatives of civil society actors rather than framed as state policies.[2] Triandafyllidou and Zapata-Barrero acknowledge that, moving eastwards on the map of Europe, in the Central and Eastern European countries the rights of native minorities are largely guaranteed, partly due to European accession requirements and monitoring. However, the provisions for integrating newcomers remain rather poor (pp. 7–10). Further, the issue of the Roma minority in the post-socialist countries stands out as a highly controversial political and a pressing policy problem.

When considering the types of multicultural policy regime in Europe, it is also essential to examine how *welfare provisions* delivered by the nation-states relate to ethnic heterogeneity. Data on this relationship are controversial. A large and often cited comparative study by Alesina and Glaeser (2004) demonstrates that there is a negative correlation between racial diversity and the level of social spending. Other authors also argue that ethnic heterogeneity has a largely negative effect on welfare spending (Sanderson and Vanhanen 2004). Mau and Burkhardt raised questions about such a neat correlation. They tested data from 16 Western European countries from the European Social Survey 2002–2003 and arrived at the conclusion that societies which are relatively heterogeneous are not necessarily restrictive in their welfare provisions (Mau and Burkhardt 2009). Others highlight both convergence and divergence across Europe by refining the welfare regime typologies, taking into account different types of migration flow, and also examining the relative importance of labour market regimes within or in addition to welfare services (Sainsbury 2006, Carmel et al. 2012).

Educational systems are understood as part and parcel of multicultural regimes. The MIPEX offers a complex insight into citizenship and migration policy regimes by embracing all members of the EU (plus other 'old' democracies). As a seventh policy area, the measurement tool includes the field of education from the second full round of assessment conducted in 2010. Education policy is understood to be composed by equal access to all levels of education for all, targeting the specific needs of migrant children and their families, providing new opportunities to all children by bringing migrant experience into the school, and supporting parents and teachers in accommodating to intercultural education. A quick review of the values of the education indicators measured in 2010 shows that the specific components of education policies in the nine countries of the EDUMIGROM research are not closely tied to each other. For example, the UK and Denmark produce their high scores by very mixed achievements in the four key areas, and likewise the relatively low overall education policy score for France is the outcome of diverse performance in the four areas. It is obvious that one cannot use the MIPEX tailored to a migration agenda to examine policy regimes in Central and Eastern Europe concerning the inclusion of native Roma. By the same token, the conceptual frame of the index may inspire multicultural policy thinkers and critics, intrigued by the very differences in MIPEX values among Central and Eastern European polities, when assessing policies on social diversity including Roma.[3]

From among the key components of the education systems, ensuring good-quality service in compulsory education for all children should be of prime interest to the cause of multicultural inclusion of minority youth. In the relevant literature (Woessmann 2004, OECD 2007b, 2010, Pfeffer 2008, Schuetz et al. 2008, Schnell and Crul, Chapter 3 in this volume), it is agreed that the timing and rigidity of streaming and tracking of students are key instruments of stratification and/or equalisation, and thus also subjects of multicultural policies. In weakly stratified educational systems, the majority of students attend comprehensive schools with late tracking and the possibility of between-tracks mobility. Further, access to post-secondary education is not predetermined by the choice of a given track. In highly stratified systems, the selection of students into academic tracks occurs early, resulting in low mobility between the tracks and educational dead-ends blocking paths to higher education. In his often cited study, Pfeffer (2008) classifies several OECD countries according to selected institutional features of their national education systems. He places the Anglo-Saxon and the Scandinavian countries in the cluster of low-degree educational stratification. In contrast, most continental European countries with their early tracking and low degree of educational mobility run highly stratified educational systems. The former state-socialist countries (including the Czech Republic, Hungary, Poland and Slovenia) are located in the middle, together with Belgium and Italy.

Based on this quick overview, one can argue that educational stratification/equalisation policy models and complex multicultural policy regimes do not generate two identical European maps when layered onto each other. For example, Sweden stands out as a pioneer on both grounds followed by the UK, which makes deliberate efforts to offer citizenship by acknowledging difference and making efforts to ensure equal opportunities in schooling. Denmark can be seen as a reluctant state in relation to social diversity issues while being committed to low stratification in education. The Netherlands appears as a truly multicultural champion with a school system of relatively strong stratification but allowing movement between tracks. Germany is a slowly moving country on the ground of multiculturalism and, until recently, a deeply committed implementer of stratification policies in education. Central and Eastern European countries with large Roma minorities tend to intensify stratification in education while showing reluctance to develop multicultural strategies.

When investigating the degree of social inclusion of second-generation migrant and indigenous Roma youths in Europe, the EDUMIGROM project encountered European multicultural policy regimes largely in congruence with the country groups and tracks noted above. The research captured three clusters of policy regimes regarding social diversity: *genuinely multicultural* (Sweden and the UK), *partially restrictive* (Denmark, Germany and France) either with old colonial or with economic migrant minority populations, and *segmented* regimes (the Czech Republic, Hungary, Romania and Slovakia), where the treatment of different ethnic and national minorities (including migrants) is diverging depending on the groups' social and political status. Nevertheless, during the course of the research it has become appealing to consider a slightly different type of European map. When examining the major types of social and political context in which educational policies affect minority youth, the historical patterns of inter-ethnic relations have been identified as one of the key contextual elements of multicultural policy regimes. This thinking has been inspired by the acknowledgement that all modern societies embrace particular degrees and domains of social difference, and embody various regimes of citizenship as the outcome of their state-building histories and historical constructs of national identities. In this regard one can identify three types of domestic condition shaping citizenship policies: the *post-colonial states* with subsequent waves of immigration in which the majority in domination has developed multilayered relationships and integration patterns towards migrants and their descendants; states embracing significant *labour migration* (and, to a smaller extent, asylum seekers and refugees) from various regions of the world from the 1960s and 1970s on, and gradually accommodating to the continued presence of migrants; and the *post-socialist states* with sizeable Roma communities (and a smaller flow of migrants after 1989) whose 'difference' from the majority population became pronounced after the collapse of state socialism and whose saliently disadvantageous status has appeared as a grave political challenge since then. This triadic understanding of broader social contexts, combined with a scrutiny of multicultural policy regimes and school practices, proved to provide powerful explanatory frames to interpret the educational experiences of minority youth in localities and schools of mixed ethnicity, language or religion.

Social outcomes of multicultural policies in education

Multicultural studies, in addition to critically explaining different political and policy choices across polities, seek to understand the link between policy interventions and outcomes. Capturing policy outcomes entails well-known methodological challenges that are by no means less formidable in multicultural policy research. In the following, the outcomes of educational policies and schooling practices on the lives of ethnic minority youths in different European polities will be assessed. This review will be necessarily limited in its scope and target.

In addition to identifying policy models of multicultural citizenship, Koopmans (2010) investigates how integration policies and welfare regimes have influenced the integration of immigrants, focusing on eight European countries: Austria, Belgium, France, Germany, Sweden, Switzerland, the Netherlands and the UK. Comparative data are produced to assess policy results in labour market participation, spatial segregation and incarceration outcomes. The results are contrary to the high hopes of multicultural theories: when combined with a generous welfare state, policies providing immigrants easy access to equal rights have produced low levels of labour market participation, high levels of segregation and an over-representation of minorities among delinquents. Sweden, Belgium and the Netherlands belong to this cluster of policy and social outcomes. According to Koopmans, this can be explained by limited incentives for host-country language acquisition and inter-ethnic contacts. Those countries that have either more restrictive or assimilationist integration policies (Germany, Austria, Switzerland and France) or a relatively modest welfare state (the UK) have achieved better integration results. The UK appears to be an exception with its relatively high segregation rates as opposed to its good performance in the other two domains (Koopmans 2010, p. 18)

It is worth referring to recent labour market participation data which seem to refute the somewhat surprising thesis on low labour market participation amidst high multicultural provisions (Kahanec et al. 2010). More importantly for our topic, and also in contrast with Koopmans' account, recent comparative research among children from immigrant backgrounds pointed out that the educational attainment of migrant students is comparatively greater in countries with lower levels of economic inequality, larger investments in childcare and a well-developed system of pre-school education (Heckmann and NESSE 2008). The OECD's PISA 2009 survey results demonstrate that, with few exceptions, first- and second-generation migrant students exhibit poorer performance than non-immigrants, the differences exceeding a score equivalent to one year of instruction. The size of the performance gap among these groups varies markedly, however, across countries. The PISA data also allow for highlighting that, among the countries which assist migrant youths to produce good school achievements and also make efforts to provide schooling that can compensate for the lower status of families, one can find the Netherlands, Sweden, the UK and Switzerland. Good academic achievements are obtained together with a greater impact of the families' socioeconomic background in Germany and France. Lower achievements with enhanced impacts of the socioeconomic differences of families can be observed in Austria (OECD 2011, pp. 90–91).

Accordingly, the countries whose educational systems are best able to compensate for a disadvantaged social background can be found in each major type of multicultural regime (restrictive, committed multicultural and in between). Among the countries with good academic achievements but with poorer equalising effects are conservative welfare regimes with restrictive or mixed inclusion provisions. None of the old European host countries is in the worst category of low achievements with low equality results (but Spain and Greece are there). The absolute difference between the reading performance scores of second- and first-generation immigrants as measured in the PISA tests is relatively high in Sweden and the UK, potentially commending these countries for ensuring education mobility for migrants, while it is low in the Netherlands and Belgium, demonstrating a modest achievement rise among their migrant families in the short run (assuming that there is no big difference in the ethnic composition of the different generations). The more restrictive countries (Austria, France and Switzerland) produce moderate results in the reading performance between generations of migrants

(OECD 2011, p. 98). The difference in the reading performance scores of the natives and second-generation migrants is relatively high in all major host nations with the exception of the UK and, to a lesser extent, the Netherlands, confirming the observations regarding the tangible inclusion outcomes of the most committed multiculturalist polities.

Recent empirical inquiries have examined particular enactments of multicultural policies in European urban settings, the social and political contexts of which positively deviate from the respective national policy regimes. These cities, however, offer suitable spaces for comparative inquiries regarding multicultural policy outcomes. By relying on Vertovec's notion of superdiversity, Crul and Schneider (2010) investigate large cities and their second-generation migrant communities. The authors pursue a combined agenda of identifying the institutional arrangements that state and municipal policies promote and examining the outcomes of these arrangements. To gauge the role of educational systems in facilitating ethnic mixing, Crul and Schneider study the same ethnic group of Turks across several polities and localities. In Germany and Austria, one can find high proportions of second-generation Turks with upper secondary degrees and a few with a college degree, while their fathers accomplished only primary education. In France, one can find a more even distribution of second-generation Turks in all three categories of schooling. The Netherlands again demonstrates mixed results with a high proportion at the college level but the lowest in the upper secondary schooling category among the countries observed. In Sweden, second-generation Turks have achieved truly high mobility in schooling with high percentages in the upper two categories of schooling (Crul and Schnieder 2010, p. 1256). One may ask the question: To what extent do these results concur with, or contest, Koopmans' findings regarding the controversial multicultural policy outcomes across Europe? Is it Germany and Austria that produce good integration results in upper secondary education for migrants, or is it Sweden with its high social mobility based on schooling statistics or is it France with its large share of second-generation Turks holding college degree providing pathways of integration for the offspring of low-educated fathers? Further research should help to find clear answers to these puzzles.

The EDUMIGROM research, which concentrated on some selected minority groups and specific school sites across Europe, offers an incomplete yet broad European picture of the academic achievements of minority ethnic youths. As several chapters of this volume argue, the overall educational performance of ethnic minority youths in the nine investigated countries looks much less favourable than that of their majority peers, with some important internal variations. The performance of second-generation migrant youth displays multiple correlations with the social capital of the ethnic group concerned, the available social assistance for accommodating to the host country environment, and the state of interethnic relations in their now home country. Coming from an ethnic minority background implies a good deal of vulnerability, even if paired with relatively good socioeconomic conditions. Furthermore, 'visible' minorities in the old democracies of Europe have poorer chances of keeping up with their majority peers in educational performance than their 'white' peers of Eastern and Southern European origin (see Szalai, Chapter 5 in this volume). There are fewer significant variations in the performances of Roma children across the post-socialist countries when posited against the respective majorities. The academic attainments and opportunities to drop out, on the one hand, and to continue in secondary and upper secondary education, on the other, are invariably less for the Roma than for the non-Roma youths in the four Central European countries of the EDUMIGROM inquiry. Do these results contradict the findings of the comparative discussion of Huttova et al. (2008), whose analysis uncovered that the disadvantaged situation of children from migrant and ethnic backgrounds was influenced by largely similar conditions and practices throughout Europe, including the structure of the educational system; the practice of tracking; segregation within and between neighbourhoods and schools; direct and indirect discrimination in the classroom; and curriculum bias? No contradiction is to be found if we link the notion of academic achievements with other important outcomes of schooling in an ethnically diverse social environment. Most notably, self-esteem, aspirations, and social ties of ethnic minority youths are also fundamentally influenced by school practices and contribute to these young people's social capital. Social capital, in turn, is crucial for the educational and career prospects of young people from migrant, national, religious and linguistic minority backgrounds and to overcome disadvantages in their social positions.

According to the EDUMIGROM outcomes, in the participating two Scandinavian countries, Sweden and Denmark, the values of equality shape not only public discourse but also ethnic minority youths' ideas about their future. Educational practices produce a fair level of equality amidst diversity and thus create patterns of inclusion with some remaining disadvantages for minority youth. These 'other' young people do not feel excluded on ethnic grounds in spite of their experiences of discrimination in education and on the labour market. It is important to note that in Denmark the equality of all citizens is genuinely believed in and pursued by targeted policies but primarily on the ground of assimilationist ideals (Carson et al. 2011, Moldenhawer and Padovan-Özdemir 2011). A very different set of social and political conditions influence the educational and longer-term ideals of ethnic minority youth in Germany. Adolescents from immigrant backgrounds see their future careers through a recognition struggle of Muslims or self-endorsement of their values and traditions. Turkish and Lebanese adolescents in the selected neighbourhoods face the choice of either accepting the strong assimilationist pressure by the majority or following the rules of their own community. Their communities are often seen by the majority as having established themselves in a 'parallel universe' of Muslim traditions (see Straßburge, Chapter 12 in this volume). At the same time, large groups of young people from immigrant backgrounds consciously pursue schooling towards occupations with a rewarding status in the mainstream (Mannitz 2011).

The EDUMIGROM research has found variegating strategies among the youth groups in the selected communities of France and the UK. In the lower-working-class environments, residential segregation is the paramount condition of everyday life and social relations. Ethnic migrant groups of compact segregation (Black Caribbean students in the UK; North Africans in France) often revolt against their marginalisation by departing early from school. Another group of the second-generation migrant adolescents try to accommodate to the mainstream by accepting a low ranking in the school hierarchy. The alternative ideal of upward mobility stems from ethnicity-based solidarity and business ties cultivated in the neighbourhoods, whereas social relations are sought with majority peers in school. A secondary-school diploma seems good enough to gain an esteemed social position in the urban middle class or as a stepping stone to higher education. This latter model has been observed in a Pakistani community in the UK. Students from immigrant origin in France often face deep discrepancies between their aspirations in their primary- and middle-school years and the possibilities which are available to them once they enter upper-secondary school (Law and Swann 2011, Schiff 2011).

It is noteworthy that the EDUMIGROM studies portray Denmark and France as further apart than do other notable inquiries into major types of multicultural regime. Denmark is known in the literature as a country which has a relatively strict migration policy and limited engagement with multiculturalism-oriented citizenship policies, but which is strongly committed to the fundamental values of equality and equity. This dual character is also reflected in education. While the achievement gap between majority and minority students is substantial (OECD 2010), this does not prevent minority students from feeling included and developing high ambitions regarding the future. They believe that the Nordic model of social ties and welfare provisions, relying on relatively broad equality and solidarity in society, provides accommodation and alternative paths for upward mobility to young people of immigrant communities, even to those living in segregated conditions. This two-sided nature may explain that in the EDUMIGROM investigations, Denmark and Sweden do present relatively close models and achievements of social inclusion, especially through in-depth inquiries into the aspirations, self-esteem and social ties of ethnic minority youths. France stands out as a peculiar case as far as multicultural policy regimes in Europe are concerned. As such, it is rarely discussed together with the UK. The two countries are seen to have fundamentally different, notably colour-blind versus colour-conscious, understandings of citizenship, welfare provisions and politics of social diversity. However, the comparative EDUMIGROM studies of ethnic minority youths have found that the post-colonial paths of France and the UK do explain certain similarities in their citizenship and social inclusion policy outcomes (see more on this by Szalai, Chapter 15 in this volume).

A close scrutiny of the everyday life, social ties and aspirations of lower-middle-class urban youth reveals that in Western democracies young people from immigrant backgrounds often readily identify with their peers in the neighbourhood. However, important differences were found by the EDUMIGROM research in the contents and forms of such identifications between France and the UK, on the one hand, and Denmark, Germany and Sweden, on the other. Residential segregation of migrants in the three latter countries is reinforced by ethnic segregation within schools and some-times also in after-school life. Overall, however, the neighbourhood tends to provide a comfortable and safe social environment for young people who value the relations with people sharing similar everyday experiences. In some cases, neighbourhood ties generate pride and frame identity; in other cases, these ties shape looser forms of sociability in spite of ethnic divisions (see Neményi and Vajda, Chapter 7 in this volume). In contrast, the vast majority of Roma in the Central European countries perceive themselves as excluded from youth cultures due to segregated living. Neighbourhoods in these communities are sources and places of intragroup sociability but not a conduit to developing self-esteem. In this respect, a paramount division between the old and the new democracies of Europe has to be recognised.

The EDUMIGROM inquiry has captured strong similarities in the social outcomes of schooling practices across the Roma communities in the four Central European countries similar to a host of other investiga-tions. Although their parents or grandparents experienced certain (mostly forced and partial) integration during state socialism, young Roma in these countries currently face tough forms of segregation and exclusion. Deep poverty, joblessness, confinement to miserable housing in segregated neighbourhoods with poor infrastructure are their everyday realities. The majority society views the deprivation and the acceptance of this depri-vation as a 'culture of poverty' that Roma are responsible for or which is ingrained in their cultural traditions (Szalai 2011). In these circumstances, not only harsh forms of segregation but neutral educational service pro-visions deepen social exclusion. As a consequence, minority youths tend to develop fragile self-esteem, limited aspirations and inward-looking social ties. Depending on several circumstances, ethnically segregated schools are sometimes viewed by Roma parents and children as places of peace and secu-rity, even if stripped from the hope for social mobility or inclusion. Against these findings, interviews and focus group discussions with parents revealed their strong preference for integrated schooling, provided that their children are not routinely faced with verbal and physical insults at school.

This limited review allows us to suggest that the performance in social inclusion policy for ensuring fair or equal access to minority ethnic youth to education is quite diverse across countries in Europe. But one can safely argue that multicultural regimes tend to outperform the more restrictive ones as far as the educational outcomes and the broader social prospects for ethnic minority youth are concerned. This does not mean that the results are guaranteed purely by good policy choices or that it is easy to maintain public support for more equitable educational services catering for social diversity.

Moving forward: Encouraging and limiting experiences

Nowadays it is difficult to engage with the literature on multiculturalism without encountering voices that report major backlashes. These voices are critically reading political arguments, policy frames and popular sentiments with increasing anxiety and invite the advocates of multicultural political theories to rearticulate or refine their positions.

When reflecting on recent political trends, two internationally renowned scholars of the subject – Parekh (2008) and Modood (2012) – have made important contributions to reaffirming the theoretical position in support of multiculturalism. Both of them discuss at length how and why the problem of Muslim communities and their recognition claims have embodied the most fundamental challenge and are at the centre of a master narrative of multicultural debates in Europe. Parekh advocates the equally important recognition and distribution aspects of multiculturalism, whereas Modood emphasises group membership as a central feature of a genuine multicultural policy regime. Modood adds that 'hyphenation and internal pluralising of national identities is essential to an integration in which all citizens have not just rights but a sense of belonging to the whole, as well as to their own group'. He also joins other scholars of migration, citizenship and the politics of minorities to propose the concept of tolerance as a potential to shape social spaces where recognition is not necessary. It is suggested that tolerance is not a passive, detached position: it is the concept and the practice of conscious non-interference in a state of affairs where one has the power to intervene. The notion of tolerance and acts of toleration will enhance the repertoire of multiethnic practices for inclusion (Dobbernack and Modood 2011, Maussen and Bader 2012).

One of the main authors of the 'backlash reports', Joppke, argues that in the 2000s, a wholesale retreat took place due to diminishing public support for and policy failures in inclusive citizenship policies. He notices a seismic shift from multiculturalism to civic integration in Austria, Belgium, Denmark, France, Germany, the Netherlands and the UK where

governments established, among others, new integration policies and programmes such as language tests, and minimum levels of competency in
national culture and norms (Joppke 2004). Modood shares this worry to
some extent in view of the riots which took place in northern English
towns in 2001, the terrorist attacks of 11 September 2001 in the US and the
growing public feelings that multiculturalism creates separate and hostile
communities (Modood 2012). He also acknowledges that fear of and hostility
towards immigrants, and Muslims specifically, are exacerbated by concerns
about security and the fear of transnational Islamist terrorist causes. Islam is
also seen as culturally threatening and/or illiberal and undemocratic in its
values.

In a recent volume discussing the state of multiculturalism in seven
European countries, Triandafyllidou and Modood (2012) also acknowledge
that the Netherlands, a forerunner in multicultural policies, has shifted
towards establishing integration courses and civic integration tests for newcomers. Due to the mounting unrest of second-generation immigrant youth,
the French government has reasserted its republican civic integration model,
banning the use of religious symbols in schools and the wearing of the
veil. In Germany, social inclusion is still an accepted objective yet the
citizenship law of 2000 is efficiently decreasing naturalisations. The UK
and Sweden are perhaps the only European countries that have maintained their commitments to multicultural policies, although they also have
made compromises in public debates. Schierup and Ålund (2011) argue
that the 'actually existing system of liberalism' has always had difficulties
in embracing multiculturalism, although there was a short golden age of
cultural diversity. The much valued Swedish model was loaded with immi-
nent tensions from the start and has operated through an ethnic division
of labour. A decisive shift occurred with the neoliberal turn in the 1990s:
integration policy has been combined with larger considerations of growth.
This view may suggest that if Sweden has been exposed to imperfections
of policy implementation and had to make conceptual compromises, less
developed multicultural regimes are even more exposed to implementation
challenges.

Vertovec and Wessendorf are ready to contest the bleak reports on
multicultural retreat in Europe. They argue that novel discursive strategies rather than actual policy reorientations can be observed. Indeed,
multiculturalism is disappearing from major policy statements in the UK,
the Netherlands and Germany. The frame of social diversity is becoming
preferred instead, which originally emerged as an individual path to inclusion in diverse societies (Vertovec and Wessendorf 2010, p. 16). Summing
up the authors' accounts in their volume, Vertovec and Wessendorf show
how in the UK a variety of skilful practices facilitate ever-increasing diversity, how the Netherlands maintains actual policies regarding migrants in
spite of harsh backlashes in public talks, and how France moves slowly

towards the recognition of migrants even though a strong integrationist stance dominates policy discourses. Denmark has never perceived itself as a multicultural society and continues to combine interest-based pragmatism and identity-based nationalism. In Germany, an official multicultural policy has never existed; the country has pursued a pragmatic acceptance of diversity. The overall judgment is that Western democracies show middling forms of social inclusion which reject exclusion yet do not embrace true recognition of diversity-based citizenship.

Based on the MIPEX, an original concept and method used to classify and monitor policies across 21 OECD countries, Banting and Kymlicka suggest that European countries have adopted some level of multiculturalism policies over the past three decades. In the last decade, there has been a tangible reduction in the Netherlands, and a modest one in Denmark and Italy. But Belgium, Finland, Greece, Ireland, Norway, Portugal, Spain and Sweden have shown resilience, and some have even strengthened their multiculturalism policies (Banting and Kymlicka 2012, p. 10). A range of European countries, mostly in Northern Europe and less so in Southern Europe, have put an emphasis on integration principles at initial entry, renewed residency and the naturalisation of migrants, and have introduced a range of tests, courses and contracts. This poses the question of whether multicultural and civic integration strategies are compatible or whether any attempt to combine them would be inherently unstable. Banting and Kymlicka contend that the compatibility of these two citizenship strategies varies immensely from one country to another. As a distinctive group, Denmark, Germany and Austria have adopted forms of integration that are compulsory and highly assimilationist. By contrast, some countries with longstanding multicultural efforts, such as Sweden and Britain, have adopted forms of civic integration policies that are more voluntary and pluralistic.

In Central and Eastern Europe, the language of multiculturalism has not become appealing in policy debates and practices except for particular circles of the liberal-leftist and human rights NGOs. The dominant discourses on ethnic, religious, linguistic and cultural heterogeneity refer to minority rights, anti-discrimination, social inclusion and, occasionally, diversity management, resonating with but not simply copying the language of the EU. This pertains to discourses stemming from a basic political position that exclusion is a public 'defect'. Major policy ideals concerning the social inclusion of Roma are characterised by a dynamic encounter between two major positions: the first uses the notion of ethnic discrimination and/or minority rights, whereas the second refers to socioeconomic (class) deprivation and welfare principles. A range of scholarly and critical accounts argue that the two axes are inextricably intertwined in the processes of exclusion and thus policy interventions should also combine a dual approach (Vermeersch 2005, Szalai 2011). This combined framing characterises the latest policy documents of the EU on Roma inclusion.[4]

In contrast with these promising hopes, the EDUMIGROM research and other inquiries reveal that in Central and Eastern European societies a significant part of the public shares the view that Roma communities can be blamed for their current miserable conditions and thus welcomes assimilation, discipline and social control-centred policies. In a fresh analysis of comparative results, Fox and Vidra (2012) argue that in Central and Eastern Europe the concept of social integration has remained dominant in educational policy regimes. The integrationist policy language holds its key position against the rising tide of right-wing, often explicitly racist political voices but also against multicultural policy ideals. There is substantial evidence to believe that the right-wing and exclusionist arguments and ideals currently have more public appeal in these countries than the multicultural one. A closer look, however, may reveal important differences in this regard across the region.

The current state of affairs suggests that European political and policy processes concerning ethnic (and religious, cultural, linguistic) divisions are not very likely to make a radical shift. One can expect policy responses that promote some muddling through by corrective instruments. This scenario resonates with the general nature of the political and policy cooperation within the EU in the area of social policy affairs. The current economic crisis and its consequences may make the problems of social exclusion even more serious and the responses slower due to severe cuts to public funds. This trend may trigger discontent and more pronounced cleavages within societies in Europe. Thus the consequences of the global economic crisis may necessitate changes more radical than expected now. But none of the potential scenarios will benefit from discrediting the frame of multiculturalism that has started to gain legitimacy among a critical mass of respected and powerful politicians and active citizens in Europe. Organising schooling along the principles of equal access to good education services to all by acknowledging the special needs of ethnic and migrant youths seems to accomplish more on a societal level in the longer run than any assimilationist or saliently stratifying system. What is more, the literature suggests that it is possible to pursue educational reforms aimed at increasing the equality of educational opportunities by decreasing the differentiation of the education system without endangering educational quality (Pfeffer 2012).

Notes

1. The MIPEX project is led by the British Council and the Migration Policy Group. The MIPEX measures 148 indicators in seven policy areas in 31 countries across Europe, Canada and the US. From 2010, education has also been part of the policy areas. For details, see http://www.mipex.eu/.
2. Interestingly, this portrayal of the Southern European countries reveals an overall slow policy development in contrast with the MIPEX by Kymlicka and Banting,

which reports some strengthening of multicultural policies in parts of these countries.
3. See the details of the conceptual frame, definition of policy areas and data on education policy qualities: http://www.mipex.eu/education.
4. See, for example, *EU Framework for National Roma Integration Strategies up to 2020* at http://ec.europa.eu/justice/policies/discrimination/docs/com_2011_173_en.pdf.

Part II

International and Intergroup Comparisons of Ethnic Minority Students' Experiences of Otherness in Schools

7
Intricacies of Ethnicity: A Comparative Study of Minority Identity Formation during Adolescence

Mária Neményi and Róza Vajda

Introduction

By relying on the findings of the EDUMIGROM study, this chapter discusses the formation of the ethnic identity of teenagers belonging to various 'visible' minorities across Europe. By analysing their narrative constructions, formulated in face-to-face interviews revolving around relevant experiences within and outside the community, we aim to explore shared characteristics and common features of the identification process. This process is conceptualised here in terms of identity models and identity strategies.

Identity models refer to background conditions, ranging from the characteristics of families and communities to the policy context and the larger political, economic and cultural environment which function as a 'web of meanings' (Geertz 1977) in processes of socialisation and individuation. Hence, by reflecting on the given circumstances, these models include sets of viable life strategies that are allowed or even supported by the internal rules and expectations of the in-group and of the majority society. It was assumed that identity models as mediated by the immediate environment, especially by the parents, can be explored in terms of ethnicity, and vice versa: ethnic identity is related to other social identities that are derived from all sorts of circumstances (gender, religion, social status, migration, political ideology, etc.). Models imply relatively static constructions providing reference points to individuals which together constitute the blueprints of identity strategies.

Identity strategies represent the manifest aspect of identity formation and are the ways in which individuals actually relate to their ethnic belonging and perceive their current and future position in society (Phinney 1992). Because our chapter is concerned with adolescents, it seemed all the more appropriate to study identity in the making as a set of responses to outward circumstances. We also propose considering the future prospects, visions and aspirations of teenagers which, in turn, reflect their understanding of their present condition. Given their age, the unfinished nature of identities is accentuated. Moreover, the ethnicity of our respondents also exacerbates the emotional charge of their self-images. In trying to grasp identities that are in constant transformation, while underpinned by solidified structures within larger (local and national, social and political) contexts, it was acknowledged that the respondents' self-identifications reflect, in particularly sensitive ways, widespread practices of ethnic (religious, national and racial) labelling that are prevalent in the given country (Verkuyten 2005).

The discussion below focuses on the perceived positive and negative aspects of ethnic belonging, its ascribed or self-ascribed nature and its connection with integration. Our analysis is primarily concerned with the extent to which minority ethnic students think that their culture, customs, behavioural rules and very existence is accepted and respected, or, on the contrary, the degree to which they feel excluded because of the given implications and perceived traits of their 'ethnicity'. By reflecting on the educational, familial and occupational aspirations of minority ethnic students, we examined whether these reinforce ethnic separation – that is, enclosure in or reliance on one's own ethnic community – or rather enhance integration or assimilation into the larger society.

Dimensions of ethnicity: A typology

Amidst the complexity of components, two sets of cross-cutting factors proved to be decisive in the development of identity strategies. The first denotes whether or not separation from the majority is a matter of voluntary choice by the individual or the minority community, or, on the contrary, whether it is a consequence of social pressures and oppression by the majority society. The second kind of distinction refers to the personal drive to express or, contrarily, to suppress ethnic difference. Obviously, these latter predispositions, again, are framed by outside conditions that not only impose constraints on the development of identity but, indeed, invest it with meaning. The combination of positions along the two factors allowed for the classification of identity strategies into four categories, using a two-by-two matrix. The four cells of Table 7.1 represent typical patterns of identity formation – namely, 'ghetto-consciousness', 'responses to slum existence', 'affirmation of ethnic (or religious) pride' and 'striving for assimilation/cosmopolitanism'.

The voluntary as opposed to the involuntary assumption[1] of ethnicity refers to the key instances determining ethnic belonging: individual agency as opposed to outward social and political forces, respectively. Along this dimension, ethnic ghetto and slum dwellers are distinguished from the residents of (mainly lower-middle-class) ethnic neighbourhoods and (usually

Table 7.1 Patterns of identity formation

	Maintenance of difference	Trivialisation of difference
Involuntary assumption of ethnicity	Ghetto consciousness	Responses to slum existence
Voluntary assumption of ethnicity	Affirmation of ethnic (or religious) pride	Striving for assimilation/ cosmopolitanism

well-off) families living dispersed among the majority society.[2] This variation is conditioned mainly by historical and cultural factors, including political tendencies, rather than merely by class or social status. Being born into a ghetto or slum provides few chances of self-determination, even if it does not prevent individual reflections on group belonging. By contrast, taking pride in one's ethnic origin or religious belonging, melting into the majority society, or the adoption of a supra-ethnic ideological stance marking cosmopolitanism all imply some degree of individual will, the emergence and viability of which is, again, determined by the dominant political ideology and the historical and cultural context. Hence preconditions in terms of social and political pressures and opportunities which shape ethnic strategies must always be taken into account. Another way of looking at these preconditions would be to differentiate between compelled as opposed to self-conscious ways of assuming ethnic identity entail that differing degrees of agency.

The other axis – that is, the maintenance as opposed to the trivialisation of ethnic difference – accentuates the fact that ethnicity, whether ascribed or self-ascribed, allows for some variation in identity strategies, especially in terms of expressing or suppressing ethnic identity. Nevertheless, being different is seldom a matter of free will but rather represents, at its best, the outcome of a conditioned choice and, at its worst, an inevitable fate. This situation involves serious struggles for the members of socially excluded minority groups who try to earn social respect and enforce their interests in one way or another. As the management of identities is always a work of both power and will, the conceptual opposition presented here refers to the two extreme poles of a continuum. The categories of our diagram are intended to indicate that ethnic identities are mainly reactive, working upon the given circumstances, yet leaving more or less room for action and self-reflection. Conditioned by the social status and situation of the given minority group within a particular historical and cultural context, and fuelled by individual or collective aspirations that are adjusted to the available patterns of identification, ethnic difference may be maintained and supported or trivialised, refused and even abandoned through the employment of identity strategies.

Ghetto consciousness

Ethnic ghettos are isolated and socially deprived urban neighbourhoods, separated from the majority society. Such segregated residential areas are characteristically populated by extended families in which parents are mostly uneducated and engaged in menial jobs. Due to the limited educational and employment opportunities and the marginalised status of the inhabitants, these places show a high concentration of social problems, such as poverty and unemployment. Life in the ethnic ghetto is characterised by permanence, even immobility, and also has a great deal of instability and insecurity. Amidst these conditions there are hardly any chances to break out. Thus, ghettos have a particular propensity for reproducing the low and excluded social status of the inhabitants, including educational disadvantages.

Among our interviewees the clearest examples of identity strategies as conditioned by ethnic ghettos are provided in the countries of post-socialist transformation and concern the Roma minority. Certain post-colonial minorities, such as Algerians in France or Afro-Caribbeans in the UK, also fit this paradigm, at least when they are relegated to stigmatised urban areas. The consciousness and attitudes of these teenagers is marked by a sense of being born into a closed and isolated community that is despised by the majority society and not valued much by the insiders either. Thus they experience ethnicity as a confinement rather than a source of empowerment, which is imposed on them and does not allow for much variation in terms of future expectations.

Given the general destitution of the area, the local schools attended by those of our interviewees who fall into this category are usually of poor quality, which induces poor school performance and provides strongly limited opportunities for further education. If at all, students continue their studies in nearby vocational schools which typically enforce strong gender distinctions. Thus girls are mostly trained to work in the less-qualified service sector as hairdressers, shop assistants or kitchen employees, while boys usually acquire qualifications in traditional industrial or building trades as mechanics or painters. Such an education ensures that these young people will end up at best in low-paid blue-collar jobs. As expressed by a Czech Roma adolescent, 'If you are Roma and you are a bit brown, you can hardly find a job.' When ethnoracial discrimination has less of a stronghold on individual expectations, the future seems to be utterly unpredictable: 'If I finish school and find a job, then it will be good enough. It might be better, or might be worse... One can't really plan the future,' said a Hungarian Roma teenager.

Given the perceived lack of future opportunities, a kind of resigned passivity and lack of ambition characterise these adolescents. Defeatism originates in the strong stereotypes held against the group which become interiorised as autostereotypes that function as self-fulfilling prophecies.

Since they are bound to fail, they had better not even try doing anything. 'I think non-Roma are different because they want to achieve some goal. Roma do not...they are often lazy, lacking goals,' explained a Czech Roma.

Even if the children from the ghetto, like most youngsters of their age group, freely entertain hopes for a full adult life at an early age, they see how futile such day-dreaming is as soon as they become conscious of their circumstances. Experiences of hostility on the part of the majority society and (fear of) discrimination make them relinquish any hopes for a better future. Their desperation increases when they understand that their fate is tied to that of their community and, subsequently, that they are unable not only to change their own lives but also to influence the future of the community. The acknowledgment of this sad state of affairs is expressed by a 15-year-old Romanian Roma girl:

> We live in the landfill. Recycled material, copper, aluminium, beer canes...I think having children in the house only involves problems and trouble. If one day dearth comes, how will you give them what they need? But you do tomorrow the same as you do today, as the wheel spins...When I was little, I wanted to become a doctor. I wanted to change my house, human perspectives, and discrimination against Gypsies. I thought if I had a high position, I could help the poor. If I had where to stay, where to work, I would do better...Obviously, you have three options: to steal, to beg, or to prostitute yourself.

Instead of communal ties, ghetto consciousness is dominated by a lack of belonging. As a result of the deterioration of community life, the valuation of traditions or ethnic consciousness does not thrive here. Hence, conventional ethnic markers such as language, customs or religion have only very limited significance, if any at all. Ghetto communities maintain very scarce inter-ethnic relations and almost no positive connections with the majority. This state of affairs is clearly signalled by residential and educational segregation. The main source of self-differentiation is represented by occasional conflicts with the majority society. Socioethnic division from the surrounding society is reinforced by symbolic barriers too. The other means of feeling unique for those who differ slightly from the in-group is by distancing themselves from fellow ghetto dwellers, manifesting in this way a kind of compensatory self-esteem. This is illustrated by the words of a Hungarian 'Romungro' boy:

> We are normal, but the Vlach Gypsies are different from us. They relate to everything differently, they talk differently, they are self-conceited...they cannot have fun without fighting and making a big row. They act as if they were kings. We are not like that, we know how to have fun and

party, we can talk to any people, and we don't care whether the person is Hungarian or not Hungarian.

Another source of compensatory self-esteem is derived from successfully coping with hardship and humiliation. This comprises the seeds of what in more favourable circumstances could become a sort of ethnic pride. Hence, even though they are the product of negative conditions, the locality and its community may become associated with a positive sense of belonging together and even some level of group cohesion can be identified.

The coercions holding the collective together result in weak self-determination that fails to produce positive self-esteem. Still, in the face of an outside threat, the ghetto community, in particular the extended family, may function as a protective shield. The lack of future prospects enhances the importance of family values and expectations so that eventually many young people decide to stay in the familiar environment and continue with the way of life seen in the family. The supportive network of the family and the role models provided by the immediate environment help in coping with difficulties and getting along in life. The lack of any perspectives and entrepreneurial spirit, coupled with the acknowledgement of having to rely on one's 'own kind', inadvertently reinforce community feelings: 'we hold together more', 'Gypsies and Gypsies are more attached...they do not look down on one another,' said a Hungarian Roma.

Affirmation of ethnic (or religious) pride

By contrast, when separation from the majority society occurs on a voluntary basis, perceived differences tend to be filled with positive content. The self-enclosure of the community in such situations is associated with an ethnic or religious consciousness owing to which the group has been able to achieve some degree of social respect or at least tolerance from the majority society. The economic profile of the typically metropolitan neighbourhoods in which one finds individuals belonging to this category is marked by self-reliance, especially in terms of employment. Given the strength of the community, national, ethnic or religious origins are often seen as more significant than citizenship. Solidarity and group cohesion are manifested in a variety of forms, including family enterprises, peer networks, religious congregations and schools managed by the community.

Typical candidates for this category are Muslims in Western European cities, including those in Germany, Denmark or France (in our sample). Besides religion, upward mobility and achieved social status may also reinforce ethnic consciousness and pride. Thus the Gabor Gipsies in Romania as well as a few other Roma families typically living in ethnically mixed neighbourhoods and belonging to the higher ranks of the working-class also belong to this group.

As in the ghetto, extended families are also present here but not because of the lack of family planning; rather as a result of accommodation to ethnocultural or religious norms which value high fertility. The family not only represents the basic element of community life but also provides a socially desirable model and a resource for the young generation. Being an important economic unit, it may also function as the basis of small enterprises run by the nuclear family or provide a supportive network formed by the extended family. Therefore it is especially due to its practical importance that the family acquires significance in the development of identity: 'I often help my father in the butcher business. All our family helps him. And he gives work to all of us,' reported a Turkish-German boy.

Education has great significance as the source of individual success and upward mobility. Children usually attend schools that are dominated by the majority yet that are sensitive to ethnicity and cultural difference or, when available, enrol in schools run by the minority. Integration into the school system ruled by the majority is generally welcome as a way to social advancement and it is not seen as involving detachment from the original community. The parents – characteristically first- or second-generation immigrants or recently urbanised Roma who have managed to attain higher social standing and better material circumstances – often represent as examples for their children in terms of career choices, further education and lifestyle. The parents' high expectations and, indirectly, the requirements set by the community become interiorised by the children. The overall impact of economic demands and community expectations supports gender distinctions: small enterprises are managed by men while the female members of the family are usually employed as assistants. As a consequence, attitudes towards schooling differ in the case of boys and girls. As girls gain less support and opportunities for self-development, they are especially inclined to adopt a broader perspective of the future that involves some degree of disengagement from the original community.

Incidentally, self-conscious Roma students born into relatively favourable circumstances manifest signs of positive ethnic belonging: 'I am proud to be a Roma...we like traditions while Romanians do not have so many traditions,' a Roma girl from Romania said. However, it is mainly well established immigrants who are likely to develop a strong sense of community. While based on ethnicity and religion, such local identities often express detachment from the country of origin and demonstrate relatively close links with the community and place of residence in the host country. Illustrative examples are provided by Turkish students from Kreuzberg in Berlin: 'In Turkey I am a foreigner. They don't regard me as an ordinary Turkish boy like themselves but as someone from Germany. Therefore they regard me as rich and special.' Or: 'My parents will definitely return to Turkey when I am grown up and have my own family. But I will stay here...Here in Kreuzberg is my home.' Or: 'I never felt discriminated against and I never was called a "Scheiß-Türke" or something like this. Here in Kreuzberg I was always part of the majority and not of a minority.' Longing for the place of birth may also determine future ambitions to return home one day: 'When you think of how it's like in Morocco – summer all year long –, I sometimes think to myself: I want to go back.' 'We are proud to be Berber, we are proud to be Moroccan,' exclaimed a Moroccan student living in Denmark who, after finishing business high school and working a couple of years as a policewoman, plans to go back to Morocco and open a business of her own, such as a store or a restaurant.

Group cohesion, the adoption of traditions, the determining power of religion and the related cultural practices – all of these factors affect plans regarding future employment, forms of marriage (for example, the acceptance of arranged marriage), the planned type of family, the number of children – in short, the conception of a 'good way of life'. A Turkish boy living in Germany stated: 'It is important to know the Koran very well to educate our children in the right way. It is important to marry within the same religion.' Although the ethnonational background may also be important in informing future aspirations, the cohesive power of religion seems to be especially strong: 'When I get married, it is very important that she has Kurdish background and my parents want that as well. Then we will share everything, religion, culture ... I don't want to break that chain,' said a Kurdish boy from Sweden. Or: 'Never ever would I marry someone who isn't Muslim. Never in the world,' affirmed a Moroccan student living in France.

In religiously based communities, shared faith often overrides other types of tie in terms of providing orientation in life and a sense of belonging. A Moroccan boy living in a Parisian neighbourhood explained:

> ... for us, the Muslim community, religion plays a very important role ... If he simply respects religion, it means that between the ages of 10 and 12 he will know the way to the Mosque. So if he knows that way, there won't be any problem. Just with his lessons at the Mosque, leaving the national education aside, we'll see that that child will be well educated compared to a child who doesn't even know about religion ... My friends are Muslim like me, an Algerian, a Tunisian, a Mauritanian, it's mixed. That's why I say the country doesn't count.

The proud assumption of ethnic or religious identity often involves active connections with the country of origin. The resulting positive ethnic identity is reinforced when the multicultural environment in the host country allows for complex attachments. A Palestinian girl from Lebanon, now living in Denmark where she is proudly wearing the headscarf, said the following about her multiple ties: 'I live in Denmark and I'm happy for it ... but I'm also still happy for where I'm coming from, like, I like the religion, I believe in Islam and the culture we have at home.' Ethnic traditions are also seen as protective: 'A girl from the Comoros has a lot of prohibitions. When you're young, you ask yourself why all these rules but when you really think about it, it's good for us, it preserves us, it keeps us from doing a lot of stupid things. Our customs are great,' said a Comorian girl living in France. The broader community can provide the same sense of security as the family: 'Sometimes when I meet other Moroccans I feel protected in some way even though I don't really know the person,' explained a Moroccan student living in Denmark.

The growing distrust and hostility affecting Muslims in the West, along with the countermodels provided by the surrounding society, often heighten a sense of difference and group cohesion, and strengthen group solidarity. At the same time, both animosity and modernising influences create divisions within the community. Hence, while acknowledging the essentially voluntary nature of the adoption of group identity and the positive contents that it involves, the coercive momentum should not be dismissed in this category. Positive group identity, at least in part, is produced as a reaction to external pressures, such as anti-immigration policies or hostile anti-minority attitudes. However, in contrast with vulnerable ghetto populations, these generally well-settled minorities are able to utilise communal resources to protect themselves.

It also should be noted that membership of a community not only depends on individual will but, to some extent, it is also prompted by certain collective disciplining mechanisms of the community. Expectations of the family and the larger community exercise pressure on individuals to the extent that group membership comes to be seen as the guarantee for making a decent life in the future. In this sense, beyond representing an attribute of personal identities, 'ethnic pride' may be interpreted as a collective response to a particular situation or group status which may be regarded either as a transitory state in terms of social integration or as a relatively permanent solution reflecting the ideal of a multicultural mosaic society.

Responses to slum existence

Slums, like ghettos, are mostly deteriorated urban neighbourhoods located on the outskirts of cities or in deprived inner-city districts. They are separated from the majority society but separation occurs on social rather than on ethnic grounds. Slums resemble ghettos due to the lack of resources, such as public services, as well as education and employment opportunities. These are also stigmatised places stricken by refusals of the majority along with their assumptions about and aversion to poverty, people's low social status, the prevailing destitute residential conditions and the marginal lifestyle. Because they lack the essential means for individual and collective development, slums become self-reproducing localities due to a downward spiral of social decline.

Examples of identity strategies characterised by slum existence can be found, primarily, in the French, British and, to a lesser extent, Danish and Swedish urban communities of high immigrant concentration. The attitudes of interviewees coming from some mixed Roma and non-Roma neighbourhoods in deteriorated and economically depressed Central European cities, where residents live in deep poverty and social exclusion, also fit this pattern.

Because of the diversity of the residents' cultural, religious and ethnic backgrounds and the haphazardness of individual lives, a wide variety of family forms fall into this category: mixed families, single-parent households, parents living in polygamous relationships, adoptive parents, relatives taking care of abandoned children and so on. Besides the lack of quality education, it is the unstable background of children that virtually predestines them to poor school performance and very limited opportunities for further education. Yet, because they desperately want to break out of their situation, many students see an important potential in education in terms of social mobility and respect. 'I don't want to work in a supermarket...Why do it if I can get education instead? I want to be something,' said a Kurdish adolescent from Germany. Such ambitions often involve a desire to break away from one's own family and people:

> I want to move to another country because I don't think my opportunities are that many here. For instance, my brother is an educated machine engineer but gets no job and has to work in the subway. The same with my father. When I look at my family, I see how it works here, said an Eritrean boy living in Sweden.

Given the lack of common cultural references, weak group cohesion and complex family types, individual identities are shaped to a large extent by experiences of discrimination and marginalisation. Severe socioeconomic disadvantage is coupled with aversion and ethnic prejudices on the part of the majority society: 'Sometimes I think that the others are afraid of Roma people.' And: 'Czech people sometimes slander them [Roma people]. It is because all of them [Czechs] think they [Roma people] are all the same and do the same things, that they steal, that they are criminals,' voiced in a variety of ways by our Roma respondents in the different Central European countries. Due to their multiple exclusion and the lack of any positive collective ties, children are often at a loss as to how to identify themselves. The words of a Somali boy in Denmark reflect the ambiguities and confused feelings associated with ethnic identity:

> When the Danes look at me, they see a perker [which translates as 'nigger']. When the perkers look at me...they would call me a Dane...It has a big impact on how I'm looked upon and what expectation I have to live up to. Most people look at me like I'm something else than what I am.

There is a strong awareness of stigmatisation, exclusion and discrimination among young people in this category which induces a sense of shame or even self-hatred. The resulting identities are unstable, effectively situational and reactive in character, and they are negative in their effects. At the same time, visible traits such as skin colour tend to fix ascribed ethnic identities, implying the impossibility of integration:

> I feel like an Eritrean because I look like one. It is very obvious with my dark skin and dark eyes. If I meet someone in the street they don't look at me like a Swede, they think I am an African or an Eritrean. Therefore, I feel like an Eritrean.

Destitution and experiences of rejection by the majority society result in a conflict-ridden life in the slum, marked by distrust and envy, rather than a sense of belonging together. Religion and culture do not play an important role in (self)-identification, though language occasionally becomes a marker of intragroup distinctions. However, inter-ethnic differences are especially conveyed by reference to stereotypes expressing ignorance, social distance and sometimes hostility, and reflecting on them often functions as a source of compensatory self-esteem. This mechanism is aggravated by the schools, where the proportion of minorities is high, while efforts to thematise cultural or ethnic difference are absent or ineffective. A girl with mixed ethnic background in one of the British sites described distinct 'types' in her community:

> 'He sells drugs, he uses knives and guns, he is not a very nice person, be scared of that person, you will get your phone robbed, he is a woman beater, he is a man slag, he cheats on his girlfriends'. That is the typical Black guy... [A Black girl] is a bitch, she's right hard, she'll bang you, don't mess with her'... [An Asian boy] is a suicide bomber, he's from the Taliban.

Yet, to some extent, inter-ethnic relationships exist within the local communities and make it possible for young people to suspend ethnicity or engage in mocking with it. This is how a Malian boy described the nuances of inter-ethnic connections in a French *banlieue*:

> There are girls that we call 'Black guys' chicks', because they only go out with Blacks... they say it's because Blacks are more tender and all that and that Arabs are violent and all.... It's true sometimes you hear 'dirty nigger', 'dirty Arab', but that's just making fun, it's just teasing, 'cause we get along. It's just humour. It's the way people laugh together in Saint Denis.

Students in this category hold visions of a future that is full of uncertainties and anxieties, and they tend to resort to a kind of escapism. They develop great expectations of living in a distant place in the same country, express a nostalgic yearning for the country of origin, or entertain utopian desires to move to a third country. 'Of course, I will have a better job and live in a different area. In a big house where the Swedes live. I would never let my children grow up in this area. I know how the atmosphere can be here,' anticipated a Kurdish boy from Sweden. An Ethiopian girl living in Sweden said: 'I have seen so much in Sweden, I want to get to know another part of the world. But I don't know yet, maybe Ethiopia.' This kind of escapism often expresses a wish to 'act white' – that is, to melt into mainstream society. It may even entail a sense of cosmopolitanism even though the wish to transcend one's narrow social context, in this case, is not so much fuelled by principles and ideologies but rather driven by disillusionment and the awareness of limited opportunities. A Tunisian girl living in France admitted:

> Personally I'm not too inspired by my origin. Some call me the corrupted girl... I may have Maghreb origin, but I'm more often with Blacks or people of colour than with Arabs... I noticed that if you get into religion too young you don't live... I would never wear the veil, I'm against that. I'm for putting it in religion but not ahead of it because it would prevent me from doing lots of things.

Striving for assimilation/cosmopolitanism

Neither traditionalism nor poverty determine the lives of minority adolescents whose families have managed to avoid, or break out from, ghettos or slums and to establish a decent working-class or lower-middle-class lifestyle on their own, without having to rely on the extended family network or on the support of the original community. While maintaining a strong ethnic identity is obviously an option in such circumstances, children often wish to break away from the original community and melt into a larger, not necessarily ethnicity-based, one that is represented by the majority population of the given country or by a supranational entity.

This complex category is typically represented by new immigrants from Asia and Africa, on the one hand, and upwardly mobile Roma families in post-socialist countries, on the other. Their drives are certainly intensified by, respectively, the prevailing anti-immigrant rules and attitudes, and the general hostility against Roma.

The parents of the children belonging here are usually significantly better educated than minority adults in the other categories, yet their educational attainments do not suffice to reach middle-class status in the host country. Thus they push their children to achieve even more in life by means of quality education and the adoption of majority values and lifestyles.

Children aspire to become professionals – such as a pilot, an IT specialist, a lawyer or a doctor – and to live in a modern nuclear family. 'I would just like to have a normal life, where you have a job and a home and feel well... I think the ideal family, as it is completely ordinary, maybe two children, like completely normal,' said an Afghan student from Denmark. Given their secular views and Westernised perspectives, these families are usually more progressive-minded and liberal in terms of gender roles and other social norms than those succumbing to traditional values (marked by 'ethnic pride') or those who suffer from poverty and marginalisation (in slums or ethnic colonies). Nonetheless, as it is usually the father who is the driving force in migration and social mobility, it is boys rather than girls who embody the family's hopes for further upward mobility.

By living in typically middle-class neighbourhoods, members of this category mingle with the majority population. Children normally attend local schools dominated by majority students and characterised by either colour-blind or multicultural educational policy. These institutions tend to reflect on and also reinforce the aspirations of 'visible' minority youths to overcome ethnic barriers, neglect religious ties and loosen community attachments. However, notwithstanding its integrative efforts, the school fails to protect minority students in this category from experiences of prejudice and discrimination from their peers or the outside society.

Such contextual features, combined with young people's personal characteristics, account for their tendency to 'act white'. The driving force behind such attitudes is a sense of incompleteness and instability concerning their social status that originates in the often frustrated 'mobility project' of the previous generations. Occasionally, it is pragmatic decisions that are responsible for relinquishing the significance of ethnicity. This is the case, for instance, when the demand for occupations associated with the ethnic community is scarce and thus young people are practically forced to step outside their traditional economic niche. Although the voluntarism of assimilation is questionable when other alternatives are rendered unfeasible, individual decisions still matter and reveal particular ways of reflecting on ethnic belonging.

These young people's future plans regarding education, employment, the choice of a partner and a family reveal a heightened sense of individual autonomy and the adoption of majority values and/or modern ideals. Besides being informed by modernist ways of thinking, the wish to loosen the ties to their ethnic community is generally motivated by a desire for conformity. Refusal of ethnic traditions is typically nourished by a kind of anxiety, reflecting pragmatic considerations regarding social inclusion, which tends to be more articulated than in the case of slum dwellers: 'I don't want to live in South Harbour in the future. I want to find an area with many Swedes. It is important that my children learn the Swedish language well, and people speaking good Swedish are really lacking in South Harbour,' explained an Ethiopian girl whose family had immigrated to Sweden. Rejection of ethnicity as an overly significant marker may be grounded in principles, too. A boy at one of the French sites, who would like to become a psychoanalyst and wishes to travel and live in different countries, expressed his thoughts as follows:

> Pride isn't really my thing... Frankly, it's not something I take to heart. I feel neither French, nor Moroccan, nor American. For me, representing a country without having a good reason to do so is stupid. A president, if he represents a country OK, he's a president, it's normal. But a guy who visits his country once a year and says he represents it – it's stupid. They just do that to make trouble and to look down on others, to give themselves some pseudo-superiority.

Downplaying ethnicity helps to break down obstacles and to establish solidarity based on other sorts of values which are more responsive to actual personal experiences and needs. For instance, a teenager planning to continue his studies in a business school said:

> [Ethnic background] doesn't matter because we are still like brothers. One is from Iran, the other is from Palestine, and the sixth is from Afghanistan. It doesn't matter because we are not in those places now... You can always have prejudice against someone but then if he's nice to you, if he's your friend, you skip the prejudice,

Students in this category typically have a large number of inter-ethnic relationships as well as anti-prejudice attitudes and display a tendency to understand and reflect upon social problems. Our Swedish respondent coming from Ethiopia remarked about prejudices against white people there: 'I think it has to do with colonisation... even though it happened a long time ago. Prejudices stay. I will live differently than my parents. I can focus more on my individuality, on what I strive for.'

As opposed to guest workers in earlier decades, today it is mainly highly qualified people (usually men) who fuel migration and make efforts to become self-reliant as soon as possible. This requires some level of accommodation to the norms and styles encountered in the host country. Given that we are dealing here largely with the children of highly qualified guest workers and middle-class Roma parents who have acquired a new style, it is no wonder that they are more self-confident than 'visible' minority teenagers belonging to the other categories with regard to their ambition to integrate into society and become recognised as equals. Whether full social inclusion through assimilation or cosmopolitanism will be achieved by the next generations or remain illusionary projects is another question. The answer depends to a great extent on the direction of larger-scale sociopolitical trends within nation-states and on the international scene.

Conclusion

Notwithstanding significant differences between the four types of identity pattern, ethnic identity is never free from pressures and constraints. This seems to be acknowledged by our interviewees as well who, being aware of their limitations, envision more or less plausible future lives. Although they frequently cherish dreams about earning social respect by excelling within their minority group or by becoming part of mainstream society, it is primarily the viable identity strategies that tend to surface in their narratives. It seems already quite clear to these young members of racialised minorities that, no matter how hard they try, they will probably fail to assimilate, especially if they bear visible identity marks (the 'stigma') and/or come from a multiple-disadvantaged social background. Ethnic minority adolescents appear to be very reflective not only concerning their limitations but also regarding their attachments. National, ethnic, religious and cultural ties have differing significances according to several factors, such as the history and nature of the community in question; the time, reason and form of migration; the economic resources and social accommodation of the community; and the cultural and political atmosphere in the host society. External determinations appear to be more powerful when one is born into a slum or ethnic colony than for those living in non-segregated, ethnically and socially mixed residential areas. This is reflected by the categories of our typology that refer to forms of 'being' as opposed to forms of 'acting'. In the more disadvantaged cases, the assumption and expression of ethnicity is more constrained by historical circumstances defining the group in question that is also characterised by low social status and/or ethnic segregation. In contrast, individual perspectives and ambitions are more decisive when the structural determinations of ethnicity are weaker – that is, when ethnic identity is not so much determined from the outside or imposed by the community itself. This is the case with self-reliant migrant communities that occupy favourable economic niches and are held together mainly by economic interactions, though cohesion is often also reinforced by religious and ethnic belonging. Urbanised, upwardly mobile Roma show similar patterns of identity formation. Interestingly, variation on the scale of ascribed versus self-ascribed identities has less to do with the content of ethnic identity: some may want to do away with a relatively stable and successful identity, while others give up, early on, the idea of overcoming the narrow confines of a 'negative', though vaguely defined, identity. At the individual level, 'ethnic mobility' depends especially on the availability of feasible alternatives as far as the employment of identity strategies defining a positive relation to ethnicity is concerned. The freedom to live and act out one's ethnicity is thus inversely related to the vulnerability of individuals.

The permanence and character of a community, on the one hand, and of individual membership, on the other, are contingent upon features of the sociopolitical environment and on outsiders' perceptions. These factors may favour or discourage internal cohesion and the inception of individual or collective 'struggles for recognition' (Honneth 1995). As far as ethnic colonies vs. slums are concerned, the expression or suppression of ethnicity is largely determined by the policies and the internal rules governing such places. What these two situations have in common is that they both allow individuals minimal opportunities to break out. Hence residents of such places act out schemes implied in the very nature of their self-enclosed community that are grounded in ethnicity in the case of ghettos and in social status in the case of slums. Endeavours aimed at the exhibition of a positive (and more complex) relation to ethnicity may emerge only when there is a sense in developing ethnic pride. That is to say, if living conditions are utterly miserable and the social environment is totally hostile, claims for respect will hardly be articulated, let alone recognised. When, in turn, the community is strong enough to ward off the stigmatising effects of ethnicity, a sense of ethnic pride may surface as it happens typically in urban ethnic neighbourhoods. Curiously, the viability of assimilation is also heavily contingent on the social acceptance of one's ethnic identity that is about to be abandoned. Moreover, assimilation is a real option only as long as the expected outcome is acknowledged by the society that sets it as a requirement. In contrast, when the very possibility of becoming part of the society is denied to 'visible' minorities on quasi-ontological grounds, such attempts are necessarily doomed to failure. Paradoxically, 'acting white' may bring about rewards even in a repressive society that bans the expression of ethnic differences, while it does not work in a quasi-liberal state if its feasibility is pre-emptively questioned on racialised or racist grounds. Cosmopolitanism, allowing for a virtually unconstrained development and exhibition of individual identities, in turn, may breed only in a truly liberal social environment as the bracketing of ethnic or national origins makes sense only when these can be displayed equally.

Notes

1. Religion and, to a lesser extent, language, common origins or intentional migration represent important elements in the construction of what Ogbu calls 'voluntary minorities', in contrast with 'involuntary minorities' formed by coercive forces, such as discrimination or segregation, or that are produced by the vicissitudes of history (Ogbu 1991). At an individual level or even in an intergenerational comparison (for example, among migrants), it is not always easy to make the distinction, as is suggested, among others, by theories on acculturation (Gordon 1964, Berry 1991, Gundykunst and Kim 2003).

2. We reserved the term 'ghettos' to denote impoverished and neglected, urban or rural residential areas, populated mostly or only by members of an ethnic group (including 'Roma colonies' or 'Roma rows' in Central and Eastern Europe), while ethnic enclaves in inner cities are referred to here as 'ethnic neighbourhoods' (Zhou 2005). 'Ghettos' and 'slums' – the two basic types of 'excluded localities' – are distinguished by the significance of ethnicity, prevalent in the former and dissolved in the latter.

8

Dampened Voices: A Comparative Look at Roma Adolescents' Discourses on Being 'Othered' at School

Margit Feischmidt

Introduction

There exists a considerable body of work in sociology and anthropology which addresses the issues of educational disadvantages and poor school performance of ethnic minority children. According to an influential paradigm resulting from an anthropological approach to the study of the educational process, significant differences in the cultural and religious backgrounds of minority and majority students provide the primary explanation for the achievement gap between these two groups. This assumption is challenged by John Ogbu, who has demonstrated that underachievement is characteristic of the members of communities who are integrated formally but who are actually restricted in their upward mobility (Ogbu 1991). Gibson's work has proved that children of identical ethnic background, or originating from the same country, can obtain different achievement levels at different schools, even more in different national educational systems, depending on the relationship of the immediate and wider social environment towards them (Gibson 1996).

Sociologists and anthropologists inspired by neo-Marxist theories have shifted the focus of education research: by reconsidering the role of schooling in achieving equality and offering a chance for social mobility for disadvantaged youth, the reproduction of inequalities and marginal positions has come to the fore (Chambers 1976, Willis 1981, Hall and Jefferson 1997). Yet from another perspective, scholars of cultural studies claim that working-class youths' opposition to the educational system and their emerging counterculture play a major role in the reproduction of their inherited class position (Willis 1981). Students' attitudes – manifested in their speech, everyday behaviour and interactions – have become the focus of a culturally oriented strand of new education research. Likewise, ethnographic investigations of youth subcultures have reflected on the multifarious deprivation of ethnic minority youth by posing the question of whether minority groups could take an active position against racism (which most often appears in combination with other forms of social oppression). In this vein, authors such as Stuart Hall and Paul Gilroy claim that the cultural politics of 'Blackness' can be seen as a response to the common experience of racism and marginalisation that produces a range of different popular manifestations (Back 1996, p. 3). Hebdidge, Chambers and others derive meanings of racism and anti-racism from style formations. However, their analyses leave aside the interactional components and the everyday experience of racism and ethnicity (Hebdidge 1974, Chambers 1976). In contrast, Les Back gave an ethnographic account of 'racism and multiculture in young lives' by claiming that, in most cases, racism is talked about in the context of lived relationships, events and experiences (Back 1996, p. 161).

The ethnographic approach and the neo-Marxist paradigm of British cultural studies have influenced scholarly work on education and minority youth in other Western European countries as well. However, they have had little resonance in research on young Roma and their educational opportunities in Central and Eastern Europe where mainstream studies have basically concentrated on the systemic aspects of education, the differences in educational opportunities, and the subsequent lack of integration of Roma into the labour market (Dupcsik and Vajda 2008). The EDUMIGROM research programme partly intended to fill this gap by giving an ethnographic account of what happens in schools and in the classrooms where ethnic minority students' marginal position, their low achievements and, in many cases, a gradual turning away from schooling are reproduced. One of the aims of our investigation was to map the social life and relations in the schools by observing the day-to-day realities of 'othering' (Jensen 2011) and by studying the processes creating categories of difference and the ways in which these categories become parts of the lives of minority youths (Cornell and Hartmann 2006, Brubaker et al. 2007).

In line with the ethnographic as well as the post-Marxist approach of 'othering', this chapter offers a comparative view of minority and, primarily, Roma adolescents' experiences and reactions to 'othering' by analysing the contents of their testimonies and also by looking at their reactions to and identification with the perceived forms of being 'othered'. The first section will study their sense of being discriminated against by the main actors of everyday life at school. The second part will focus on the manifest and latent racialising contents in adolescents' inter-ethnic encounters.

Actors, activities and explanations of 'othering' in minority students' discourses

In the context of minority students' discourses about experiences of being 'othered' in their school and social milieu, I will first present the most frequently mentioned topics and arguments that accompany this phenomenon and introduce the ways in which students' experiences are interpreted.

'Othering' in students' discourse about school activities and relations to teachers

Although it is central in studies on ethnic minority students, the difference in achievement by ethnicity is less interesting for us in this discussion. We will only consider how these differences are ethnicised or racialised in students' discourses.

In this context, elements of an ethnicised dichotomist system could be revealed by which learning implies 'acting white' and refusing to learn correlates with 'acting Black'. A Slovak Roma boy said: 'Whites want to learn, they want to get something, most of them. They care about school. But this is a Roma character. They do not learn. This is their worst character.'

However, we also found more complex ways in which strategies of educational incorporation were influenced by students' perceptions of ethnoracial and/or social differences. Most ethnic minority students in our study think, just like their majority peers, that the school 'is about competition, successful are those who study and behave appropriately, and unsuccessful are those who don't learn or don't behave properly,' as a student from a migrant background in Denmark remarked. While committed and competitive minority students are found among economic migrants in Sweden, Denmark and partially in the UK, very few Roma speak in similar terms. A Roma girl in Slovakia, who is quite successful in school, emphasises the structural barriers that she has to face: 'that I am first of all a Roma and a Roma woman has never achieved anything'.

Some students feel comfortable in the school even though they are not committed to its official goals. They take advantage of it as a social space which helps them to create and maintain social relations beyond the neighbourhood and their families. A similar phenomenon could also be observed among second-generation migrant adolescents from post-colonial backgrounds, and it manifested itself in the investigated schools at the Central European sites too. These young people with a pronounced attitude towards networking are less concerned with their teachers than with their classmates. Their efforts to create friendships and peer communities help to differentiate them from those who are committed to learning. Ethnic or racial categories are often applied in their struggle to legitimise their alternative approach.

Many Roma students say that they do not like the school as such; instead of aspiring to meet the academic requirements they like to hang around together. If this preferred social activity can take place in school (usually the same peer groups are involved), they remain in school longer. Students in troubled classes, who are in constant disagreement with the teachers and who, at the same time, do not find partners for togetherness among their classmates, might easily feel alienated from school and develop an oppositional strategy (Szalai 2011).

One of the most common subjects of minority students' conversations – as of students' in general – are the teachers and their judgements. It is important to mention here that most of the students in our study declared that they felt safer in their schools than in broader society and they usually regarded their teachers as more just and fair than most adults in the outer world. Complaints by minority students about being treated differently by their teachers were rare in the Western communities of our inquiry. Unjust acts of teachers were openly denied in France and reported to happen accidentally in German schools. However, complaints about teachers' unjust treatment were much more prevalent in the case of Roma students at our Central European sites.

Most of the British, French, Danish and Swedish school staff seemed to be conscious – although to varying degrees – of the relationship between school and society, including the role of the teachers in managing the conflicts and injuries arising from the relations between students from different social and cultural backgrounds. At the same time, most of their Central European colleagues teaching Roma students declare that they do not care about their students' social problems. Moreover, they seem to reproduce – intentionally or not – the worst anti-Gypsy attitudes of the dominant society – be it in Hungary, Romania, Slovakia or the Czech Republic. Roma pupils from a Slovak school talked about a teacher who often commented on the disorder when he entered the classroom by saying 'I feel like I'm in a *Gypsy* village!', by which he meant that he found the classroom messy and smelly. In all four Central European countries, students complained that cases of harassment among students (whether verbal or physical) were not punished at all by the teachers. Teachers usually do not even notice these incidents because – as the interviews with teachers suggest – most of them think that the school is 'not about changing cultural habits and presumptions'. The perceived cultural dichotomy between teachers and students is certainly less powerful when members of the ethnic minority are also represented among the teachers. We assume that minority students in our French, Swedish, Danish and, in part, also in our British schools feel more comfortable and relaxed because in these educational units one-third to half of the teachers are themselves of ethnic minority origin.

Students' complaints about 'bad teachers' are often expressed by the leaders of oppositional groups who think that they are more readily punished than their majority peers for the same act. The fact that students who have a negative image of the teachers have a decisive role in the narrative construction of the anti-school, anti-establishment position is very common in schools and not only in the schools of our study. However, the memory of 'bad teachers' was also widespread in our adolescent communities among students committed to school. Many Roma and some German Turkish students claimed that negative experiences with some of their teachers broke their school career. A Slovak Roma girl recounted how she was the only Roma in her class and was humiliated by her teacher in front of her classmates. She then went to a grammar school, only for Roma, where her teachers were more helpful and her classmates kinder. This is a typical story supporting the perceived advantages of the minority-only schools, which nonetheless offer fewer opportunities for acquiring social and academic competence and hardly ever offer careers for upward mobility.

The 'good teachers' are also present in ethnic minority students' discourse, albeit less frequently. Among the children of the better-educated economic migrants there are students who are grateful that they have the opportunity to study and that they get the necessary support both from their parents and their teachers. The latter can provide such unbiased help because they 'don't make a difference,' as one of the Danish students from an immigrant background stated: 'the teachers look at who you are, not which country you are from'. Although a Hungarian study emphasised the significance of teachers in the career of the first generation of professional Roma women (Kóczé 2010), such commitment was unfortunately rarely mentioned in our Central European minority communities. In one of the Hungarian schools which ran a special programme supporting talented Roma children, a very strong positive relationship has developed between a couple of students and their teachers. Some students (both on the Hungarian sites and particularly in one of the Slovak schools) spoke about 'good teachers' providing support to students' extracurricular activities, either in music or in sports.

'Othering' in peer relations and students' talk about extracurricular activities

By looking at inter-ethnic relations and their variations in a range of Western and Central European communities, we were able to observe how 'othering' affects peer relations and how cultural and religious differences are presented in the domains of leisure and age-specific activities. The great majority of ethnic minority students stated both in interviews and in the question- naires that they had friends from the majority group. At the same time, adolescents from the majority hardly ever mentioned friends from among their minority peers. Hence one assumes that minority teenagers spoke more of their desires than of actual close relationships with classmates from the dominant group. As for the inception of these relationships, it turned out that the organising framework of friendships and gangs was often the neighbourhood that embodied a combination of the marginalised socioeco- nomic situations and the immigrant backgrounds of the involved minority youths. While a common 'us' includes many different ethnic minorities in Sweden, Denmark, France and the UK, where young people mostly describe themselves with reference to multiple identities, the descendants of immigrants in Germany do not consider themselves as Germans but rather as Muslims. The Central European young Roma adolescents are even less likely to have a common identity that they would share with their majority peers as Hungarian or Romanian citizens. Their state of separateness is all the more worth noting because their formal citizenship was never disputed and in many cases they demonstrate strong cultural assimilation.

Cultural differences affect inter-ethnic peer-group relations, first of all if they derive from different religious practices and family norms. Compared with their German majority peers, Turkish and Arabic youths in Berlin have different time frames for leisure activities. They more often spend evenings with the family, their peer socialisation involves more social control from adults and prevents them from alcohol consumption, and they tend to meet in more gender-separated groups. From the beginning of adolescence, these differences seem to gather increasing significance. In the eyes of the Muslim youth and teenagers, the major distinction between them and their German, French or British peers is their different understanding of the gender roles and partner relations. Consequently, not only do liaisons between Muslim girls and non-Muslim boys (and vice versa) become prohibited but also a culturally defined distance and difference between Muslim and non-Muslim girls as well as between Muslim and non-Muslim boys becomes more and more important (Straßburger et al. 2010). Nevertheless, this is certainly less significant for those young people for whom religion is just a symbolic issue that does not regulate their choices. Although the most distinct gender roles and norms are defined by Islam, different understandings of gender roles manifest themselves concerning Roma as well. In the case of a Romanian Roma group (the Gabor Roma), a fundamentalist neo-Protestant church together with a very strong patriarchal ideology are the main guardians of ethnospecific gender distinctions. Though they generally accept public education, the attitude to school has different implications for boys and girls. The girls do not pursue their education beyond the lower secondary level. There are many cases in which Roma girls abandon school because of traditions which make them marry at the age of 12 or 13.

The ethnocultural proscriptions which prohibit any intimate relationship between Roma and non-Roma peers are sometimes even stronger than the religious differences, and these (re)produce the perception as well as the social reality of caste-like hierarchical relations. Financial constraints and the segregated place of residence are additional factors limiting students' possible options of leisure activities. Many Roma boys living in villages or slums, who would like to engage in different sports, cannot afford this. The separation of places for leisure activities, or rather the exclusion of Roma boys and girls from the common facilities, are the most powerful forms of 'othering' which our interviewees perceive as a major sign of discrimination against them. In one of the studied localities in Slovakia, we observed that there were several discos that Roma were prohibited from entering (Kusá et al. 2010). The same is true of the Hungarian sites. At the same time there are certain locales – clubs and pubs – where young Roma tend to congregate while these are considered by non-Roma people as the most dangerous places in town.

One of the most important and sensitive issues regarding the perception of 'othering' is that of students' participation in extracurricular activities, especially class trips and outings. In the Western communities the problem arises from the general expectation that, regardless of their social, ethnic and religious background, all students should take part in a few days of outdoor activity regularly organised at the end of the academic year. Ethnic minority students, and especially their parents, argue that these organised leisure activities remove young people from the control of their families and afford the children more freedom than they would normally have at home. They feel that the school interferes with their private life in a way that they cannot accept. This is most problematic for Muslim families who think that teachers do not regard Islamic rules as acceptable or important.

The situation is exactly the opposite in the Central European schools. In Slovakia, as well as in Romania and at one of the sites in Hungary, Roma students do not attend any of the extracurricular activities (including the ones which take place in the school), but for very different reasons. In these countries the graduation ball after the concluding year of primary school has a similar important and symbolic role as the study trips in German-Muslim youths' relations. In one of the Slovak schools, the telling example of an excellent male student was revealed who did not take part in this festivity. His explanation was that he did not go because nobody would have danced with him. Others, both in Slovakia and in Romania, said that in fact they did not want to participate because these events were boring; nobody liked them. Or another, very common explanation made reference to the self-segregation of minority students and their parents who either cannot afford the expense of extracurricular activities or assume that they will encounter negative experiences that should be cautiously avoided.

Racism as students' explanation for experiencing 'othering'

To what extent do minority students recognise that what happens to them at school, in their peer groups or in their neighbourhoods is not accidental but is rather part of a system? This is an important question that one should address when discussing minority students' discourses on 'othering'. Students articulated two major systemic explanations for being perceived as fundamentally different and being discriminated against on this basis. The first one points to racism and leads them to consider that their experiences of 'othering' are the consequence of the working of a racist social structure, a racist environment, or are the products of a racist majority. The other systemic explanation refers to a cultural framework. According to this, minority adolescents feel that their experience of 'othering' is due to the majority's perception of their fundamentally different habits, values and cultures.

We identified rather different interpretations in the nine countries studied concerning students' general discourses on discrimination and racism. In some countries, such as France, young people reported having very few experiences of racism while in others, such as Hungary, racism became the major explanatory factor for Roma youths' experiences of difference. Referencing majoritarian racism in the discourse of minority students is not only a derivative of their concrete and direct experiences but also of the general discursive context. In France, the official ideology does not accommodate the recognition of ethnicity and it also denies the existence of racism in school. Moreover, the fact that one-third of the teaching staff in the schools under study has an ethnic minority or immigrant background similar to that of their students probably contributes to reducing the significance of negative generalisations. The opposite is true in Hungary, where minority students tend to explain their failures by pointing to discrimination and anti-Gypsy sentiments. Such feelings are widespread among adult Roma as well and generally reflect the widespread ethnoracial fundamentalism among the majority of the Hungarian population.

Due to differences between the social composition of ethnic minority communities and those of the dominant groups, and also to the varying relations between them, the perceived relevance of racism can be different even in the case of different groups within the same country. In the UK, neither our teenage Pakistani interviewees nor their parents brought up the issue of racism as a matter affecting their personal lives. On the contrary, many of them emphasised that life in the UK offered better opportunities for young people than in Pakistan. At the same time, many interviewees from the Caribbean community were hyper-aware that ethnic disparities still continued to exist and that these worked to their detriment.

Those who consider racism to be relevant to their situation reported encountering such manifestations in four areas. The first domain is the general public discourse which affects them the most through stigmatising their residential neighbourhoods. Stigmatisation of the neighbourhood is closely connected to the issue of criminality, which is one of the worst and most oppressing forms of racist perceptions, notwithstanding certain real dangers which are faced by young people who are growing up in ghettos. The second area of racist manifestation is the media which often produces a degrading, dehumanising image of 'problem minorities'. Negative images of both Muslim immigrants and Roma limit the chances for the social recognition of minority youth, even in places where individuals belonging to these minorities do not have to face daily public manifestations of racism (Szalai 2003). This is the case with minority students in Copenhagen who reported investing enormous efforts into distancing themselves from the perceptions of immigrants as responsible for gang violence, social problems and religious fundamentalism. The third issue raised by our young interviewees is that of discrimination on the labour market. Many have grown up hearing stories from their parents and relatives about being rejected or fired because of their skin colour or their foreign accent. In certain countries, notably the Central European ones, such testimonies are reinforced by age-group specific grievances arising from encounters with anti-Gypsy and racist youths and music subcultures. These symptoms, representing the fourth strong manifestation of refusal and discrimination, are widespread in the post-socialist region, being particularly virulent in the North-Eastern part of Hungary but also in Slovakia and some parts of Romania. Students attending segregated 'Gypsy' classes within formally integrated schools face daily reminders of their fears by way of the symbols and representatives of skinheads and extremist right-wing subcultures in the streets and bars, as well as in school.

Minority students' perceptions of the culturalisation of 'othering'

We encountered three types of cultural approach regarding the presence of ethnic minority students on the part of the institution. The most common school policy is a culture-blind approach which reflects the meritocratic and universalist perspectives of the educational systems in Europe. Less popular is a culture-conscious approach, be it in the form of a multicultural policy – as in the UK or Sweden – or by applying an ethnocultural perspective as a couple of Central European and German school-experiments demonstrate. In addition to these two official cultural policies we observed how a third form of hidden culturalisation of social distinctions transpired through teachers' discourses and behaviour, notably those working in Central European schools.

Many students said that they found majoritarian reactions concerning their particular religious or cultural habits to be demeaning. The most common complaint in the Western European immigrant communities was the prohibition on wearing the headscarf. A young German Turkish woman recalled with bitterness that teachers in primary school had criticised her headscarf and ordered her to remove it during sports: 'One female teacher was so brutal. She once even forced me to leave the sports hall without my headscarf.' Now in the *Gymnasium* she is allowed to wear a headscarf: 'They accept it. Therefore, I like to be here. Teachers here are used to us.' Other students are harassed by teachers who frequently bring up discussions about misunderstood features of the Muslim culture, such as arranged or forced marriage, partner relations, sexuality and family life in Islam. Often such teachers do not show any intention of entering into an open discussion but rather they want to assert their own perspective. In two Danish schools, minority students also complained about their teachers' tendency to talk about cultural differences in a personalised way by referring to immigrant students in class as examples. Although this happens with the best intentions, certain students feel that such initiatives on the part of the teachers undermine their attempts to become similar and to hide their cultural habits in the school environment.

The cultural peculiarities of ethnic minority students are not regarded with condescension in all of the public schools. Many schools, such as the above-mentioned German *Gymnasium*, have developed a kind of multicultural policy. However, in the critical eyes of adolescents, the negative aspects of multiculturalism are predominant. For instance, the British case shows that, although there were schemes in place which sought to recognise and promote diversity and to increase inter-ethnic community cohesion, in practice they were not utilised effectively as learning resources and thus tended to increase distinctions on cultural grounds (Swann and Law 2010).

While the Central European schools were the least likely to give any significance to minorities' cultural peculiarities, very few students complained about this. This is most probably the consequence of longstanding assimilationist policies applied by the respective states amidst the concurrent and wide support of the non-Roma majorities. One of the schools hosting a large number of Roma students in South-Western Hungary started to deal openly with issues of Roma identity. Since many Roma teenagers feel ashamed of their origin, the school put special emphasis on stressing the positive values of Roma culture. A 'Gypsy club' was organised once a week in order to teach all students dances, songs and tales from the minority culture. This activity was soon terminated due to a lack of financial support and interest. Paradoxically, the initiative had started at a moment when most of the local Roma population, notably young people, had already been acculturated and therefore had lost the affective emotional ties to their language and specific traditions.

The performative reactions of minority youths to 'othering'

Focusing on the interactions between minority and majority peers, we studied how 'othering' was realised and replicated in three performative contexts: (1) through the verbal conflicts and insults among youth; (2) during acts of teasing and joking; and (3) when showing off one's anti-school position through youth and ethnic subcultures.

A glance at these inter-ethnic occurrences highlights very clearly that being different is not a continuous experience or an omnipresent issue in minority young people's lives and social relations. The issue comes up intermittently, most often through ritualised forms of communication. Interestingly, the experience of 'othering' presented in the preceding section is played out in these situations and reveals how different categories and systems of difference (gender, class and ethnicity) intersect and take on special meanings in particular interactive contexts.

Verbal conflict, insults

Analysts of working-class youth have introduced the idea that school represents an arena in the life of students where they not only reproduce their current social positions but also develop new rebel positions and cultures (Willis 1981, Hall and Jefferson 1997). There exists a conflict-driven relation between the followers of an accommodation strategy and those who adopt a strategy of resistance. The school as an arena for the opposing parties and their struggles not only offers a space to act out the conflicts between the conformists and the rebels but also makes it possible to reproduce the general conflicts and contradictions of the larger community from which the students come.

Les Back believes that incidents of racist name-calling among British youth lead to flight from multiethnic peer space and result in moments of heightened 'race' consciousness. In a different Central European multiethnic environment, Brubaker et al. (2007) also found that conflicts and insults demonstrated the manner in which ethnicity became salient in everyday relations.

While French youth acknowledged the ambivalence and the playful character of verbal conflicts, in the Central European localities, similar exchanges between Roma and non-Roma peers were considered rather as verbal abuse. Some teenagers painfully recalled situations in which they were called 'Gypsy'. 'I did not tell anything to anybody. It was that way. It was such a peculiar feeling. Then it has stopped when I have grown older.' Another student remarked on how it felt very unpleasant and frustrating when her schoolmates regularly treated her differently because of her darker skin: 'It is disgusting this shouting... For instance, if a Roma girl walks around, they start to shout at her: "Gypsy goes, look at her, Gypsy!" However, if a white girl walks around, it is normal, nobody cares.'

Some of our young Roma interviewees spoke of 'radical peers' as fomenters of anti-Gypsy instigations. A Slovak Roma girl recounted how in her primary school there were often quarrels, usually started by 'radical schoolmates': 'The teachers either did not know about it or did not want to know, or did not believe it. Therefore the conflicts were not handled.' Outside school, more conflicts and physical attacks were provoked by a group of skinheads from the village. The Hungarian Roma teenagers living in a ghetto district also complained about the verbal insults which they had to endure from their 'racist' Hungarian peers.

Ethnicity is not evoked during the conflict but rather immediately after it when the idiom of race or ethnicity provides a readily available explanatory framework for the dispute. Whenever a conflict takes place among students that involves Roma youth, the latter immediately resort to an ethnic interpretation. We occasionally witnessed contradictions between the interpretation of Roma students and our ethnographic observations. While Roma students in Hungary reported frequent conflicts between Roma and majority peers, none of the conflicts that we witnessed during our field observations appeared to have any direct and evident ethnic or inter-ethnic motivations or implications. However, all quarrels were readily ethnicised and made to fit into this explanatory framework. In one instance, a clumsily thrown snowball caused a fight. While boys from Class A played among themselves, one of the snowballs hit by chance the head of a boy from Class B. This was immediately interpreted as a deliberate ethnic offence in which a Hungarian student had attacked a Roma boy, who promptly answered the insult by beating his offender. All of the Roma and non-Roma youths who were present when this story was recounted agreed that the conflict had taken place for ethnic reasons, thus demonstrating how both the minority and the majority contribute to the fixation of such interpretations (Kovai 2012).

Teasing and joking about 'otherness'

Several years ago we studied the relevance of joking relations in the everyday construction of ethnicity (Brubaker et al. 2007, p. 285). In line with Les Back's ethnographical description of 'duelling play' in everyday relations among youth in London, we found that joking in inter-ethnic situations was a practice whereby young people tested the limits and the potentials of their personal relationships versus group belongings.

French students reported frequent teasing among classmates and usually tended to minimise the role of ethnicity in the interpretation of these events. Our interviews show that urban minority youths find kidding and teasing to be the most acceptable ways of facing and treating 'otherness'. The manifestations of such teasing can vary to a very large degree, the most common subject of teasing being skin colour, as illustrated by the following excerpt from a focus group discussion with Roma youths in Hungary: 'but we have our little jokes ... Like, for example, chocolate boy ... , like that ... That's how we show Feri we like him'. (Feri is a successful Roma student who is popular among his peers, not so much because of his academic achievements but because of his sporting prowess and masculinity).

When students are teasing each other about their skin colour in an ironic way, they subvert racial meanings and create an anti-racist stance. However, teasing relations may also reproduce social and racial inequalities – for example, if the protagonists of the jokes obviously differ in status. Ethnic jokes have a special meaning in deeply divided societies since they reproduce inequality in a mild, delusive way, appearing harmless to the dominant majority while often being offensive to the affected minority. The following example from Slovakia illustrates this very general relationship. A Slovak

Roma boy was describing his positive relations with a 'good' non-Roma classmate with whom he spent a lot of time. 'He is more often with us than with whites.' However, he and his Roma friends feel embarrassed when they see that their non-Roma friend is laughing at jokes about Roma or comes up with remarks which make Roma ridiculous. The Roma boys emphasise that they share their embarrassment with him: 'When he is with us, we ask him why he has laughed at such jokes. [We tell him], you are either with us or with them' (Kusá et al. 2010).

Performing 'otherness' by showing off

The third performative reaction to 'othering' is typical of students who adopt an oppositional stance. Such attitudes of opposition become meaningful within a larger context as manifestations of a culture of resistance. Resistance to school is materialised in a continuous fight between a certain category of students and the institution. Through such struggles, those who resist accommodation strive to appropriate physical and symbolic spaces from the school in order to introduce their own rules and gain control. They resort to truancy in order to undermine the educational objective of putting people to work. We met the highest rate of truancy and drop-out among Roma students in the Central European schools. This is an individual strategy of opposition which, in some cases, is also supported by the students' family. However, in most of the cases, minority students and likewise their majority peers resort to collective strategies of opposition, targeting the educational system in its entirety. Through their clothing, their manners of speech and their ways of amusing themselves which are different from what is considered by the school as the norm, they express their resistance to the institution. We have found that young people living in the multiethnic Western European ghettos manage to find effective performative tools and opportunities to show off and to develop reactive positions against their structural inferiority. By contrast, Roma teenagers from our Central European communities who feel rejected by the school do not develop clear and articulated reactive positions against the educational system. It was interesting to see how far ethnicity became relevant in fuelling certain reactive positions and how it was instrumentalised in order to create a kind of 'identity politics' against racism.

Conclusion

In conclusion of our discussion about minority students' experiences of 'othering', it can be established that there are two major types of discursive position which ethnic minority students can adopt: downplaying and overcommunicating 'othering'. There are social factors which influence these discursive positions, such as the students' perceived chances of inclusion and social mobility, as well as their relation to the educational system. Our comparative empirical material shows that undercommunication of 'othering' seems to be coherent with an attitude of accommodation, while overcommunication of 'othering' correlates with an oppositional stance towards schooling.

To avoid or to downplay the experience of 'othering' is what minority students tend to do when the difference that they are supposed to represent in terms of religion, language or culture is too far from their everyday practice and therefore does not prove relevant for their self-understanding. The students engaging in this strategy are preoccupied first and foremost with topics that are common to minority and majority youths alike: these are age-related issues for the most part. Additionally, the strategy of 'downplaying' implies an enduring conscious effort on the part of the minority teenagers who would like to be accepted and appreciated by the school system and/or by their peers, and to this end they try to hide elements from their personal history that they think might impede such efforts.

Downplaying the experience of 'othering' is strengthened by an attitude of subordination of all other interests to those of schooling and to efforts to get ahead. This attitude is found among second-generation economic migrants and some youths from post-colonial migrant backgrounds. Successful students who are often striving to accomplish the upward mobility project of their families through a promising school career, as well as those who report having more friends among the majority, certainly are less affected by and therefore less preoccupied with 'the differences' assigned to them, and more inclined to hide or downplay their experiences of unwelcome 'othering' (including injustice and discrimination on the part of representatives of the majority – be they teachers, parents or peers).

Possessing social and cultural capital which brings minority students closer to the school and offers them some protection against being defenceless to 'othering' was emphasised in many cases, most of all by ethnic minority youths in Sweden, Denmark and the UK. At the same time the Roma students of Central and Eastern Europe have virtually no opportunities to downplay their experience of 'othering', except those few adolescents who come from a solid middle-class social and economic background and who are integrated into their non-Roma environment in terms of both their residence and their schooling.

Overcommunicating 'othering' and emphasising discrimination is the most common strategy of Roma youth in the schools and communities of all four Central and Eastern European countries. Personal stories about abuse and discrimination are central to their narratives. Though less essential in a personal sense, we met narratives of discrimination and the tendency towards overcommunication in Western cities with large immigrant communities too. However, an important difference derives from whether young people can or cannot find their own voice to react against the perceived 'othering'. The self-assertive capacity can be strengthened from two directions: either from the ethnic community which provides minority youth with enough safety and powerful symbolic capital to build reactive strategies, or from the peer community which empowers them with the social capital deriving from the class- and neighbourhood-based inclusive relations. When none of these capitals are at their disposal, minority youth become defenceless and downtrodden by the majority discourses. This is what characterises the situation of Roma adolescents and shows, at the same time, the most remarkable difference between the relative social positions of Roma and post-migrant youths.

9

Educational Strategies of Minority Youth and the Social Constructions of Ethnicity

Bolette Moldenhawer

In the European epoch of the knowledge society, education has become increasingly important. It is both a central pillar of the welfare society and a decisive resource of social mobility and positioning that together explain the outstanding importance of academic qualifications. The increasingly complex conditions in education are part of the currents of social mobility generally, and ethnic mobility in particular. In this chapter, I consider the experience of education among young people from ethnic minority backgrounds, their descriptions of success or failure, and the role of their socioeconomic positions, gender and ethnicity in shaping their achievements. I shall examine how minority students view their future and see education as a factor in shaping their pathway to adulthood. The field material providing the basis for the discussions consists of interviews with students in their concluding year of compulsory education and also with their parents. The observations of different minority groups in the nine countries participating in the EDUMIGROM research programme will reveal a variety of educational strategies that cut across ethnic backgrounds and national contexts, and are influenced by a series of factors, such as socioeconomic positions, residential segregation of schools, and various forms of racism and discrimination.

The chapter is organised into three main parts. The first delineates the theoretical-analytical framework by describing the key concepts of Bourdieu's theory of practice (Bourdieu 1997). This is followed by a description of John U. Ogbu's approach (Ogbu 1978, 1987, 1991) to young minorities' sociocultural adaption and cultural model of schooling.[1] The second more analytical part deals with educational strategies from the perspective of experiences, attitudes and prospects of schooling among young minorities. I have identified three strategies: a strategy of commitment, a strategy of instrumentation and a strategy of opposition. The analysis is shaped by what

I call a continuum between these three strategies. The third and concluding part places the empirical findings in perspective.

Theoretical-analytical framework

Bourdieu's theory of practice comprises three major concepts: habitus, strategy and capital. Learning associated with a particular class of condition of existence produces *habitus*,

> systems of durable, transposable dispositions, structured structures predisposed to function as structuring structures, that is, as principles which generate and organise practices and representations that can be objectively adapted to their outcomes without presupposing a conscious aiming at ends or an express mastery of the operations necessary in order to attain them. (Bourdieu 1990, p. 53)

In other words, habitus accounts for a social agent's practical sense; it is a form of 'second nature' that gives a so-called 'feel for the game' (Bourdieu and Wacquant 1992, pp. 120–121). This 'feel for the game' is what enables an infinite number of 'moves' to be made, adapted to the large number of possible situations and contexts which no rule, however complex, can foresee.

Even more central to the work of habitus is Bourdieu's notion of *strategy*, which will be used analytically to understand the educational strategies of minority youth, and how their perceptions, appreciations and actions in education are conditioned by the embodiment of immanent necessities as perceived and translated from the social world. In fact, a key feature of Bourdieu's analysis of strategies is the persistent incorporation of objective chances in the form of subjective hopes and mental schemes, be it in schools, on the labour market or in politics. The ongoing dialectic of subjective hopes and objective chances can yield a variety of outcomes, ranging from a perfect mutual fitting (when people's desires are objectively destined) to radical disjunction (when people's desires are objectively non-destined) (Bourdieu and Wacquant 1992, p. 130). The presumption embedded in this notion of strategy is that the actions that people perform to realise their goals may have principles other than mechanical causes or the conscious intentions that call forth a practical mastery of the game and its risks.

Bourdieu uses the concept of *capital* to explain people's capacities to 'play the game', and the resources that they accumulate and exchange in order to maintain their positions within a social field. He describes different forms of capital: economic, cultural and symbolic capital. Economic capital is a term for real monetary forms that result from possessing this capital. It carries a certain importance but draws its actual value from the symbolic dimension.

Cultural capital, on the other hand, exists in several forms but is mostly tied to an embodied form of cultivation. Moreover, cultural capital, in its institutionalised form, refers to formal education, and in its objective form to the property and cultural techniques, routines and procedures (for example, legitimate knowledge, technology, art and institutions) that act to legitimise the cultural goods (Bourdieu 1997). An important dimension of the analysis to come is the fact that the different forms of capital can be converted to one of the other forms, the conversion to symbolic capital being the most powerful, because it is through this form of capital that the other forms are unconsciously seen and recognised as legitimate (Bourdieu and Wacquant 1992).

To better understand the social practices among ethnic minority groups, I also draw upon the work of John U. Ogbu and his explanation of differences in school success or failure which are historically determined. To him, the historical background of a minority group's incorporation is a crucial factor in understanding why they have different attitudes and expectations towards the immigrant community, the majority ethnic group and the school system. He operates with two types of minority group, distinguishable by the manner of their incorporation into the receiving society. He calls the first group 'involuntary (non-immigrant) minorities,' who are 'people who have been conquered, colonised, or enslaved...who have been made part of the U.S. society permanently against their will' (Ogbu and Simons 1998, p. 165). The other group is referred to as 'voluntary (immigrant) minorities', whose community consists of 'those who have more or less willingly moved to the United States because they expect better opportunities (better jobs, more political and religious freedom) than they had in their homelands or place of origin' (p. 165). Voluntary minorities consider social discrimination to be a temporary phenomenon and develop a 'pragmatic trust' in society and its educational system (p. 174); they consider cultural and linguistic adaptation to be positive appendages to their identity, and they develop 'a strategy of "accommodation and acculturation without assimilation" ' (Gibson 1993, p. 438). Involuntary minorities, on the other hand, see discrimination as continuous and inherent in a racially stratified society and they develop an oppositional stance to assimilation requirements. They consider cultural and linguistic differences to be 'makers of collective identity to be maintained, not merely barriers to be overcome' (Ogbu and Simons 1998, p. 175) and they continue to resist adaption because it constitutes a threat to their cultural identity. Although this categorisation of voluntary and involuntary minorities cannot be transferred directly to the minority groups whose educational strategies are discussed in this chapter and whose ancestors had been incorporated with a certain mix of voluntary and involuntary elements via post-colonial migration (as in France or the UK) or economic migration (as in Denmark, Germany or

Sweden) (Szalai et al. 2010), Ogbu's approach is an important aid to understanding why minority groups respond differently to the school system.

To approach ethnicity, I consider forms of cultural difference that act as a marker of social difference. I, among others, am inspired by Fredrik Barth's notion of ethnic boundaries (Barth 1969), which, contrary to the view of ethnicity that stresses shared culture, favours a more relational approach, emphasising that group membership and commonality is identified in contrast with the perceived identity of other racial and ethnic groups. The basic idea behind this notion of ethnicity is that the content of ethnic categories is socially constructed rather than grounded in any objective, essential biological reality (Moldenhawer 2011). Given that inter-ethnic and intra-ethnic group relations are dynamic, the analysis to come will show how ethnic categorisations can have different cultural meanings in different national contexts. Attention will be paid to experiences and attitudes towards education among minority youths across Europe, given that they are in a position from which they cannot expect to easily convert their cultural capital (in embodied form) to symbolic capital – that is, as recognised educational skills.

Experiences and attitudes towards education among minority youths across Europe

After providing a brief overview of the socioeconomic positions of the students interviewed, I shall present my analysis of the main factors which account for the differentiation between the three educational strategies and cut across ethnic backgrounds and national contexts. These factors are immigration and socioeconomic backgrounds, school models of inclusion and patterns of discrimination.

Socioeconomic positions

The students' socioeconomic positions are differentiated on the basis of the parents' labour market status and level of education. The vast majority of the young people from Roma backgrounds live in underprivileged conditions with no regular jobs, and most of them have little or no education. Among the students whom we interviewed in Denmark and Sweden, a significant proportion are also regarded as socially disadvantaged. The majority of the parents are unemployed or earn minimum wages, while others are self-employed and rarely educated past primary level. Some families do, however, manage to achieve a more favourable socioeconomic position and leave the socially disadvantaged districts. The pattern among families in Denmark and Sweden, as well as among some Roma families in Central Europe, is indeed that they do their best to move away from the segregated areas as soon as their socioeconomic situation improves. In Germany, the socioeconomic position of half of the interviewed immigrant families of Turkish and Lebanese backgrounds is also heavily influenced by either unemployment or a compromised employment situation that does not provide the necessary minimum income for a decent living. The minorities of a post-colonial background whom our study approached in France and the UK are generally more settled in terms of residence and labour market position. In France, the sample includes mostly minorities of Maghreb and Afro-Caribbean backgrounds, while in the UK it is mostly minorities of Afro-Caribbean and Pakistani backgrounds who were interviewed. The majority of the Pakistani families live in socially deprived areas with labour market situations varying from jobless and blue-collar workers' positions (such as taxi drivers) to professionals. In the French sample, only a few of the parents are regarded as qualified professionals, such as nurses, engineers or policemen. At the same time, it is outstandingly true in the French case that the range of educational qualifications is much wider among the immigrant parents than among the non-immigrant parents because many of the former have worked as qualified professionals in their country of origin. They have not, however, succeeded in finding jobs at a similar level in France. This means that the position that they occupy in France masks the variety of professional qualifications and cultural capital in its embodied form.

Educational strategies

Strategies of commitment

Students who consider schooling as a necessary means of social mobility and also as a guarantee of obtaining a secure life apply a strategy of commitment. Governed by expediency and 'the logic of necessity,' they work hard to reconcile the disjuncture between their minority position and educational positioning.

The dominant pattern among Roma students within this category is that they consider the presence of white students within ethnically mixed schools important because white students encourage them to strive harder. These Roma students describe how the majority of their own kind with little educational aspiration can hinder their intensive study progress. In these ethnically mixed schools with a colour-blind approach, no ethnic group is discriminated against whether positively or negatively, and no classes or curricula involve cultural or linguistic differences. Even though Roma students in such schools prefer to use categories other than their own ethnicity when talking about their families and self-identity, this does not entirely remove ethnicity from their everyday life and their tendency to group together.

In the case of Romania, the so-called Romanianised Roma have developed an identity formation strategy of 'assimilation' with the aim of identifying with the mainstream, on the one hand, and achieving educational success as an instrument for Roma emancipation, on the other (Vincze et al. 2010).

Considering the Hungarian case, only a minority of the Roma students follow this strategy. Among those who are defined as the 'integrated' type, there are high-performing students attending ethnically mixed classes who manage to achieve recognition in education simply by working hard. Being a Roma is not, however, a fundamental part of their self-image. For these Roma students, efforts towards social integration and strong identification with the mainstream culture are developed as a necessary response to social forces of discrimination (Feischmidt et al. 2010).

In the Slovakian case, almost all of the excellent Roma students come from families of a more solid economic status. Even though there are relatively few high achievers among this group of students, there is no shortage of talent: all students with good grades plan to continue onto higher education and to get a university degree (Kusá et al. 2010). In general, all high-achieving Roma students receive the necessary moral support from their families. However, they also share the structural inequality and continuous awareness of racial and ethnic stigmatisation of the entire Roma population. As 'involuntary minorities' they suffered oppression and discrimination for generations, which explains why they have to give up their original identity instead of considering cultural and linguistic adaptation to schooling to be positive appendages to their identity.

In countries of economic immigration, such as Germany and Denmark, there are students with a Muslim background who are indeed devoted to the strategy of commitment. In the Danish sample, these students are mainly Arabic speaking and from ethnically mixed or 'minority' schools with a diversity-conscious approach. These Muslim students of both genders with lower-middle-class parents feel comfortable about schooling and strive for prestigious higher-education programmes. They describe themselves as well-behaved and high-achieving students, and they appreciate teachers who set high standards and push them to achieve. Descriptions of 'doing well' in school are closely linked to high grades, taking an active part in lessons and completing homework assignments which they are more conscientious about than the average student. While 'Muslims' as 'the others' tend to be referred to as such in the society at large, within the school context this label is neutralised and they are perceived as high achievers, which is more flattering. Moreover, they emphasise the importance of having what they call 'the right friends', who might be minority youths with different ethnic backgrounds, aware of the importance of doing well in school. As one Muslim girl of a Turkish background put it, 'If you take care of yourself and do your homework and participate in the classes, then it doesn't matter what country you come from. It is up to the person to show who she or he is and not so much the talk about their background' (Moldenhawer et al. 2010). Another important feature that distinguishes these teenagers from the abovementioned Roma students is the fact that they are historically incorporated as voluntary minorities. For these students, linguistic and cultural differences are important as markers of collective identity to be recognised. Consequently, they are grateful for the educational opportunities available to them in the immigrant society compared with their emigrant societies. They succeed in converting the family's cultural resources (cultural and economic capital) into new forms of (symbolic) capital in situations closed to their parents who often work in unskilled jobs despite possessing valuable educational capital (Moldenhawer 2005, Erel 2010).

Fieldwork in Germany found that minority students were generally strongly influenced partly by the school system of early tracking and partly by ethnic school segregation. However, some Muslim students whose parents have acquired educational capital abroad and for whom quality education seems natural, have ignored the advice often given by teachers to continue education at a lower level (in the *Realschule*) than they wish for (in the *Gymnasium*). They perceive the teachers' attitude as being discriminatory and recount how they have been shamed in public for being 'non-German.' One Muslim girl of a Turkish background described how her primary school teachers had opposed her decision to opt for the *Gymnasium* because she was wearing a headscarf. One teacher expressed his opposition very clearly: 'You will never succeed there!' (Straßburger, Chapter 12 in this volume).

For the students in this category, it is common to view higher education and access to a prestigious profession as a way of showing their parents gratitude for what they have done in terms of immigration. These students strongly subordinate other interests to those related to schooling in an effort to achieve even more than the school and their parents expect of them. They therefore feel responsible if they fail, which results in a strictly disciplined lifestyle. For female students it could be the case, for example, that they have social obligations at home to structure their leisure time, while male students are more likely to spend their leisure time in communities where religious norms and principles are an integrated part of their daily lives. It is a paradox that they make decisions related to success based on objective options that are not actually available to them but that they insist on anyway. The fact is that it is these young people's strong belief in their own opportunities that helps them to overcome obstacles on their path. They are driven by a pragmatic view that makes their chances to succeed in the future appear greater than those actually are, and it is this attitude that allows them to succeed in realising their opportunities. By prioritising the education system more or less completely, with no regard for school models of inclusion, they become the system's best customers (Moldenhawer 2005). Generally, they keep in close contact with their nuclear and extended family since their success is considered as the success of the family as a whole; it is their way of repaying their parents. They can expect some academic support from family members depending on their parents' level of education (cultural capital in its embodied form). They may also receive emotional support and substantial encouragement from the family. The interviews reveal an unmistakeable pattern of confidence among the students in their own ability to realise their dreams – that is, to study and work hard in school. Even if the students speak about discrimination in general, like the Afro-Caribbean girls in Mac an Ghaill's study (1988), they do 'not merely fulfil negative expectations. Instead, they responded to such experiences in a more hidden way, which reflected their commitment to obtaining educational qualifications' (Stevens 2007, p. 160).

Strategies of instrumentation

Minority students from lower socioeconomic backgrounds with a predominantly instrumental strategy do not possess the same sort of self-confidence that they would achieve success in school. Roma students, in particular, who live in underprivileged conditions with no regular jobs, receive poor education and suffer from social exclusion. For the most part, they attend segregated schools (most prevalent in the Czech Republic and Slovakia) or ethnically mixed schools applying internal separation (most prevalent in Hungary and Romania). In these schools, Roma students are stigmatised as mentally or socially deprived. Segregation deprives Roma students not only from quality education and meaningful inter-ethnic personal relations but also from their dignity and self-esteem. Paradoxically, no professional groups or actors are working against this form of educational segregation. Roma parents, for example, tend to choose these segregated schools because they consider them as 'safe' and relaxed environments, despite knowing that their children are faced with lower expectations and a less demanding curriculum than at other schools. This could in fact be viewed as a rational adaptation to what the parents experience as unequal objective opportunities. What the parents want out of the educational investment are qualifications and well paid jobs for their children.

The Romanian fieldwork identified similar cases of Roma students who recognise the symbolic value of schooling and wish to continue their studies after compulsory education but place more importance on maintaining good and trustful relationships with teachers and school professionals (Vincze et al. 2010). Nevertheless, their experiences at school are not always positive. Although they are ambiguous in their attitudes towards the school and the educational choices they are faced with, they are concerned about what will happen if they leave school; their immediate worry is that they will lose their friends and the existing connection with this environment. However, they are tired of school and find it difficult to see the potential of their education. The most pressing question to ask is why to continue if it leads to nothing, or if they lack the ability to continue. They also seem to be less well organised with regard to their spare time and are more interested, on the whole, in spending time with their peers.

In Slovakia, regardless of the different educational strategies for 'survival', Roma students generally display an unwillingness to learn and study at home (Kusá et al. 2010). They are more relaxed about their marks, admit that they prefer to associate in class with other Roma who have similarly relaxed attitudes towards learning, and manage to maintain a high level of personal self-esteem despite their poor school results. On the other hand, Roma students value good relations with their teachers even though they do not formulate ambitions of upward mobility. They prefer to have a normal life, a secure independent means of living and a means of providing for their future Roma family. Another important finding is that these students do not reject Roma students who do work hard and manage to perform well at school.

In the Afro-Caribbean and Pakistani communities in the UK, there are examples of students who are heavily influenced by their parents' downward mobility in terms of status and standard of living. Pakistani girls, in particular, value working hard at school while embracing traditional gender roles. Especially in ethnically mixed schools with a diversity-conscious approach, the school manages to transmit enough hope and aspiration to counterbalance feelings of disappointment. In addition, the students describe how the categories of either 'Black' or 'Muslim' are seen as different markers of identification. While 'Black' in the UK became a marker of political and social identification under the banner of racial disadvantage and discrimination during the 1970s and 1980s to counter 'the exotica of difference' (Hall 2009, p. 206), 'Muslim' has recently been singled out as one of the more problematic markers of identification (Alexander 2009, p. 218). The students especially describe how the rise of 'Islamophobia' has impacted negatively on their future life projections. The frequent association of Muslims with terrorism and their subsequent stigmatisation creates an identity depicted as being in conflict with British culture.

Research has demonstrated that especially Muslim students from Pakistani backgrounds have been singled out as educational 'problems' and that they form part of an 'underclass' (Archer 2003). The Pakistani students in our study do indeed confirm that this group tries to opt out of social and cultural barriers in society at large by pursuing education as a prerequisite for acquiring a better social position.

In the Danish and Swedish cases, minority students who display a strategy of instrumentation consider education as a means of escaping social marginalisation rather than of social mobility. They are from varying ethnic backgrounds and attend 'minority' schools in segregated ethnic communities characterised as 'problem areas' (Moldenhawer and Øland 2012). Previous research has shown that young immigrants with a weak socioeconomic status find it difficult to gain symbolic value from their educational capital compared with young people of a Danish or Swedish background (Moldenhawer 2009, Lundqvist 2010). In countries of immigration (such as

Denmark, Sweden, Germany and France), the term 'immigrant' is used as a further group-specific category of distinction between the (often white) majority population, on the one hand, and the diverse immigrant population, on the other. In Denmark and Sweden, the term 'immigrant' was coined in the 1970s as an administrative category, replacing the previously used 'foreigner' (Alsmark et al. 2007, Jønsson and Petersen 2010). However, it did not take long before 'immigrant' had become associated with generalised stereotypical conceptions of 'the others' and different types of social problem (Horst and Gitz-Johansen 2010). Being categorised as an immigrant is generally associated with difficulties in all societal arenas, such as the labour market (unemployment and ethnic discrimination), housing (housing segregation and a high concentration of immigrants in socially disadvantaged neighbourhoods) and education (lower grades and a lower probability of transition to higher education). One further implication of this social division is that children of immigrants are also considered to be 'immigrants', or 'second-generation immigrants', even though they were born in the receiving society and have lived their entire lives there.

The students whom we interviewed attend schools that have become 'minority' schools as a result of the powerful residential segregation typical of the urban district where they are located. In these schools, the students' thoughts about ethnicity are taken seriously. This, however, does not change the fact that the students are concerned about the compromised learning associated with classes composed of ethnic minorities rather than majorities. They stress the importance of teachers who make them feel safe, recognised and comfortable, but at the same time they describe it as a problem when teachers occasionally have low expectations and do not offer real opportunities to them for improving their results. They are acutely aware that they have to work twice as hard as their majority peers because of their immigrant background. A distinctive strategy for trying to overcome ethnic inequalities (that is, the social categorisation of immigrants as 'problems') is the development of alternative aspirations, such as the desire to move abroad after graduation. For instance, some students whom the researchers met in the course of the fieldwork in Sweden, especially Black students from Ethiopia and Eritrea, describe this as a way of escaping marginalisation and the limited opportunities in Sweden (Kallstenius and Sonmark 2010).

In contrast with students who display a strategy of commitment, these students are regarded as socially disadvantaged on the basis of their parents' lower socioeconomic positions. Without appropriate cultural capital or relevant social capital, they 'may easily find themselves in the "wrong" place or in the "wrong" course with all the risks of drop-out that that brings into play' (Ball 2006, p. 232). In addition, they are more likely than the former group of minority students to suffer from discrimination and the social categorisations of 'Roma', 'Black', 'Muslim' or 'immigrant' and to be viewed as 'problems'.

Generally, this group of students is less able to make a decision about their education. Even though they are aware of the symbolic value of educational qualifications, they find it difficult to put all of the possible choices into perspective. In other words, their perception of education is influenced by how they are perceived and categorised by society, in terms of discrimination, ethnic segregation and social marginalisation. This group of students fails to overcome the disjunction between subjective hopes and objective chances. They do not have the same capacity, or desire, to 'ignore' the societal obstacles outside school. Consequently, these students are conscious that school is a critical judge and that they must work extremely hard to be judged on the same terms as students of a majority background. As a result, they are less able to recognise the distinguishing features of the school than the students outlined within the strategy of commitment, and thus assimilate to the conditions, taking them as given. As minority students whose families occupy subordinate positions, they are desperately aware of their position and what they are up against (Moldenhawer 2005).

Strategies of opposition

Students from disadvantaged families living in segregated neighbourhoods tend to make choices based on an oppositional strategy. This disadvantaged student population perceives education as a foreign world. Many such students, primarily of Roma origin, can be found in the least desirable classes at segregated schools. In Hungary, for instance, ethnic inequalities are effectively maintained by separating classes with a specialised curriculum from average classes, and by subtly and ambiguously classifying students as either 'Gypsy' or 'normal' students (Feischmidt et al. 2010).

Some of the most marginalised members of minority groups perceive the social, political and economic barriers against them as part of their undeserved oppression. The more they experience discrimination and unequal treatment in education, the more they turn to an oppositional frame of reference. Such minority students from the most troubled classes, who are in disagreement with teachers and who reject the dominant system of assessment, easily feel that they do not belong to the school system. This is the case for some of the minority students in France where educational failure is linked more closely to oppositional anti-school behaviour and unwillingness to optimise studies than to limited potential (Schiff 2010). Consequently, minority students are more inclined to blame the (vocational) schools and the teachers for their failure than majority students who are more grateful to the schools for keeping them, despite their potential personal failings and limitations, such as dyslexia or other cognitive impairments. In France, the serious difficulties that minority youths and residents of the *banlieues* (suburbs) continue to face in relation to education are not described in terms of racism and discrimination, however. Due to the republican principle of equality which opposes differentiation based on ethnicity (Brinbaum and Cebolla-Boado 2007, p. 446), major 'racial' and 'ethnic' distinctions are instead being made between the *jeunes des cités* ('ghetto youth') and 'the others' (Schiff, Chapter 11 in this volume). At the same time, it has been argued that a crucial feature of ethnicisation in France is 'the refusal to address the obstacles race creates for the racialized people' (Tissot 2007, p. 368). Rather than describe the problems that immigrants face in terms of racism, immigrants are considered to be 'problems' related to socioeconomic background, the influence of an anti-school peer culture, a difficult home environment or insurmountable cultural differences.

In the German case, the students of a Turkish background are perceived by teachers as 'foreigners' or 'outsiders' who should be taught to adapt to the dominant culture. In these 'minority' schools with a colour-blind approach, an oppositional school culture and lack of discipline emerge among Turkish minority students, likely as a result of their limited educational opportunities. The reaction can also be seen as a justified expression of cultural norms and habits to foreign members of the dominant culture. As demonstrated by the interviews and focus group discussions with these students, they feel the need to protect their ethnic identity against the encroachment of the German teachers who are trying to 'force' them to assimilate.

Educational strategies of opposition have been noted among minority students with roughly similar social class membership to that of students structured by a strategy of instrumentation. The difference is that these students tend to perceive 'education' as a hostile and foreign world, and themselves as victims, particularly of segregated, stigmatised and marginalised school institutions, but also of society as a whole. As long as they have no choice in terms of social positioning, other than to continue their education, they tend to hold teachers and the school system responsible for their failure. Even though their parents have been historically incorporated as voluntary immigrants, their children see discrimination as continuous and inherent in an ethnicised and racially stratified society, which explains their opposition to assimilation requirements. As the above analysis suggests, it makes a difference whether a minority group is bound together by relative success or by stigmatisation.

Educational strategies across national contexts: Concluding remarks

The analysis has clearly demonstrated that the symbolic value of education as the route toward a desirable future influences minority youths' experiences, practices and aspirations. It is apparent that the students express, albeit in different ways, a strong belief in the significance of education which they see as the most obvious entry path to the labour market. Bourdieu and Ogbu's concepts were introduced to understand the varying patterns of experiences, practices and aspirations related to educational incorporation. In the continuum between strategies of commitment, instrumentation and opposition, I have drawn attention to the ways in which minority youths across national contexts construct a variety of conceivable futures. The questions of race, ethnicity, gender and socioeconomic position are central here to understanding their educational prospects and future in society. To illustrate and contextualise each educational strategy of identification, I used data from a small number of cases from a variety of national contexts. I am not suggesting, however, that the analysis applies to all minority students who were interviewed in the course of the EDUMIGROM research, let alone the entireties of youth communities from immigrant backgrounds.

This chapter has shown that experiences of discrimination, and social and ethnic differentiation in education across national contexts can affect minority students' future career prospects in different ways, especially if they attend school in socially disadvantaged environments. Regardless of the varying forms of ethnic 'othering', it is apparent that the students perceive being categorised as 'Muslim', 'Black', 'immigrant' or 'ghetto youth' as a stigma and a disadvantage. It is, however, the students who display a strategy of opposition who suffer the most from discrimination and the social categorisation of 'othering'. Although these specific forms of discrimination are considered to be types of inequality in themselves, they are also deeply embedded in the history of immigrant incorporation within each of the national contexts of the study.

The analysis also reveals how minority students position themselves differently as a result of different educational strategies in different national contexts and social status hierarchies. In particular, the students who display a strategy of commitment towards accommodation make decisions related to educational success based on subjective hopes for 'overcoming' the barriers of objective opportunities. They consciously subordinate other interests to those of schooling in an effort to achieve even more than what is expected of them, which is why they feel responsible if they fail. However, the students who display a strategy of opposition and are heavily influenced by their parents' experiences of social disadvantage, marginalisation and segregation do not see school as a source of hope and aspiration to counterbalance feelings of disappointment. These students perceive education as a hostile and foreign world, and they hold the system responsible for their failure. The students who are in between and display a strategy of instrumentation are generally more uncertain about whether they will 'make it' in education. They are more concerned about the way they are exposed by society at large in all three terms of discrimination, ethnic segregation and social marginalisation. In comparison with the students who are more likely to overcome the disjunction between subjective hopes and objective chances, these students more often suffer from a desire to 'ignore' the societal obstacles outside school.

To conclude, it has been demonstrated that the strategies of the different groups of minority students can be interpreted as a kind of conversion strategy which transforms their continuous investment in education into a form of symbolic capital. This chapter has thus provided a picture of how minority students are exposed to the ever-increasing requirements of education and how they try to accommodate to a world of enduring social inequality.

Note

1. Young minorities are categorised as 'visible' minority students who we distinguish from students of either a majority background or an immigrant background who 'visibly' do not appear as strangers. This counts for students of Roma backgrounds in Central and Eastern Europe, and for those pupils of immigrant and post-colonial backgrounds in the communities in Western Europe who (or whose ancestors) are of non-European descent.

Part III

Ethnic Differences in Schooling in National Contexts

10

Racism, Ethnicity and Schooling in England

Ian Law and Sarah Swann

Introduction: Ethnicity and the framing of public and political discourses

The UK has always been ethnically diverse with a population developing from complex historical migration patterns and periods of conflict, conquest, state formation, empire and decolonisation. Specific movements relevant here include sporadic in-migration of Gypsies and the importation of African slaves and servants from the sixteenth century onwards, mass migrations of Irish and Jewish people in the nineteenth century and post-war economic migration to Britain from the Caribbean, the South Asian subcontinent, China and Africa. In the post-war period, there has been both increasing mixing of ethnic groups and 'superdiversity', which have created an ethnically complex society. The differences in economic position, migration history, political participation and perceptions of social citizenship are significant across minority ethnic groups in the UK and they are becoming increasingly evident. Recent debate has highlighted the problem of hyper- or superdiversity where professionals and managers face substantial dilemmas in responding to the needs of culturally complex societies.

Most migrant groups have been subject to racism, xenophobia, hostility, violence and practices of restriction and exclusion during the process of migration and settlement. Diverse and highly durable forms of racist hostility provide a constant source of tension and conflict, including anti-Gypsyism, Islamophobia, anti-Black racism and anti-Semitism. Despite significant developments in policy and procedures across many institutions, there is a 'racial crisis' where increased understanding (theorising) and evidence of discrimination, inequalities and exclusions accompanies ongoing entrenched racism. Sources of inter-ethnic and intercultural conflict are cultural, political and economic, and they include opposition to the recognition of difference and superdiversity, contested control of territory and land (particularly for Gypsies and Travellers), and disputes over access to social housing, schools and other resources (Cemlyn et al. 2009). Newly articulated forms of hostility, hatred and grievance have been suffered by refugees, asylum seekers and other migrant groups. More widely, everyday cultural ignorance, miscommunication and misrecognition of difference lead to offensive behaviour, affronts to dignity and lack of respect, all of which have led to various forms of conflict.

Migrant and post-migrant groups have also been subject to and active in achieving varying levels of political and cultural recognition, acceptance of racial and ethnic difference, inter-ethnic marriage and cohabitation, and incorporation into political, economic, cultural and social spheres of activity. The Afro-Caribbean population tends to be economically disadvantaged and socially assimilated, in terms of cohabitation and marriage patterns, and with some significant degree of political incorporation; the Pakistani population tends to be in a position of greater economic marginality and poverty, with more social distinctiveness, due partly to social closure, and less political incorporation. Both of these latter two groups had the right to settle in the UK, to acquire citizenship and to participate in electoral politics due to previous British colonial relations and obligations. A continuing linkage between Blackness, violence, masculinity and dangerousness, and the ensuing high-profile misrepresentation of young Black men in the news media, have been exacerbated by both government and media responses to a series of shootings, stabbings and related violent incidents in the UK. National controversy over Black male youth has focused on the problems of gangs and gang-related violent crime, underperformance in education and the labour market, school exclusions, over-representation in the criminal justice system, absentee fathers and low aspirations. In response, it has been argued that there are a large number of young Black men who have high conformist aspirations and strong aspirational capital (Yosso 2005, Byfield 2008, Finney 2011) but who succeed, due partly to institutional racism in school environments including receiving harsher punishments, being over-represented in the lowest-ranked teaching groups and being taught by less experienced staff, with lower expectations and entered for the lowest 'tiered' examinations (Gillborn and Mirza 2000, Rollock and Gillborn 2010). National controversy over Muslim male youth has also been increasing. Muslim boys, once regarded as passive, hard-working and law-abiding, have been recast in the public imagination in recent years with hostile images of volatile, aggressive hotheads who are in danger of being brainwashed into terrorism, or of would-be gangsters who are creating no-go areas in towns and cities of the UK, and preying on white girls (Shain 2011).

The Equality and Human Rights Commission's recent triennial review of fairness in the UK confirmed the extent of racial and ethnic inequalities, with Black Caribbean and Pakistani babies being twice as likely to die in their first year as Bangladeshi or White-British infants, and also pointing out that, by the age of 22–24, 44 per cent of Black people are not in education, employment or training, compared with fewer than 25 per cent of white people (EHRC 2010). The relative vulnerability of minority ethnic groups in a variety of market contexts means that the current economic recession and associated cuts in welfare are having, and will have, a greater negative impact on these groups. Almost half (48 per cent) of young Black people are unemployed compared with the 21 per cent rate of unemployment amongst white men with mixed ethnic groups having the greatest overall increase, rising from 21 per cent in March 2008 to 35 per cent in November 2009 (IPPR 2010). Lower employment means more poverty. Ethnic minority women experience higher rates of poverty than white women and a recent report has argued that the economic recession presents two major risks: first, that minority ethnic women will be locked into their destitution for the foreseeable future and, second, that anti-poverty approaches marginalise the needs of minority ethnic women by failing to recognise and address those needs, and that they are being pathologised and ignored (Moosa and Woodroffe 2010). There is a deteriorating policy climate in the UK where, amidst greater concern for white working-class sentiments of exclusion and resentment, it is increasingly difficult to prioritise fundamental race equality and ethnic diversity objectives (van Dijk 2002).

Ethnic differences in education and the public/political agenda

Education has often been the highest-profile policy field where changing national and local government priorities have been signalled and implemented. From 1945 to the late 1950s, racial discrimination legislation was seen as unnecessary despite strong popular racism. These issues and ethnic diversity were largely ignored in government policy. From the late 1950s to the late 1960s a cross-party political consensus emerged that advocated strong racialised immigration controls and weak protection against discrimination to manage the perceived destabilising effects of minority migration. In education, assimilation was a key goal with a focus on dispersal and English-language teaching. Cultural pluralism and integration came to dominate policy rhetoric into the 1970s with an emphasis on minorities changing and adapting to 'fit in'. Increasing community-, ethnic- and religion-based and anti-racist protest led to the popularisation of multicultural and anti-racist education across local education authorities through the 1980s, but schools had great freedom to ignore these developments if they wished, and many did. From 1986 onwards there was a weakening of these movements and a government drive came forth to curb and push back multicultural developments (Tomlinson 2008). The introduction of a National Curriculum which failed to acknowledge race and ethnic diversity is indicative of this position (Law and Swann 2011).

New Labour from 1997 onwards signalled a change of direction with an explicit focus on the significance of issues of racism, but this more progressive stance lacked a fundamental understanding of racism and equality issues (Somerville 2007, Gillborn 2008). Following 11 September 2001, government policy moved from 'naïve' to 'cynical' multiculturalism (in other words, it departed from promoting the values and organisations concerned with different minority cultures with little commitment to equality towards a view that this was misguided and primarily led to increasing divisions between communities which then required action to promote social cohesion), and signalled a return to integrationist and assimilationist priorities with an increasing perception that multicultural policies had failed by encouraging greater ethnic division. In the wake of the urban disturbances of 2001, much policy discussion has focused on the goal of community cohesion. To some extent, this has replaced an earlier emphasis on social exclusion and inclusion, in part because some analyses of those events suggested that self-segregation of minority ethnic communities was a factor in undermining cohesion. Following the 7 July 2005 Islamist suicide attacks on London civilians, the rights and perspectives of the white majority became increasingly asserted with calls for stronger intervention to improve integration, community cohesion, security and contemporary assimilation, summed up by Gillborn (2008) as 'aggressive majoritarianism'. In education, this is exemplified by attacks on wearing the veil by Muslims in school as part of a new guidance on school uniform codes which emphasised security, integration and cohesion and which was then quickly interpreted by the media as 'a school ban on veils'. Here, looking different is seen as a 'common sense' threat to national society and local community cohesion. This indicates a deteriorating policy climate and one in which it is increasingly difficult to prioritise fundamental race equality and ethnic diversity objectives, and which shows greater concern for white racist sentiments (Law and Swann 2011).

Cuts in public expenditure and ramping up the neoliberal agenda of choice and competition in education, developed under New Labour, are the two key drivers of current government policy on education. Expansion of the academies programme, creation of 'free schools' and severe budget cuts mark out some of the central actions of the new government in this sphere. The further restructuring of secondary education in this way is likely to have a detrimental impact on ethnic minority groups, as in Sweden. Cuts are leading to the dismantling of the complex raft of policies, initiatives and programmes concerned with addressing ethnic minority achievement, and issues of racial and ethnic diversity in schools. In a recent survey on the current position of Ethnic Minority Achievement Grant services that embraced half of all local authorities in England, 80 per cent of the respondents had experienced or were expecting to experience restructuring and/or the reduction of posts through forced or voluntary redundancies in the near future, and nearly a third of the authorities had already completed or finalised plans to delete or reduce their Ethnic Minority Achievement Services (NALDIC 2011). Common negative impacts on schools included a reduction in pupil support and availability, and a rise in costs of valued additional school-based work, such as interpretation or home school liaison; a shortage of knowledgeable specialists when demand is rising; and a disproportionate affect on less well-funded schools in which ethnic minority pupils are concentrated. The biggest deterioration reported was in the quality or availability of support for ethnic minority pupils and students.

The attempt to scrap the education maintenance allowance by the government was partially reversed but still substantial cuts will be undertaken. This will impact differentially on ethnic minority students as a much higher proportion of some minority groups had received this support (43 per cent of all 17–18-year-old full-time students received EMA whereas 67 per cent of Black African and 88 per cent of Bangladeshi students were in receipt of this allowance).

The move away from prioritising issues of racial and ethnic equality in educational policy is clear in the silence on many of these issues from the Department of Education, and it reflects the explicit rejection of multiculturalism and policies to address ethnic diversity by the prime minister. The Department of Education website now contains practically no information or guidance for schools on matters of ethnic minority achievement, which is very different from the mass of reports and guidance made available to schools under New Labour. Overall, this new climate of muscular majoritarianism and strengthening neoliberalism resulting in the decimation of progressive interventions marks a political acceptance of increasing racial and ethnic inequalities, an indifference to the racialisation of education, and hostility to race- and ethnic-specific policies and programmes.

Segregation and integration are 'chaotic concepts', and their misrecognition and misinterpretation provides fertile ground for 'myths to grow' (Finney and Simpson 2009). There are many myths associated with schooling in the UK, including a current government view that multiculturalism has facilitated segregation and that minority ethnic groups prefer segregated schools. Multiculturalism, in terms of the recognition of the human needs that arise from ethnic diversity in social policy, and anti-racism, in terms of the recognition of the need to challenge the fundamental basis of racial hostility and associated violence, have not led to increasing spatial, structural or cultural segregation, and these objectives remain legitimate policy goals. Despite the political rhetoric, ethnic managerialism, recognising the need to respond to ethnic diversity in the provision of public services and applying 'new public managerial' strategies to this issue, is prevalent across all sectors – for example, the sanctioning of faith schools, and adapting institutions, law and professional practice (Law 1997, Modood 2010). Also, the failure of institutions to adequately identify and respond to differing needs does lead to poor-quality service provision and reproduces patterns of exclusion, as in the case of the failure of secondary education in relation to Gypsy and Traveller children, and the very limited attention to issues of racism and ethnic diversity in the National Curriculum (Ball 2009).

Race relations law in the UK defines segregationist practices as direct discrimination, treating people less favourably because they are a member of a specific group, and cases of, for example, segregation of minority ethnic children in special remedial English classes which deprive them of learning from the National Curriculum have been found to be unlawful.

There is a strong desire for ethnically mixed schools among both white and minority ethnic families (Weekes-Bernard 2007), although a minority of both white and minority ethnic parents do prefer schools where their child is part of the ethnic majority in the institution. The pattern of ethnic composition of schools and the underlying ethnic segregation arise largely from differentials in income and wealth, and decisions in the housing market and the resulting mismatch between the choice of schools and outcomes (Finney and Simpson 2009). Here the statutory legal duty placed on schools to promote both 'good race relations' and 'community cohesion' – for example, in contexts where there are concentrations of either white or minority pupils, and also where there is evidence of inter-ethnic conflict – is of particular importance. Further, all minorities, including Muslims, want to live in mixed neighbourhoods, and they are generally worried about increasing residential concentrations in certain areas as caused by those who move out. Paradoxically, both increasing suburbanisation and increasing inner-city concentrations which characterise the housing outcomes for all minority ethnic groups result from both increasing socioeconomic polarisation within minority ethnic groups and 'white flight'. White middle-class children often have little interaction with children from other backgrounds. These children rarely have working-class friends and their few minority ethnic friends are predominantly from middle-class backgrounds. It was clear from our fieldwork (see below) that there has been little social mixing despite the ethnic mix in some schools as a whole, confirming the persistence of embedded ethnic and racial divisions.

So, in response to the segregating tendencies in education, it is paramount to address the attitudes of white children and young people, as well as ethnic differentials in child and adult poverty through the tax and benefit system, the minimum wage and implementation of the race-relations legislation. Persistent disadvantage and complex barriers to both work and benefits are experienced by minority groups. The emergence of destitution amongst some asylum seekers, rising unemployment differentials, and failure by the Department for Work and Pensions to implement statutory race equality strategies (Law 2011) are all further signs that indicate poor prospects for the future and the likelihood of increasing ethnic differentials in both poverty and in income and wealth, and hence the reproduction of current patterns of ethnic polarisation in schools. The relative vulnerability of minority ethnic groups in a variety of market contexts means that the current economic recession and associated cuts in welfare are having, and will have, a greater negative impact on these groups and also on school outcomes.

Fully implementing the eradication of direct and indirect racial and ethnic discrimination in schools and other educational institutions could go a long way towards dismantling segregationist practices – for example, in differential examination entry and setting, across schools. Race relations legislation has placed a statutory responsibility on schools in this regard since 1976. There have been successful formal investigations and court cases but currently the lack of leadership, data collection, accurate analysis and action within schools on issues of racial and ethnic equality indicate that this is a low priority, and this reflects the prevailing reticence to grasp these issues effectively at the national (and international) level. Racial and ethnic inequalities, racial and ethnic hostilities, and patterns of racial and ethnic segregation in education are known and broadly understood, yet still they are largely ineffectively dealt with in political, policy and professional contexts. Yet a post-ethnic, post-racial society is being built as declining racist attitudes, increasing mixed-ethnicity friendship groups amongst young people, increasing ethnic mixing in residential neighbourhoods, and the demand for ethnically mixed schools are evident as positive social trends in the UK. These trends are constrained, counteracted and frustrated by the powerful effects of hostile political rhetoric and divisive structural forces, such as the marketisation of education and increasing child poverty. Despite the constraints of politics, policy and markets, everyday multiculturalism is a living, powerful social process which will not be denied. The next section examines case study evidence exploring these issues.

New research on schooling and ethnicity

General patterns of ethnic inequality in education determined the selection of minority ethnic groups for this study. These were Gypsies, Roma and Travellers, Afro-Caribbeans and Pakistanis. Two cities in the North of England were chosen as sites for the research. The bulk of the research was carried out in 'Northcity'[1] and most of the qualitative research with Gypsies, Roma and Travellers was carried out in the second city location. Northcity was the main site and here a quantitative survey of 434 Year 10 pupils in three multicultural secondary schools was first carried out in 2008–2009. This city has more than 0.5 million inhabitants and a fairly typical pattern of ethnic diversity with 11 per cent Black and minority ethnic population, of which the Pakistani and Afro-Caribbean groups were the largest. All three schools, noted above, had about one-third minority ethnic pupils but varied widely in their intake from inner city areas (93, 68 and 23 per cent, respectively) and hence by their socioeconomic profile. The quantitative survey provided both background data and information on key aspects of inter-ethnic relations as perceived by the pupils. This was followed up by qualitative research which included focus-group discussions and in-depth personal interviews with students, school personnel and parents, further interviews with community and educational informants, classroom observations, case studies of schools and minority ethnic groups, and ethnographic fieldwork relating to youth and community cultures. The purpose of this stage of the research was to investigate the factors and motivations behind varying school performances and diverging educational careers, the impact of ethnicity on everyday life in school, experiences of being 'othered' and perceptions of identity. Very few of the Gypsy, Roma and Traveller Year 10 pupils on school rolls were in school and hence included in the quantitative survey, , further, the local population was fairly small and access was hard to achieve. For these reasons, a different city location was chosen for a qualitative community study of these groups. This second city location also has a fairly typical pattern of ethnic diversity. It also contains more than 0.5 million people, and over 500 Gypsy, Roma and Traveller children have been identified here.

New evidence regarding the importance of ethnic differentials in school experiences, patterns of informal ethnic segregation and the significance of inter-ethnic and peer hostilities in school life has been produced from this research. This study identifies the negative impact of gang and 'gangsta' culture, racial stereotyping and streaming on educational experiences. The findings also challenge any connection between ethnicity and low educational aspirations, apart from the case of Gypsies, Roma and Travellers where high drop-out and high levels of disaffection with school are particularly marked. The experience gained in English schools shows that despite significant achievements in developing integrated, non-discriminatory educational systems, persistent patterns of hostility, segregation and inequality remain.

Negative perceptions and experiences among Pakistani and Afro-Caribbean pupils confirm ethnic differentials in life at school. There are significant ethnic differences in pupils' perceptions of their school. Pakistani pupils were least likely to view school positively, although most of them did feel positive about their school work. Also, a significant group of pupils felt that they were unjustly treated in terms of their individual academic performance, particularly Pakistani pupils (31 per cent compared with 28 per cent of whites and just 20 per cent of Afro-Caribbean pupils). About three-quarters of Afro-Caribbean pupils felt that they had experienced unfair treatment because of behaviour. This factor would therefore seem to strongly shape Afro-Caribbean pupils' feelings about the school and is significant in light of the fact that, at national level, they are most likely to be excluded from school. Combined with contextual factors, such as the fact that pupils in this group were more likely to have suffered a dramatic life event, this has adverse social implications. School should be a safe, non-confrontational space for pupils, which is achieved through school climate and ethos. Most teachers would say that they do not treat pupils in a discriminatory manner (that is, treating some pupils differently than others), although it is perhaps too simplistic to lay the blame entirely on teachers' persisting racial discrimination (Gillborn 2008). Everyday informal ethnic segregation was common in school. Although much research has focused on teacher-pupil relationships, what emerged strongly in this study is the need to consider pupil-pupil dynamics. While the relationships pupils have with teachers seem to be generally positive, apart from criticism of unfair treatment, social relations between pupils proved to be more fraught with tensions and conflicts. Working-class pupils living in the inner city were more likely to report a negative social experience than middle-class pupils living on the outskirts (90 per cent compared with 60 per cent). Hostile groups were identified in classrooms among white, Pakistani and Afro-Caribbean pupils (21, 26 and 26 per cent, respectively). Between a fifth and a quarter of all respondents reported hostility, and this warrants further investigation into how pupils define their identities by drawing boundaries between themselves and others. Pupils perceived bullying to occur between peers living in different neighbourhoods and between peers of different ethnicities.

Pupils self-segregated themselves according to ethnicity to varying degrees in all three schools. There was also the added dimension of a predominantly white middle-class catchment. As in so many other studies of teenagers in school, social groupings and peer networks were easily identified and made visible through discussion of cliques. Particular groups hung around in particular areas of the school. Pupils openly discussed social groupings in each school. Dress styles and music tastes were sites of 'coolness' which characterised pupils' discussions of social groupings. Pupils reported socialising with peers from a range of different ethnic backgrounds, and for many the role of ethnicity was not recognised or acknowledged but in practice it operated to differentiate their everyday social experience. There was also a general reticence amongst teachers about discussing and addressing issues of racism and ethnicity.

Emos and chavs[2] were universally disliked. This was a pattern which emerged through all schools but to varying effect. Emos and Goths invoked a particular type of white ethnicity which sat uncomfortably with all Pakistani and Afro-Caribbean pupils interviewed. In understanding why emos were a peripheral group, four main dimensions of this identity emerged. First was the salience of ethnicity, 'it's mostly white people'. Identities were marked by particular clothing choices: 'They just wear dark clothes, grow their hair right long and everything they wear is black.' Some pupils displayed blurred identities: 'there are some people where they are kind of goths because they like listening to the rock music and that, but they don't dress themselves like goths, I don't know they just like listening to rock music and all that.' The boundaries which demarcated social identity could be fluid and could be experimented with. However, it was pupils who fell fully into emo identity who provoked discussion. Emo tastes were marked differently with preference to listening to heavy rock metal rather than the mainstream's preference for R 'n' B music. Emos were at the polar opposite of chavs, which was another branch of 'white' identity embodied by pupils. Chavs were constructed as a version of working-class white identity. Pupils' descriptions fit Tyler's interpretation of 'disgust reactions' received by 'the grotesque and comic figure of the chav' (Tyler 2008, p. 17). 'Hardness' was a term widely used to delineate prestige to physical strength ('he's reet hard') and on corridors, chavs would talk of 'banging people out'. However, Afro-Caribbean pupils in particular associated white chav identity with physical weakness and empty threats. In lessons, chavs were viewed as being the group most likely to get into trouble in school. White identities were also seen as under attack: apart from perceptions of emos and chavs, white boys in one of the schools complained of being called 'white bastards'. White middle-class boys felt that they had tried to forge friendships with Afro-Caribbean boys but these were often rebuffed, and this reflects both the pull of Black culture on white identities and the disjunction between these cultural groups.

Inter-ethnic hostility was particularly focused on Pakistanis. The main area of inter-ethnic antagonism was not between white and Black pupils but between Afro-Caribbeans and Pakistanis – a phenomenon that was not identified adequately by earlier research but which came through in a clear way when analysing a range of evidence and observations of a number of interactions within the investigated schools. Sometimes these divisions came out seemingly playfully but they were always instigated by Afro-Caribbeans against Pakistanis. However, this was a feeling in all three schools, which suggests a wider social division between the two groups than school-based issues.

Afro-Caribbean and Pakistani groups were strongly aware of negative and hostile stereotypes and attitudes about themselves. Pupils had very definite ideas in identifying stereotypes for Pakistanis and Afro-Caribbeans. This is a point which featured in equal measure across all three schools. Since stereotypes have social implications and can provide a picture of how different groups are perceived, it is useful to consider how pupils believe they are seen. These young people had learned and were exposed to the fact that people occupy different structural positions in society. For Pakistanis, their choices were often limited to working in the service industry. For some pupils, limited ethnic stereotyping of their identity provided the motivation (and internal resistance) to 'prove them wrong'.

Pakistanis were also commonly linked with terrorism. One Pakistani girl reported comments like 'He's a suicide bomber, he is from Taliban' for both boys and girls. Being viewed as having an identity that is at odds with British cultural norms meant that Pakistani pupils felt more prone to stigmatisation. Pakistani ethnic identity could thus constrain future life projections.

Being Pakistani with its linked associations of terrorism meant being labelled and set apart.

The stereotyping of Afro-Caribbeans was viewed completely differently. Unjust stereotyping of the Afro-Caribbean community arose frequently in discussions with pupils from this group filled with a sense of outrage. Stereotypes for Afro-Caribbean boys in particular were highly negative, such as 'being drug dealers, criminals, being in jail' or 'not getting any GCSEs [national exam passes at age 15–16]' and 'mess[ing] up their lives'. Blackness and African-ness were seen as symbolically threatening, with their associations of drug culture, crime, violence and therefore danger (MacPherson 1999, Graham and Juvonen 2002). Although there is a sense of empowerment which comes from being conceived of as a dangerous entity, this also functions as a form of disempowerment. Afro-Caribbean girls considered the masculine stereotype in terms of actors in potential romantic relationships. This too presents a negative image: 'he is a woman beater, he is a man slag, he cheats on his girlfriends: that is the typical Black guy,' said an Afro-Caribbean girl. Afro-Caribbean girls shared some of the same stereotypes and, despite being aware of ethnic groupings within school, pupils displayed ambivalence and lack of understanding about why these occurred. Probing into the underlying reasons received recurrently a uniform 'I don't know' response.

Neighbourhood location was a significant marker of identity. Pupils saw their neighbourhoods as an important context, and unpacking their perceptions and experiences of where the boundaries around particular places lay emerged as an important identity activity. Neighbourhoods are made up of people and communities bound to given places, and there is great stability and cohesion in such familiar settings.

An important analytical strand of identity and place lies with belonging and memory through public sites. This gave an interesting angle on how ethnic identities mesh and intersect with spatial location. The material culture of Northcity's industrial past seemed to resonate with Pakistani respondents as interviews and conversations often highlighted both their family's role and the collective contribution that the Pakistani community had in Northcity's past. For one high-achieving Pakistani girl, her connection to Northcity was deeply rooted in narratives of her grandfather's working life in heavy industry. When shopping in the centre in the east of the city, her presence in Northcity today was represented in statues of industrial workers which for her reanimated her grandfather's past life and created for her a sense of spatial meaning. This illustrates the ways in which minority ethnic pupils made deeper connections to neighbourhoods, to cities and to the UK with the family often playing an important role in preserving a sense of rooted connection and 'cultural imagination'.

Neighbourhood location, postcode gangs and masculine 'gangsta' culture are imported into everyday school life fuelling violence/bullying, which undermines attainment (reported by 43 per cent of pupils in one school and 28 per cent in another). The physical divide between neighbourhoods was entrenched further through the existence of postcode gangs in the wider community. An important part of identity for both Afro-Caribbean and Pakistani pupils, and particularly for boys, was bound up with allegiance to areas: 'It's basically if you live in Northcity4 you are with Northcity4, if you live in Northcity3 you are with Northcity3.' It was physically evident in graffiti around the schools, which as an act prompted competition: 'there is "Northcity4" and "Northcity5" written all over, then someone writes across "Northcity3", then some people put threats up, then someone crosses that off and puts "Northcity4" there'. Trying to ascertain whether postcode gangs were linked to ethnicity received mixed responses. For some these were associated with minority ethnic groups only. Some white pupils did, however, align themselves to the 'Northcity3' gang. Pakistani respondents felt uncomfortable being in a particular street location after-school hours because this meant waiting at a bus stop with the threat of physical and verbal abuse from the immediate white community. This shaped their decisions about whether to stay for after-school clubs. Overall, many of the group alignments were bound up with ideas of 'hard' masculinity, and involvement in gangs marked the transition to adulthood. It was a way to assert identity; nevertheless, the seriousness of the implications of this cannot be underestimated since there had been shootings in Brunsmere linked to gang wars. Visual reminders of this were very much evident: 'If you walk past the barbers now when the shutters are down you can see the bullet holes.' It served as a stark reminder of what a Pakistani mother said: 'If you have not got your mind over matter you can get pulled in to things but it is your choice... you go the right way or the wrong way.' Pupil involvement in postcode gangs cut across disaffected and conformist identities in school.

Three other key findings characterising how minority youths relate to education were identified. First, institutional processes of streaming fuelled dynamics of inclusion/exclusion, but there is evidence that some pupils could negotiate differing roles – for example, across 'boffin' (achievement-orientated) and 'gangsta' (street-orientated) positions which challenged the binary of academic achiever/disaffected. Second, over 70 per cent of pupils from all minority ethnic groups strongly recognised that education was a key means of improving life chances and, despite widely varying home backgrounds and school experiences, aspirations were high with no significant ethnic differentials. However, over a quarter of pupils did not take this view, and this educational disaffection across all groups needs addressing. Lastly, highly complex and differentiated positions, strategies and perceptions were articulated by young people in relation to their experiences of school and community life. Young people's yearning to escape being 'othered' was strongly voiced with some able to articulate narratives of emancipation and liberation from differential and discriminatory treatment.

But many felt locked into and unable to escape a tangled web of constraining circumstances and social worlds with serious consequences in terms of declining educational aspirations and drop-out from the educational system altogether.

Policy implications

The policy implications of these findings confirm that there is a pressing need to prioritise the objectives of racial and ethnic equality, antiracism and multiculturalism in educational experiences, institutional arrangements and achievement, and to actively develop and support programmes, initiatives and interventions to achieve these objectives in mainstream schooling. There are many ways in which individual schools, local education authorities and agencies can and have been responding to these challenges. Diversity was emphasised in the schools examined here by focusing on the surface manifestations of ethnicity, which served to socially articulate and preserve differences through 'boundary maintenance' rather than offering cohesive provision. First, it is necessary for schools, local educational authorities and agencies, and central government to acknowledge and recognise the nature and extent of racial and ethnic inequalities and exclusion. The likelihood that these concerns and objectives will be downgraded in the current economic context is of serious doubt given the real prospects of increasing racial and ethnic inequalities amongst children – for example, in poverty and material conditions. Second, it is necessary to actively develop and support programmes, initiatives and interventions to achieve the objectives of racial and ethnic equality and multiculturalism in mainstream schooling (Crick 1998). There is still a great need for stronger leadership, creative innovation and transformative change on these matters. At a national level, the strengthening of multiculturalism (Modood 2010) and a renewed commitment to racism reduction and anti-discrimination (Law 2010) are urgently needed.

Reducing ethnic differentials in school experiences should be a key objective in certain respects, particularly for Pakistani pupils in their perceptions of the unfair treatment of their school work, in the classroom and in their general perceptions of schooling, and particularly for Afro-Caribbeans in their perceptions of unfair treatment of their behaviour. Ofsted (the official body for inspecting schools) has a key role to play here in adequately addressing this issue in inspection regimes. Head teachers and governors have a statutory duty here to eliminate racial and ethnic inequality and racial discrimination, and to promote good relations and cohesion between all groups.

Reducing informal ethnic segregation and peer-to-peer hostilities in all areas of schooling is still urgently required, and particular attention needs to be paid to inter-ethnic hostility between Afro-Caribbean and Pakistani pupils, and racial stereotyping of Gypsies, Roma and Travellers, Afro-Caribbeans and Pakistanis. Here, supporting pupils in consciousness raising, and understanding and dealing with issues of stigmatisation are vital. The Education and Inspections Act 2006 inserted a new Section 21(5) into the Education Act 2002 introducing a duty on the governing bodies of maintained schools to promote community cohesion which came into effect on 1 September 2007. The wealth of UK good practice in 'racism reduction' (Law 2010) outside school contexts, and in school (for example, Knowles and Ridley 2006, Runnymede Trust 2007) provide a valuable evidence base of successful interventions. It would also be valuable to allow pupils the space to understand about the Afro-Caribbean, Pakistani and Gypsy/Roma presence in the UK, specifically in relation to the local contexts. Although all of the schools examined here promoted Black History Month, there were not any learning activities developed around this. White ethnic identities are currently often left out of these sorts of 'ethnic' provision but should be included.

There must be an ongoing commitment to the professional development and training of both teaching and non-teaching staff working in multicultural schools. Too little assistance is provided to teachers to help them to observe and construct the meanings and knowledge that guide their actions in the classroom. Teachers appear scared about the issues of race and ethnicity which seems to stem from hyper-awareness and insecurity. Measures to address this could include training days and workshops with parents and community members where they break from the everyday insular routine and are able to learn about the ethnically diverse groups that they teach in a very practical way. Greater attention needs to be paid to how teachers working in inner-city schools are trained and hired, and how they manage with the distinct challenges of inner-city teaching in ethnically diverse classrooms. There are two achievable options here. Option A is a postgraduate certificate in education (PGCE) specifically aimed at teachers wanting to teach in inner-city settings. This differs from the 'mainstream' PGCE as greater emphasis is placed on understanding pupil behaviour and the specific challenge of classroom management. Option B is to ensure that a statutory requirement of gaining qualified teacher status is that all trainee teachers must successfully undertake a placement in an inner-city school. Following this there must be an ongoing commitment to the professional development and training of both teaching and non-teaching staff working in inner-city schools. Too little assistance is provided to teachers to help them to observe and construct the meanings and knowledge that guide their actions in the classroom. Measures to address this could include offering a mentoring scheme or offering opportunities for team teaching where they break from insularity and can learn from others' professional practice through action and reflection in a very practical way. It would also be of benefit for all teachers to be offered the opportunity to 'see outside the box' and observe practice in a range of other types of school. For instance, teachers working in inner-city schools may observe teaching practice in the differing contexts of independent schools, pupil referral units, academies, faith schools and special schools to gain a broader level of social insight in order to be equipped to trial new methods and make change in their own milieu. Such experience would equip teachers with an understanding of how different groups of pupils of the same age perform in different settings with different organisational and social contexts. This could generate higher expectations of the pupils in their classes and it could also bring forth ideas for innovating lessons. To ensure a better understanding of teaching ethnically diverse groups of pupils, the content of the PGCE should also develop skills, knowledge and understanding of group dynamics in such settings and it should also address racial hostility, and ethnic and religious identities in school.

Reducing the influence of postcode gangs and masculine 'gangsta' culture on young people and everyday school life is a further key task for schools. Schools in this study were generally sensitive to the issues surrounding postcode gangs and some had taken a clear stance of zero tolerance, but much more work needs to be done to develop effective interventions to achieve the dissolution of such formations. The Department for Children, Schools and Families has issued guidance and a toolkit for action for schools in dealing with gangs and group offending (DCSF 2008). Further, there are useful lessons set out in the experiences of the Tackling Gangs Action Programme which was carried out in 2007 (Home Office 2007). There are also a variety of other toolkits and guides – for example, *Gangs at the Grassroots* (Brand and Ollerearnshaw 2008). Work must continue around boys' damaging and limited models of being masculine in the context of postcode gangs and also in addressing attitudes and patterns of behaviour that demean girls and women. Schools are well placed to address gender issues through specific units of work which explicitly discuss conceptions of gendered identity. Programmes may be either gender-specific or gender-relevant but they should address social justice issues which allow pupils to build and explore individual identities, and also girls' assertiveness and issues of sexual exploitation.

Also, reducing institutional processes of streaming and setting which fuels pupil and teacher dynamics of inclusion and exclusion is needed as they have little impact on increasing attainment, while they can reduce educational aspirations and attainment, and they can also be detrimental to child development (Blatchford 2005).

A key challenge for policy-makers at the national level is to find ways to promote the motivational disposition which encourages aspirations through education and learning. There is a fundamental mismatch between schools and disaffected pupils. Some of the pupils within this study were caught up in a culture that sees learning and intellectual activity as anti-identity and/or views school, for whatever reasons, as simply not a priority. While interventions in disaffection usually focus on 'fixing' the pupil, focus must also be drawn to the role of the curriculum and pedagogy which currently remains standardised and uniform. This exists as a consequence of school evaluation and pupil assessment which emphasise a narrowed range of outcomes. It is logical that a flexible, permeable and responsive continuum of support and provision is needed to target the most challenging young people based on their particular continuum of need. A flexible and creative response is needed which offers an alternative to traditional education to meet the demands of challenging pupils. This requires more innovative measures than just tweaking the timetable. There is a need for a pedagogy that captures and sustains pupils' interest in learning. The goal of educational work with disaffected pupils should be one of social justice, and schools should provide the space and resources for pupils to broaden their horizons and improve relationships. What this encompasses is self-actualisation. Schools are unable to affect the social circumstances in which pupils are living; but policy could do more to offer a curriculum which permits young people to make choices, to build self-confidence, and to see the connections between learning and a better life.

Notes

1. Northcity is a pseudonym for the city in northern England that served as the main site for the fieldwork of EDUMIGROM research in the UK.
2. Emos, or adherents to emotional hardcore culture, derives from selected US punk rock bands and often involves a stereotype of being particularly emotional, sensitive, shy, introverted or fear-ridden. Chavs, a pejorative term, has been used to stereotype white working-class youth culture in the UK.

11

Experiencing Ethnicity in a Colour-Blind System: Minority Students in France

Claire Schiff

Since the turn of the twenty-first century, French society has witnessed both an increase in residential socioethnic segregation and the rebirth of an assimilationist political discourse which condemns even relatively mild public expressions of cultural difference or of ethnic or religious group identification, especially when they emanate from post-colonial or Muslim minorities. Although France is one of the European countries with the largest proportion of students from non-European backgrounds (INSEE 2010), its citizenship model and its secular republican school system have traditionally avoided the recognition of racial or ethnic differences (Jennings 2000, Simon 2003, Simon and Amiraux 2006). This potential discrepancy between the dominant political discourse, which reaffirms the importance of colour-blind republican universalism, and an increasingly multiethnic society is particularly salient in lower-class urban public schools receiving numerous students of migrant origin. Indeed, young people attending these schools must navigate between the pervasive influences of a national ideology that regards ethnicity as irrelevant, and local contexts in which diversity has become an integral part of everyday life. It is my aim in this chapter to offer an insight into the inconsistencies and contradictions between, on the one hand, a school system which strives to keep alive the belief that individual merit is the sole motor of educational success and, on the other hand, the evidence of an increasing overlap between ethnic origin and educational inequalities, both in terms of access to resources and in terms of academic results and trajectories.

Only relatively recently have French social scientists grappled with the question of the impact of ethnicity on the school trajectories and experiences of minority youth (van Zanten 2012). The overall picture is a mixed and rather contradictory one. Indeed, large-scale studies on academic performance and achievement tend to show that ethnicity is not in itself an explanatory factor for school failure. In fact, students' immigrant origins are often associated with high aspirations and higher than average rates of entry into the non-vocational streams in secondary education, when the impact of social background is kept constant (Vallet and Caille 1999, Felouzis 2005, Brinbaum and Cebolla-Boado 2007). In contrast, more qualitative research, carried out in the socially disadvantaged neighbourhoods in which the more visible non-European minorities tend to congregate, reveal situations in which ethnicity is associated with anti-school behaviour and oppositional subcultures which are potential sources of conflict between pupils, as well as between pupils and teachers (Payet 1995, Perroton 2000).

The diverging trajectories of students of minority origin within the French secondary school system can be linked to the combination of relatively broad options for entry into non-vocational higher education, on the one hand, and heightened risks of exclusion in the forms of early school drop-out and streaming into dead-end vocational schemes, on the other hand (Crul and Vermulen 2003, Tucci 2010, Felouzis et al. 2010). Because the French school system encourages high hopes of success, and regards academia as the only stepping stone to social mobility, working-class students in general and minority students in particular often feel intense frustration when they encounter obstacles to the pursuit of their studies. Keeping in mind these general characteristics of the French educational system, as well as the influence of its colour-blind citizenship model, this chapter presents the results of a qualitative approach to ethnicity in school environments which examines the grounded social realities by exploring the more local and contextual determinants of the meaning and uses of youthful inter-ethnic relations and modes of identification.

Exploring the contextual determinants of ethnicity

When students speak of themselves and others, many factors inform their sense of belonging, factors which may be endogenous or exogenous to their school. They speak alternately as children of immigrants, as French youth, as residents of a certain neighbourhood, as pupils of a particular school or as members of a specific class group. The words of Tarik, a vocational student, provide a telling example:

> I feel French intermittently, and I feel Algerian intermittently. I feel French when I'm in school, when I'm working... when I'm looking for a job, with my suit and CV. Obviously when I have to integrate into French society, I can't show up with the Algerian label. But when Algeria was qualified [for the soccer world championship] at the Champs Elysee, I was Algerian, hundred per cent. Because it's our origins before all else. For me it's a new page beginning compared with my family. There was my family behind me, all the Algerians behind me, so France-Algeria, I can't

hesitate: I'm Algerian first. But when I'm home in my neighbourhood, I feel African, because I speak with Moroccans, Tunisians, Senegalese, Malians. I don't reject anyone. But let's face it, if there's a gang of ten, there will be four Arabs, four Blacks, one French, one Chinese.

Here Tarik is saying in essence that while his past is Algerian and his future French, his everyday life is multiethnic. In many of the working-class suburbs of large metropolises, such as Paris, the 'established group' is nowadays largely made up of second- and third-generation youths of an immigrant background whose sense of belonging is increasingly defined by a sort of cosmopolitan localism, rather than by references to specific national identities (Crul and Schneider 2010). In more provincial and less multiethnic urban environments, however, minority youths are likely to maintain their outsider identity in relation to those of the majority group. By comparing the experiences of students schooled in the very different local contexts of Bordeaux, where the population of immigrant origin is relatively small, and of the Parisian suburbs of the highly multiethnic Seine-Saint-Denis district, we were able to consider various dimensions of these local urban and educational contexts and to reflect on their impact on the manner in which students construct and deconstruct ethnic boundaries.

While the working-class suburb of Paris is characterised by a much larger than average proportion of residents originating from the African continent, the urban agglomeration of Bordeaux has a relatively limited minority population compared with other French cities of a similar size. In choosing two such contrasting sites, we wished to observe the manner in which schools recruiting students with similar social and academic profiles might differ in their treatment of ethnic minorities, depending on whether they constituted the majority of the population or simply a significant minority. We limited our choice of schools to those in which the student population was overwhelmingly of lower-class origin, in order to neutralise as much as possible the important effect of social class (which has been widely analysed in the literature). We also chose to carry out the study at the high-school level and to interview students enrolled in various programmes leading to a variety of different degrees, ranging from the two-year vocational certificate (Certificat d'Aptitude Profesionelle and Brevet d'Études Profesionnelles) to the general scientific Baccalaureate. While the schools are very different with regard to size, ratio of girls to boys, programmes offered and general atmosphere, they are all attended mostly by students who would have chosen a different school had their academic results permitted them to do so.

Our study aims to understand the construction of ethnicity and the nature of ethnic relations in the French context among working-class youth enrolled in low-prestige urban schools. Our aim is to shed light on the manner in which the various actors participating in such institutions experience and understand ethnic differences. How are ethnic or racial categorisations played out in schools receiving students who have often been negatively selected due to a variety of factors, such as low social status, poor academic performance and residence in disadvantaged urban areas? How do students make sense of the apparent contradictions between the values and practices of a school system which makes a point of ignoring their cultural and ethnic characteristics, and the fact that certain minority groups are clearly over-represented among students enrolled in the least desirable schools and streams?

Ethnic diversity in the Parisian periphery: World city or urban ghetto?

In popular and media images, the department of the Seine-Saint-Denis epitomises the French version of the 'ghetto'.[1] It is located to the immediate north-east of Paris, at the centre of a vast and densely urbanised area formerly designated as the 'red-belt' because of its longstanding tradition of Communist local government. The department is historically associated with the traditional industrial working class and more recently with concentrations of migrant communities from the African continent, who first began to settle there during the 1950s and 1960s, following the end of the Algerian War of Independence.

The Communist Party, which has lost most of its popular support in national elections over the past 15 years, has managed to maintain its dominance over municipal politics in the area since the end of the Second World War. Individuals of African origin are particularly well integrated into the municipal services aimed at local youth, judging by the fact that eight out of ten of the directors of the local municipally funded youth programmes serving the various neighbourhoods of the cities under study have African surnames.

While the proportion of migrants nationwide is just under 8 per cent, among residents of the department it is close to 25 per cent. Since the beginning of the 1990s, the departments' residential areas of high public-housing concentration and higher than average poverty and unemployment rates have served as initial settlement areas for newly arrived immigrants from sub-Saharan Africa. Yet there are in fact very few neighbourhoods in which non-European residents are in the majority (Préteceille 2012). The high concentration of these groups in certain schools is due more to the differential educational choices and strategies of majority and minority families than it is to the effect of increased residential segregation (Schiff et al. 2011). The parents of majority origin students are more likely to send their children to private, predominantly Catholic, schools. Based purely on visual impressions gathered during our multiple visits to the schools, the proportions of Blacks and Arabs appear much higher among the student population in the two schools observed than one would expect based on their share in the local resident population.

In the department, most upper secondary schools are multipurpose and offer a combination of general, technical and vocational training. For this reason, students with different academic profiles are more likely to be schooled together than in Bordeaux, where the separation between vocational and non-vocational schools is more pronounced.

Proximity and socioethnic distinctions in a provincial city

It is one thing to be a student from a 'visible' minority in a city such as Saint-Denis. It is a rather different experience to be a minority youth in a provincial city such as Bordeaux, where the immigrant population is relatively small and where there is frequent mobility between different parts of the agglomeration.

With its rather low level of urbanisation and limited numbers of immigrants (7 per cent for the department), Bordeaux is not regarded as one of the most cosmopolitan cities in France, nor is it viewed as having any particular social problems relating to its immigrant or minority population. The signs of social exclusion and strained urban relations are much less visible than around Paris, judging by the very minor incidences of urban rioting which took place during the nationwide wave of urban unrest in the autumn of 2005.

The city has been a bastion of moderate right-wing conservatism since the end of the Second World War, while a number of socialist-led municipalities have more recently taken over several of the more industrialised suburbs located immediately on the right bank of the Garonne river where one finds a much higher proportion of subsidised low-income public housing. This has tended to reinforce the physical and social separation between the older middle- and upper-middle-class neighbourhoods of the historic centre and the newer, more working-class, periphery, which has become increasingly ethnically mixed with the arrival of migrants from Morocco and Turkey over the past 20 years.

In contrast with the observed Parisian suburbs, which have managed to integrate the minority population into the local fabric of public institutions, in the municipalities of the Bordeaux agglomeration one finds few minority individuals in local government or in positions of responsibility in the local network of publicly sponsored social services and grassroots organisations. They, in practice, all appear in the 'world cultures' sector that covers the more traditional organisations serving as representatives of a particular national community (the Senegalese, the Comorian and so on) or which promote specific 'exotic' cultural or artistic activities. They are absent from the sectors concerned with youth, housing, schooling, or social and leisure activities.[2]

With the completion of the tramway line linking this area to the centre of Bordeaux, and the development of a substantial number of new office buildings and small-scale industries and commercial establishments, these suburbs have undergone a general improvement of their urban environment over the past ten years and have begun to attract a new category of more middle-class residents. Yet they have not managed to shed their reputation as disadvantaged, 'difficult' areas relative to Bordeaux proper, which retains its 'bourgeois' reputation despite the presence of several pockets of poverty.

The smaller size and close proximity of the unequally desirable urban neighbourhoods in the context of a provincial city such as Bordeaux tends to exacerbate contrasts and to render the processes of distinction and stigmatisation a more salient feature of everyday social relations and local identities, especially for younger residents of the right bank, who travel much more frequently than their Parisian counterparts between their homes and the central city.

Finally, another important contrast between the two sites concerns the structure and organisation of the local educational market. The Academy of Bordeaux is characterised by rather polarised opportunities for secondary educational training. It comprises a set of high schools offering programmes mainly leading to the general academic Baccalaureate, on the one hand, and several trade schools with rather contrasting reputations leading to the short vocational degrees, on the other hand. Opportunities for students to enter the technical streams, leading to the intermediary level technical Baccalaureate, are limited. This latter stream is well known to constitute one of the major and most efficient middle-range opportunities for children of a working-class background to obtain a degree leading to specialised higher education and is often a more effective route for professional social mobility than the general streams. Hence the educational context appears more favourable to the social mobility of disadvantaged urban youth at the Parisian site, while the urban environment is much less threatening in and around Bordeaux.

The contrasts between the two sites in terms of their urban and sociological realities, but more importantly in terms of their identities in relation to the issue of ethnic diversity and their educational infrastructure, makes the comparison between the experiences of secondary-school-aged youths in Bordeaux and the Seine-Saint-Denis an interesting venue for exploring the effects of objective and subjective dimensions of ethnic distinctions and inter-ethnic relations.

The influence of the local context on students' inter-ethnic relations and identities

In and around Bordeaux, students of immigrant origin interact with members of the dominant group on many different occasions outside as well as inside school. In such a context one's classmate or one's next door neighbour can easily represent the 'Other' and daily interactions constantly offer students the opportunity to test their identity and to confirm their membership in various communities, be they defined by ethnicity, residence or social class. In the vocational school, located in one of the more stigmatised housing projects of the area, local, academic and ethnic hierarchies actually overlap to create a situation in which minority students enrolled in the most undesirable classes have become intensely aware of their multiple disadvantages. Such a situation encourages them to develop attitudes and strategies aimed at inverting the dominant hierarchies by overplaying the role of the 'bad boy'. The following excerpt from an interview with Hakim, a second-generation Algerian student of a vocational class in Bordeaux, clearly demonstrates this:

- We observed the class all day, and there were moments when it was very tense between students.
- No, it's just for fun, it's always like that. Like when we're in the neighbourhood [*cité*], we laugh like that, and since there are several of us from different neighbourhoods [low-income projects], we're always having fun like that. It's our character to provoke each other, it amuses us. Sometimes teachers take it well and have fun with us, some don't, it depends on the teacher's personality. I've already been called 'dirty Arab' and all, but I take it with a smile. But if a teacher hears that he's gonna look for the fault in order to write a report on the student. Like [a Portuguese student], he was excluded because he made a racist joke about another student. Even if the other one laughed, the teacher looked for the little problem in order to kick him out. He got a report and was excluded. Basically the class is serious, but it's always at a moment when the teacher is gonna say something that makes us laugh, that's gonna make us think of a student from the class. For example, at a moment he will talk about Algeria. I come from there, and if the teacher says: 'Algeria was colonised by the French', for example, the others are gonna laugh and say: 'Yeah, you were slaves and everything'. And that's when the problems begin. For some little thing like that.
- But doesn't it get bad sometimes?
- No. Not between us, the guys from the *cité*, it never gets bad between us. It's especially those who come from the countryside, they're not used to it. So among themselves they get nasty. They want to act like us, but then they can't take it like us. They say we're the worst, but we understand when we're joking. In fact the class is divided in two. There are those who want to have fun, and those who are strict with themselves. It's like they're afraid to have fun.

Here the distinction between 'us' and 'them' combines references to residential categories (low-income 'projects' vs. small town), to students' behaviour in class (fun-loving vs. studious) and to ethnic origin (Arab vs. French).

In the Parisian periphery, such multidimensional distinctions were rare. Precisely because most students are of minority origin and/or come from disadvantaged urban neighbourhoods, social and residential differences do not clearly overlap with ethnic categories in these schools. The two schools investigated in and around Saint-Denis appeared more as spaces that were relatively protected from the harsh difficulties of urban life. During interviews, students often mentioned problems relating to drug-dealing, gang violence, police brutality and controls, cramped and uncomfortable housing condition, delinquency and muggings, which made life within the confines of the school appear to be relatively peaceful compared with the outside.

Although the objective dimensions of social life are much harsher for students living in the Parisian periphery than they are for students from Bordeaux, from the point of view of their subjective self-image they are less affected by negative comparisons between neighbourhoods, schools, social classes and ethnic groups. Indeed, in the less anonymous provincial environment, minority students are constantly reminded of their low social status by the very fact they are much more frequently in contact with members of the more privileged classes. Easy access to the centre of town, the fact that even in the least desirable schools and classes they remain in the minority, and the generally rather 'bourgeois' identity of the city all combine to make social, ethnic and residential distinctions more salient. By contrast, in the Parisian suburbs, segregation paradoxically shelters young people from confrontation with the 'other', which may remind them of their disadvantaged status. Even the few white youth attending the schools tend to be regarded as 'one of us' since they have usually grown up in the same urban environment as minority pupils. For most students, white (or as they say 'French') middle-class society appears thus as a rather remote and distant entity. Indeed, teachers from both schools in Saint-Denis noted that it was only when they went on outings that students' status as an ethnic minority coming from stigmatised neighbourhoods became an issue. Only when they are confronted directly and collectively with the outside world do they become acutely conscious of their identity as 'ghetto youth' (*jeunes de banlieue*). A teacher describes the situational changes:

> Something which was particularly noticeable in certain classes, in the vocational ones in particular, was that what was rare was the 'Gaulois' as students would say [term for white or French]. But in fact among them, it wasn't a problem. Between them it wasn't a problem, that there were

classes with a majority of either West Indians or Africans. And I remember a visit to the Futuroscope which was funny, really funny, because it's precisely when we go somewhere else that they are stigmatised. That's why the real problem is to take them out. I often go to the theatre with my students, and I love the theatre Gerard Philippe [in Saint Denis]. Precisely because we're among ourselves. I've witnessed awful scenes. One of the rare times that I took my students to Paris, not even to the Comedie Française, but to the Athénée at Saint Lazare, we went to see a play. Which spoke about racism in fact. At the end of the show, there were lots of classes in the audience, but it wasn't my students who were misbehaving. But there was a lady who went to see my students, because, of course they're all black. And so people like that shouldn't go to the theatre. I wasn't there, but my students came to tell me about it. I was talking with someone from the theatre and I didn't find the lady afterwards, in order to tell her just what I thought of her. But those looks, they exist all the time. We don't feel them so much because they are not addressed to us. But it's all the time, all the time. When they go into the metro, people move away (female literature teacher, majority origin, Saint Denis).

And another voice on the same subject said:

It's really the thing that comes back all the time. They feel stigmatised when we go to the movies, when we take them to Paris to see an exhibit, they feel like people look at them differently. But they overplay the 93 [postcode for the department of the Seine-Saint-Denis] when they go to Paris, and it drives me crazy. Once we went to Rolland Garros, and I said to them: 'OK, you have to take off your caps, pull down the leg of your pants.' In the metro I say: 'Stop talking ten times louder than everybody else. You wear on you the fact that you come from the *banlieue*, but you do it on purpose. You can't complain about the fact that other people look at you. You do everything for them to look at you.' 'Yeah, but he's staring at me, they say. 'But it's normal, you're the only one they can hear' (female physical education teacher, majority origin, Saint Denis).

When comparing the experiences of students in the vocational schools of the Seine-Saint-Denis with those of their counterparts from Bordeaux, we see that the relationship between the school and the outside world of the *cité*, or local street life, are somewhat inverted. In the latter case, the school functions as an entity which exacerbates and fuels students' oppositional identities, encouraging them to act out such traits. The following quote from the discussion we carried out with a group of eight minority and majority students from the two classes observed in a boys' vocational school in the suburbs of Bordeaux illustrates the negative images associated with the school and with these classes, and how they permeate social relations even outside school:

- You see the look of this high school, there's nothing to do here. It doesn't make you want to work. There are no outings, there's nothing. That's the truth. We're the only two classes of the school who never did any outings [general agreements all round].
- *And why is that according to you?*
- Because we're too turbulent!
- *You mean it's a kind of punishment?*
- Yeah! [all together].
- Maybe if they made some efforts, we would too, and we'd have outings.
- This high school has screwed us more than once.
- Yeah! [all together].
- Last time we won some tickets to the movies, because there was a contest with each class, and we were all supposed to get passes. Well they told us that since we were... it means little assholes, well the passes, we know where they went...
- They found some excuse not to give them to us.
- Because it hurts them too much here to give us the passes.
- There are even teachers who told us: 'You're so turbulent that we can't take you out.'
- They're afraid to take us out because they think something will happen.
- Take the example of yesterday [a few good students from the class enquired about transferring to a more prestigious school]. When you said you were from here, right away you're cooked. Even when we speak to people in the trade: 'Where do you come from? Oh, OK...'
- *And it's the high school, it's not the neighbourhood?*
- No, it's because the school is next to the neighbourhood.
- It's got a nasty reputation for sure.
- It's first of all the whole neighbourhood around it, and after that everybody knows that the high school is right in the middle.
- *But there's also school A* [more prestigious neighbouring school].
- All the Gaulois [whites] are there.
- *But actually most of the students here don't come from the projects* [low-income housing areas], *which is not the case in Saint Denis where they all do.*
- How to explain? If you stay here for a year you take on the personality.
- Right. You arrive with a brain, and when you leave it's empty. If you have a best friend who's always getting in trouble, and even if you're an angel, if you're with him all the time...
- Saint Denis is known for what? For their hot neighbourhoods, the riots, the burning cars. In Bordeaux, we are known for what? Because we're

in the middle of the projects here. And so it's got the reputation of being hot.

- *But when you go to the centre of Bordeaux, you don't say that you're students here.*
- All they need to do is ask in order for the atmosphere to change immediately.
- How many times that has happened to me? She says: 'Where do you go to school?' I say [name of town] I don't even say [the name of the school]. I say 'Right. I'm from over there.'
- Yeah it counts. We don't say it too much if we want to pick up a girl from the centre of town. For the good rich girls, it counts.

In the least desirable classes, the social norms of the 'ghetto' become references even for those who live in residential areas which are semi-rural and socially mixed. Indeed, students clearly feel that in order to be respected by their peers they have to adopt a certain posture associated with the stereotype of the urban ghetto youth, when in fact their out-of-school life resembles that of ordinary lower-middle-class provincial youngsters more than that of students of similar socioeconomic status who live in the public housing complexes in Saint Denis. In this latter context, the high school becomes in fact a place where the rigid rules and harsh social relations of the 'ghetto' can be softened and circumvented to a certain extent, and where students feel less pressure from the peer group to conform to their local, ethnic and gendered identities.

One of the teachers from a boys' vocational high school of Saint-Denis mentioned a conversation she had overheard among her students which underscored the weight of the social pressures of juvenile street culture exerted on those who live in the surrounding public housing projects – pressures which appear to be less intense in school:

In fact I just hear their conversations in the hallways and when they are settling down in class. The influence of the older kids [from the neighbourhoods], and it really scares me. Because I often hear them say: 'Yeah, because the older guys, the older guys from the *cité*.' It's Sekou who said that, who's six foot two, big, black, and really well built, and who acts like the boss in the high school, but clearly when you hear him talk, you see that it's the older guys who control him outside. And I heard him the other day talking in the hallway and saying: 'Well yeah, I wanted to do this, but the older guys told me to get in the car with them, and I didn't dare say no, so I got in, and now I'm in deep shit.' And that sort of thing they don't feel at all in the high school, but when they're in the neighbourhood, they must feel a hell of a lot of pressure from some of the local youth.

One of the major lessons of our comparative approach was that, despite similarities in students' social, cultural and academic characteristics, significant differences between the two sites in terms of the local urban contexts, the ethnic school mix, and the position and status of the schools and neighbourhoods relative to other schools and neighbourhoods in the area all have a considerable influence on the way inter-ethnic relations and identities are formed and evolve. While the minority students encountered in Bordeaux were much less exposed than their Parisian counterparts to the ills of urban life, such as gang violence, police brutality, limited mobility and overcrowded living conditions, they also appeared more deeply affected by the stigma associated with their inferior position relative to that of young people living in more middle-class areas and who attend more prestigious secondary schools.

Peer-group relations as reflections of school policies and teacher–student relations

The objective dimensions of the schools observed, such as their resources, the quality of the infrastructure and buildings, and the employment and training opportunities that they offer, do not necessarily determine their reputation and the general sentiments of attachment or rejection, and of comfort or discomfort, which students express when they speak about their high school experience. Because we are dealing with an age group that is engaged in a process of identity construction and that is very concerned with what others think, and because most of the students encountered feel belittled by their failure to conform to the standards of academic success set by the very elitist French school system, they strongly aspire to be respected and accepted both by peers and by adults. The content of their course of study or their chances for future employment seem to weigh less on students' judgements of their school experience than the general atmosphere and cohesion of the school, the degree of solidarity among classmates and the benevolence of teachers.

The two schools in our sample, one in Saint-Denis and one in Bordeaux centre, in which students clearly felt most at ease and in which social relations were relatively peaceful, have managed to foster a sense of belonging and trust by developing a kind of social life and a way of communication among teachers and students within the school which were not simply centred on academic issues. These are the schools in which extracurricular activities, exchanges with parents, outings and the awareness of students' difficult home-life situations are the most developed. In these schools, students thus feel that they are not judged solely according to their position within the hierarchy of classes and streams, or according to their performance and their behaviour in class. They feel that the school is a place in which they are likely to find support and help to deal with difficulties that are not strictly academic. One might say that an important aim of these schools, or at least of a significant proportion of their staff, is to create a space for even the lowest-performing students and to attempt to reconcile those who have been negatively selected by the system with the educational institution and its personnel. Although one boys' vocational school in Saint Denis was by far the most rundown and lacking in resources, and it received the largest proportion of very disadvantaged students, it appeared relatively peaceful to most of the students interviewed. The following excerpts provide good illustrations:

The reputation was that it had no girls, only boys. That it's dirty, that you have to speak Arabic, all that. That the high school is gonna cave in. In fact the atmosphere is pretty good. Because there are no fights or anything. It's surprising because all the people here, how to say, they're a bit dangerous, let's say. Almost everybody comes from a housing project (Uros, first-generation Serbian boy).

Even if it's a high school in Saint-Denis, in the *banlieue*, there's a certain harmony, everybody gets along. There is really a kind of understanding among everyone in this school. Each time you need some help... you can always find someone who will help you... There are very rarely fights in this school. When it happens it's because of some really trivial thing, and it's over quickly (Oussama, second-generation Moroccan boy).

In two other schools, which offer a variety of unequally desirable vocational schemes, student–teacher relations appeared much more tense and volatile, and peer relations more competitive and aggressive. In these schools, more stress is laid on the formal and academic dimensions of schooling, teachers' concerted work is relatively limited, and relations with parents mainly take place on an individual basis when a student is failing academically or has disciplinary problems. The concerns of the administration about improving the schools' reputation and maintaining order result in prompter temporary or permanent exclusions of troublemakers. Adults appear mainly as questionable authority figures, to be either feared or contested, and whose treatment of students is often regarded as unfair or condescending. Although students have a very different appreciation of individual teachers, they hold a generally negative view of the school personnel as a whole. In such a context, conflicts and power relations between students are exacerbated as a response to their feeling of inferiority and according to a logic that adults are sometimes at a loss to understand and to control. As stressed previously in the group discussion, in the boys' vocational school there exists a clear hierarchy between classes and streams, and low-performing students, particularly those of minority origin, are tempted to adopt a very oppositional stance and to impose the values of a peer-group street culture which denigrates those students who most conform to teachers' expectations and who are identified as 'outsiders'. The former head of this school described such obstacles to her attempts to diversify the student body and improve the reputation of the school:

> I experienced some things that were really difficult professionally speaking. For example kids from one junior high school [located in a socially mixed more rural area]...I worked very well with the principal who did a great job on tracking. So her students who arrived in vocational 10th grade were disciplined. When I would go inform them about our high school, the lunchroom was full, meaning 250 students who were there with their teachers, and we wouldn't hear a word. We would not have been able to do this elsewhere. So then when they arrived here, they had this shy attitude, a bit of fear about coming here. But it was close by and the principal had said it was a good career to do electro-technical work here. The families trusted her. I can assure you that there were students who had to leave my school because they were scapegoats. They weren't the worst, they were average students, with real vocational projects. So they had to drop out, because they were really the scape-goats, the victims. They had to pursue elsewhere, because they were even attacked outside. Because they didn't know how to get along, they didn't know how to defend themselves. The others had noticed the one who raises his hand in class, who really wants to succeed, who acted the same as in junior high school. Who hadn't changed his attitude when transitioning to high school. Or the smallest kid, the skinny one, the isolated one. I had five or six cases like that. So even if you work with the families, in the high school, word gets out. Well I saw that the recruitment from that junior high school dropped.

Although instances of bullying and victimisation among students take place in all of the schools observed, they are most pronounced in the schools in which student–teacher relations are most aloof and formal, and where students feel judged by teachers mainly according to their academic positions and performances. Ethnicity or race does not appear to be a cause in and of itself of interpersonal or group conflicts between students, but rather as a vehicle through which they act out competitive relations and express identifications and distinctions which are in flagrant opposition to institutional norms and values. While we could detect no direct relation between the level of verbal or physical violence among students and the ethnic or social composition of the school's student body or of a particular class, it appeared quite clearly that the general atmosphere of the school and the more or less cohesive nature of student–teacher relations had an impact on these phenomena.

Inside the schools, ethnic identification of the self and the others, inter-ethnic tensions and demands for recognition of cultural or religious differences are very much a function of the manner in which students relate to their schooling and how they feel about themselves as students. Compared with their peers in the more prestigious programmes, students from the least desirable classes and those who feel most constrained in their educational prospects tend to refer much more openly to their ethnic, national or religious origins as a source of pride, and to denigrate their peers using racial terminology. This does not mean that the better-performing students have a weaker ethnic or religious identity than those in the most dead-end programmes, but simply that they do not feel the need to assert such an identity as a means of compensating for their inferiority within the educational hierarchy. For them, ethnic, cultural or racial identities remain unaffected by their educational experience and their view of themselves as students.

Conclusion

The school experience of minority students reveals many of the problems inherent in the functioning of the French school system, such as negative selection, limited communication with parents, a lack of integration between in-school training and the realities of the job market and, last but not least, the entrenched belief that social and professional destinies are entirely dependent on academic credentials. It also reveals some of its successes.

Based on the existing literature and on our fieldwork observations we can safely say that there exists no outright racial or ethnic discrimination against minority students in terms of grading and tracking, or in terms of the treatment of students in class. Although some teachers may harbour racist sentiments or hold negative views of minority students, they appear to be exceptions to the norm. In fact, we were struck much more by teachers' voluntary ignorance of the issue and by the almost total absence of any mention or discussion of students' ethnicity in normal everyday school interactions and in official discourse. Because the focus of the research was precisely the issue which is most ignored by French schools, we often had the feeling that institutional representatives were literally blind to certain phenomena which appeared flagrant to us, such as the unequal distribution of ethnic groups across streams or the over-representation of students of African origin among early school leavers or the lowest-performing students of certain classes.

To the extent that these realities are not the consequence of in-school discrimination, this ignorance may serve a positive function of keeping alive for students and teachers alike the idea that success is not dependent on factors such as ethnicity. Yet however much they try, schools cannot shield themselves entirely from the realities of the outside world and from the effects of ethnic discrimination in the workplace, residential segregation and heightened anti-immigrant sentiments. While the shared values of republican neutrality and colour-blindness prevent teachers from expressing individual judgments about students based on considerations to do with cultural or ethnic differences, it does not prevent students from voicing their feelings of injustice, and their difficult relationship with authority or peer competition in terms of racial or ethnic discrimination. The contrast between a student body for whom ethnic, racial and religious distinctions are an integral part of social interactions and a vehicle for expressing a range of feelings and opinions about one's self and the others, on the one hand, and the republican school culture in which such references remain largely taboo, on the other hand, creates a deep cultural divide between students and teachers in the most disadvantaged urban schools. As we have seen, such schools can serve as a safe haven for those who are most exposed to the harsh realities and strict social controls of the 'ghetto'. Yet they can also become spaces which exacerbate students' feelings of exclusion, thus encouraging bullying among students. These reactions can be viewed as a way of inversing the dominant hierarchies and norms of success through a process which transforms the victim of larger social forces into the victimiser at the peer-group level. The problem of this invisible form of youth violence, much less spectacular than the highly publicised urban riots and local gang fights which make the news, concerns majority and minority students alike and is only beginning to be treated by school personnel as a problem that they have to address.

In the highly elitist French school system, students frequently experience transition into a vocational stream as a form of 'punishment' inflicted upon those whose academic performance and behaviour do not fit the norm. This sentiment is particularly pronounced among the descendants of migrants from the African continent whose parents have suffered disproportionately from deindustrialisation and the economic crisis, and who overwhelmingly view schooling as the only means for their children to escape from their inferior condition. Their disappointment and sense of failure are proportional to the hopes and aspirations placed in the school system.

A better articulation of the links between vocational programmes and the job market, and the development of apprenticeship programmes that offer true training and employment opportunities would undoubtedly serve to improve the attraction of such streams. It would also be beneficial to improve communication between representatives of the educational institution and immigrant families who, while they place great store on schooling, have very little knowledge of the actual workings of the system and of the range of existing programmes and opportunities. Increased communication with parents would also serve to dispel many of the misconceptions that teachers often have about families who appear so far removed from the dominant cultural norms. Throughout our fieldwork, we noted that the distance and lack of communication between the school personnel and parents created a space within which students could develop strategies that were detrimental to school success, such as playing on teachers' stereotypes about immigrant parents' supposedly harsh educational style in order to avoid sanctions or extra work. The fact that parent–teacher exchanges often take place in a formal context, under the gaze of students and in response to some failure to conform to the norm, means that each party is tempted to overplay their 'official' role as disciplinarian rather than engage in a dialogue with the aim of unravelling the often complex processes which lead students to become disengaged with their studies or to display oppositional behaviour.

Notes

1. There is an ongoing debate among scholars in France as to whether such neighbourhoods should be regarded as 'ghettos' (Lapeyronnie 2005, Wacquant 2008).
2. In stark contrast to this absence, the proportion of children with African names or faces is significant among those who have been elected by their fifth-grade classmates to be part of the Children's Municipal Councils. They number 12 out of 60 in Bordeaux and 15 out of 20 in the right-bank suburb.

12

The Interplay of School and Family and Its Impact on the Educational Careers of Ethnic Minority Youth in Germany

Gaby Straßburger

One of the most striking features of the German educational system is the strong influence of the parents' background on students' educational success. A secondary analysis of the PISA study of 2000 showed enormous differences between ethnic groups after tracking. Students with a migration background pursued their schooling in the lowest type, *Hauptschule*, more often than their German peers (28 per cent vs. 15 per cent) while they entered a *Gymnasium* (grammar school) significantly less frequently (31 per cent vs. 39 per cent) (Konsortium 2006, p. 296). It appears that the interplay of school and family has a huge impact on the educational career of ethnic minority youth. Based on field research carried out in Berlin in 2008–2009, we will discuss this relationship in detail for students with Turkish and Lebanese family backgrounds.

In general, the decision about where to continue schooling is based on the primary school teachers' recommendations. Yet teachers tend to evaluate similar performances of students in different ways depending on parents' social background.[1] If families belong to the middle or upper classes, the likelihood that they will be advised to attend a *Gymnasium* is 2.5 times that in other cases. In addition to such social selection, when performance and the influence of socioeconomic status were controlled, the PISA data showed that migration background strongly influenced the primary school teachers' recommendation. Students with parents who were both born in Germany were recommended for a *Gymnasium* 1.7 times as often as their peers with parents who were both born outside Germany (Konsortium 2006, p. 165). Obviously, the practical availability of education opportunities in Germany depends not only on socioeconomic resources but also on the family's migration status (Sachverständigenrat deutscher Stiftungen für Integration und Migration 2010).

The German system demands a lot from students' parents.[2] They are expected to actively engage in school life and to support their children in preparation for lessons and exams, and in follow-up course work. The higher the educational background of the parents, the better they might respond to the school's expectations. The better their understanding of the educational system and its internal mechanisms, the better they might support the educational career of their children. Parents with an immigration background, however, often lack the crucial educational attainment or the knowledge of the German system.

This chapter is based on intensive field research carried out in various neighbourhoods in Berlin. By comparing two schools which represent the two ends of the educational ranking, it highlights the roles and relations of the main actors involved: students, teachers and students' parents. The study aims to shed particular light on the role of the parents' background, resources and perspectives. Although they are important for educational success in Germany, these aspects may still be regarded as a *terra incognita* when it comes to minority families of Muslim background.

The discussion is divided into three parts. The first describes our empirical research and presents the main characteristics of the sample, mainly consisting of students and parents of Turkish and Arab backgrounds. The second part examines the importance of family background for educational success. By analysing the paths that led the students to attend the schools under study we show how tracking is influenced by parents' awareness and their means of support. Then we turn our attention to the interactions of teachers, students and parents in order to see how teachers respond in different ways to the ethnic composition in their schools. Following this, we will discuss the experiences and consequences of 'othering' along ethnic lines and their influence on students' identity formation. Finally, the conclusion sums up our main findings regarding the interplay of school and family, and its impact on educational careers. In addition, we will draw on recommendations that are outlined in the first report of the Expert Council of German Foundations on Integration and Migration.[3]

The research

Our fieldwork[4] was carried out in 2008 and 2009 in schools in two typical immigrant districts of Berlin. The neighbourhoods of both schools are part of an urban development and social work programme led by the city administration in order to improve the socioeconomic conditions of the local population. Education plays a crucial role in this process. As long as the local schools have a bad reputation, many members of the middle classes flee the neighbourhood when their children reach school age, or at the latest after grade six when tracking takes place. This is true not only for the German middle class but also for the (emerging) middle classes of the immigrant population.

One-third of all students in Berlin have a non-German first language. Turkish and Lebanese represent the largest linguistic minorities. They also appear to be disproportionally affected by the exclusionary school system since they belong to the category of students whose performances are typically low.[5] Moreover, they appear to be the main targets of a public discourse which increasingly categorises them as 'Muslims'.

As mentioned above, in order to draw a differentiated portrait of such students, we opted for schools which represent the two ends of the educational ranking. We started by studying an integrated comprehensive school (*Gesamtschule*) that could be regarded as the typical type of school for students with Turkish and Lebanese backgrounds in Berlin since most of them attend schools at this level. Then we went on to observe a grammar school (*Gymnasium*) to obtain an insight into the situation of successful students with Turkish and Lebanese backgrounds.

We have intentionally chosen schools in which we could contact several students of Lebanese background. Therefore we had to go to schools where the share of German students was very low since schools which are attended by many Lebanese are typically avoided by students who have access to other, more prestigious institutions. Due to this recruiting strategy, both schools were located at a position in the educational market which is lower than what should be expected as typical from this type of school. However, although neither of these two schools can be regarded to be typical of the types of school that they represent, they are nevertheless typical of schools which are attended by students of Lebanese origin.

The *Gesamtschule* which we investigated receives 500 students, more than 80 per cent of whom have a Turkish or Arab background. The studied *Gymnasium* has 535 students, around 80 per cent of whom have a migrant background. Six years earlier the share of such minority students was not even half this size.

We interviewed 9 teachers and 28 students, of whom half were female. Most of the students were aged 15 or 16 years, and 17 among them had a Turkish and 7 a Lebanese background. In addition we spoke to 11 Turkish and 5 Lebanese parents.

Although all of the students were born in Germany, only five of them may be regarded as third generation since in each case both of their parents grew up in Germany. The others are offspring of families in which at least one parent immigrated. This is the case in all of the Lebanese families who came to Germany as refugees and successfully obtained asylum. In these families, the parents were usually already married at the time of immigration. In contrast with the Lebanese, all Turkish families were formed in Germany. However, nine mothers and two fathers grew up in Turkey and joined their spouse in

Germany after marriage. Yet even if in some families both parents grew up in Germany, the language spoken at home remained Turkish or Arabic.

Many parents who immigrated as adults do not know much about the German educational system, which is quite different from the Turkish and Lebanese systems. Thus they have to rely on the information that they gather from their children, while second-generation parents who are mostly of Turkish origin have a better insight into the German system, having been part of it themselves.

The importance of family background for educational success

In the Berlin school system, *Gesamtschule* and *Gymnasium* represent opposite positions. When children leave the undifferentiated primary school in order to enter a secondary school, their parents or legal guardian can either decide to send the child to an integrated comprehensive school (*Gesamtschule*), which is open to all children leaving elementary school regardless of their performance, or to continue education in an intermediate school (*Hauptschule*), a secondary high school (*Realschule*) or a grammar school (*Gymnasium*), depending on the child's previous performance in elementary school.[6]

The decision about where to continue schooling after primary school is based on the recommendations formulated by the primary school teachers. Every student is classified into one of three distinct categories: the best are advised to apply to a *Gymnasium*, others a *Realschule* and those with the weakest results are recommended to enter a *Hauptschule*.

Paths leading to the *Gesamtschule*

Among our teenage interviewees, 12 were recommended by their primary school teachers to attend a *Hauptschule* but opted for a *Gesamtschule*, which is open to students with all kinds of recommendation. Some did so explicitly in order to avoid the *Hauptschule* since their parents had heard about its very bad reputation and wanted to ensure a safe environment for their child. Another reason which is mentioned less often was the fact that the career options in a *Gesamtschule* are – at least in theory – much wider than in a *Hauptschule*. An explanation that was often given by the students and their parents was the fact that the *Gesamtschule* was close by and occasionally that elder siblings or friends were at the school.

Paths leading to the *Gymnasium*

Two students who were advised to go on to a *Realschule* opted for a *Gymnasium* instead. Figen told us that her teachers in primary school – in a 'better' neighbourhood where she was the only non-German in class and the only girl with a headscarf in the entire school – were absolutely against her decision to go to a *Gymnasium*. They told her: 'You will never succeed there!'

But her parents strongly supported her and so she managed to enrol in the *Gymnasium* which her mother and aunt had already attended.

Samia too rejected the advice to go on to a *Realschule* and followed the example of her elder brother who was the pupils' spokesperson of his *Gymnasium*. Her father, a philosopher, supported her early on by talking with her about her professional aspirations. When she told him that she wanted to become a teacher, he replied that she had to be very hard-working in primary school to be able to go on to a *Gymnasium* and enter university afterwards. When she finally got a recommendation for attending a *Realschule*, her parents and siblings encouraged her to disregard this and aim for a *Gymnasium*. She ultimately became one of the most successful students in her class.

Ali, Hikmet, Arif, Ayhan, Mesut, Mona, Gül and Raja were advised to go to a *Gymnasium* and did so. Most of them had relatives (uncle, aunt, cousin) or friends who were at a *Gymnasium* and could therefore rely on their experiences. For Mona, who was the only one in her immediate surrounding who was heading to a *Gymnasium*, this was, however, a real challenge since she only had one cousin who had finished at the *Realschule*. Nobody in her family ever went to a *Gymnasium* and many of her relatives could not even imagine that one of them might cope with it. She says: 'Their eyes are always on me. Will I really master it?' Her parents, in contrast, have always strongly encouraged her. They referred to two aunts of Mona's living in Denmark who had studied there and started an academic career. The relatives living in Berlin serve as the negative counterexample. Mona cites her father asking her: 'Do you want to end up like them?'

As we can see from these examples, active parental intervention is often of decisive importance when the recommendation of the primary school teachers does not meet the parents' evaluation of the student's performance. As we will see in the following, parents' abilities to intervene and their means of supporting the educational career of their children differ widely and clearly correspond to the type of secondary school attended.

Parents' means of support

Some of the parents of students attending a *Gymnasium* attended the studied *Gymnasium*/high school themselves, have a university degree, are married to an academic or have siblings who have a university degree. In these families it appears natural for the children to attend a *Gymnasium* too. Ali and Hikmet's mother attended a *Gymnasium* but left when her best friend did so. Their father had been a teacher in Turkey before he joined his wife in Germany. The mothers of Mona and Gül were in high school in Lebanon and Turkey, respectively. The father of Samia was a philosopher in Jordan. Children who grow up in families with such educated parents develop the ambition from early childhood to enter an academic career. Yet this does not mean that it is easy to achieve such a goal, at least if their parents grew up in another country: the migration process interrupted their career and forced them to start from scratch. However, the expectation that they are capable of becoming an academic seems to be passed on to the children. These families – if 'family' is understood in an extended sense including aunts, uncles and cousins – have the cultural capital and consciousness to thoroughly support the child in accomplishing homework and school preparations. Besides the sometimes necessary technical assistance, they provide emotional support and open the child's mind to a professional career.

Other parents whose child attends the *Gymnasium*, such as Esin, the mother of Figen and Aygül, are inspired by the idea that their children might obtain a better situation than their own. They take note of their own negative school experiences in Germany and put a lot of energy into supporting their children. Although they do not have the cultural capital of the first group, they are, nevertheless, well aware that the children need their support in order to be successful at school, and they are convinced that they can promote their children through different means, such as sitting by their side when they do homework, and telling them not to give up too fast but to take their time. In addition to this kind of emotional help, we have learned about material support that is given to the offspring. Esin, for example, was proud to say that her daughter, Figen, had a room of her own and is liberated from household duties. She should focus her full attention on school affairs. If she wants any book her parents will buy it, and if she requires private lessons Esin will not hesitate to pay for them.

The belief that they have an active impact on their children's career is lacking among those whose children attend the *Gesamtschule*. Some of these parents say that although they really wanted their children to be successful in school they did not listen to them. Another issue brought forward in this group is that parents cannot help their children if they themselves do not have the required knowledge. As the interviews make clear, this group of parents is lacking the knowledge not only about the things taught at school but also to evaluate the career options of their children and to support them to find their way. Furthermore, most likely they also lack a network that might be activated when important career decisions, such as tracking after primary school, have to be taken and related practical problems have to be managed.

Families of students in the *Gesamtschule* in Moabit are relatively poor, many fathers are unemployed and most mothers have never worked. The educational level of the parents is rather low and only some are familiar with the German educational system. Thus they are hardly able to help their children with homework and they most probably lack the knowledge and networks necessary to influence their children's academic career in a positive direction. Many cannot imagine having an active impact on their children's career. This opinion of the parents is shared by the students. Yet most of the students in this group stated that their parents were interested in their academic success and told them to study hard.

A tentative conclusion at this point would be that the differences between the resources of the parental home of students enrolled in the *Gymnasium* and the *Gesamtschule* suggest that schools not only fail to counterbalance the uneven distribution of socioeconomic means and cultural capital but also further aggravate these structural differences.

In what follows we turn our attention to the interactions of teachers, students and parents as they describe how teachers in the *Gymnasium* and the *Gesamtschule* respond rather differently to the ethnic composition in their schools.

Teachers' thoughts about the influence and responsibility of the school and the family

Teachers in the *Gesamtschule* regard the families as being underprivileged by pointing to the fact that around 80 per cent of the students' families receive social welfare benefits. While the idea of a *Gesamtschule* was to bring together students of different socioeconomic and educational backgrounds, this objective has become increasingly distant in recent years.

Diversity is missed regarding not only the composition of the student body but also the academic performance of the students. A *Gesamtschule* should ideally be attended by one-third of students who were advised to enter a *Hauptschule*, by one-third who were recommended to attend a *Realschule* and by one-third who were recommended to continue in a *Gymnasium*. However, in this school the educational level of the newcomers has for a long time been closer to that of students at a *Hauptschule*. Especially in the eyes of the German middle classes but also of the emerging middle classes of the immigrant population, the school is regarded to be not much better than a *Hauptschule*. If they send their children to a school in this borough they probably choose another one among the available *Gesamtschules*. Those are attended by many more students with better recommendations, and the share of German students is higher.

Most teachers in the *Gesamtschule* feel frustrated by such a downgrading and view it as a burden which makes teaching very difficult. Many of them regard the decline in the general academic level of students as the outcome of various factors. One is the unfavourable change in the socioeconomic conditions in the surrounding neighbourhood, while another is the shift in the ethnic composition of the student body towards children from immigrant backgrounds. Students of Turkish and Arab origins represent altogether more than 80 per cent of the student body. Germans are clearly in the minority; most classes include only one or two students without a migration background. Most teachers view the language problems of migrant students not merely as a consequence of the ethnic composition of the neighbourhood but also as caused by the families themselves. Turkish and Arab families are described as 'living in a parallel world' which does not provide children with the resources needed to succeed in wider society. Out of the seven teachers interviewed, there was only one young female teacher (Ms Regius) who expressed clearly that the problems were caused by socioeconomic rather than ethnic or cultural factors: 'There is no difference between German families and migrant families. The problem is the underprivileged situation of both of them. Our children grow up in a non-academic environment.' Her colleagues, however, tended to blame the victim and to argue in culture-bound terms:

In Turkish and Arab families values are different; education is not so important. Parents don't educate in a consequent manner. Thus, children come late, don't bring with them the material needed or even stay away from school. Especially girls have to care for the household and don't have time to work for school. Families always stick to their communities not enabling their children to see something new. They pamper the children and give them a lot of material goods, like expensive mobile phones or computer games...

Some teachers even criticised the family's decision to have many children: 'Parents sometimes tell me that they have many children and can't take care so much of each of them. This is an excuse I can't accept. Of course, it is difficult to educate so many children, but why didn't they think about that before?' (Ms Kaiser). Or they blamed parents for marrying the 'wrong' spouse: 'The language problems get worse and worse, and this is mainly caused by spouses who come from Turkey not knowing any German' (Mr Peter).

All in all, many teachers in the *Gesamtschule* do not regard parents as being partners in solving educational problems but rather as an important cause of such problems. They feel that they are being blamed for the failures of the family. 'We can't make up for their mistakes' is a message which was given in many variations: 'The bad performance of the students is not our fault. Nowadays we are more and more expected to do things which were in the parents' responsibility before. This can't go on like this. We have to give it back to the parents' responsibility' (Mr Cesarin). 'We are already doing more than what might be expected. Often we are forced to take the parents' role' (Ms Schott). 'Parents often want their children to be good in school and they expect us to make that come true' (Ms Kaiser).

Teachers in the *Gymnasium* evaluated the family situation in a rather different way. They acknowledged the success of many students from Turkish or Arab backgrounds because they were well aware of the fact that most of their families cannot support them in learning. One of the teachers, Mr Yücel, summarised his impressions as follows: 'Although their environment – parents and peers – is not leading to success, many succeed. They work enormously hard to catch up with what is required. This is a great achievement.'

Like their colleagues at the *Gesamtschule*, teachers at the *Gymnasium* complained about the dramatic change in the ethnic composition of the school's student body. However, they evaluate it rather differently: 'The ethnic imbalance is unfair. Our students are structurally discriminated against by it,' states Mr Schiller. They regard the actual ethnic composition as problematic in different aspects. Since Turkish or Arab students are in a majority position, the school is less attractive to those groups, Germans and non-Muslim students, which would be needed in order to create a better balance. 'It's a vicious circle,' says Mr Schiller, who would even opt for an ethnic quota system in order to overcome this problematic situation.

As in the *Gesamtschule*, the quasi-absence of German classmates contributes to severe problems regarding linguistic competence. Teachers in both school types complained that they constantly had to explain expressions which would be easily understood by students in other grammar schools. They told us that many students left the school before they reached the final grade. For this reason they describe their school as being closer to a *Gesamtschule* than to a *Gymnasium*.

When we asked about their contact with the students' parents, we received different reactions. While Mr Schiller complained that half of the parents did not attend the parents' evenings ('especially those who have "difficult" kids never come'), Mr Yücel would favour an outreach strategy: 'If parents don't come we should approach them. Especially teachers with migratory background – such as him – might be a bridge between the parents and the school.' He pleads for a change in the teachers' mind that would encourage a new understanding of what the school is responsible for:

> We have to accept that the parents of many students won't be able to evaluate the way the educational system and career strategies work in Germany. Most parents can't make appropriate suggestions to our students. Therefore it is our responsibility to provide information on career options and paths.

Comparing the statements of the teachers in the two schools, we see that they reflect rather different attitudes concerning responsibilities and desirable interactions between the school and the family. While most teachers simply complained that parents of Turkish and Arab backgrounds did not show enough interest in their children's school career and did not seek contact with the school, others favoured an explicit turn in teachers' attitudes towards reaching out and suggested a change in the definition of the schools' responsibilities. This would, according to them, have to include tasks which are often seen as being the parents' duty.

However, we should not jump to conclusions about differences in types of school (*Gesamtschule* vs. *Gymnasium*) but rather assume that the attitudes of the teachers interviewed in these two schools reflect a typical debate in German schools that is not restricted to certain types of school.

Experiences and consequences of 'othering' along ethnic lines

There is a second subject besides that of parents' evenings which is a typical cause of conflict between teachers and Muslim parents. This is the issue of participation in class trips:[7]

> Often girls are not allowed to attend class trips although they are obligatory. I won't ever accept this. There is no excuse! I won't stop efforts to get the parents' approval until children may attend. I don't care if I have to call the parents or if I have to visit them at home!

Ms Cittavecchias' powerful engagement with class trips is typical of some other teachers, too. At the same time, it is mirrored by the strong resistance of migrant parents.

Being aware of this, we presented a scenario concerning a conflict about a class trip during a focus group discussion with mainly Arab mothers of students at the *Gymnasium*. As expected, it caused great excitement. Most mothers felt very embarrassed by teachers who did not accept that they were reluctant and mostly refused to let their children go. Their main point was the lack of control that makes it impossible to protect the children. Many mothers were sure that teachers could not replace parental control and protection. Two reasons were mentioned: the class is too big to have an eye on everything that is going on, and German teachers would just not care about things that are important to Muslim families. They might even invite them to do things which would not correspond with Islamic rules, such as going to a discotheque.

The mothers' arguments against class trips are based on the idea that there are two value systems – the Muslim vs. the German – that contradict each other at certain points. The children themselves seem to be still too weak to resist if the influence of German values becomes too strong. In everyday life there is a balance of power and parents may protect their children from doing something wrong. This protection cannot be ensured, however, when children are out of reach for several days.

As we could observe during our field research at the two schools, students were often faced with discussions about issues such as the headscarf, arranged or forced marriage, and family life in Muslim communities. Many felt bothered by teachers who bring up these topics without showing any intention of entering into an open discussion. Muslim students argued that such teachers simply wanted to demonstrate that they have the power of defining the proper way of life in Germany.

However, the effect of such experiences of 'othering' is a petrification of group identities. In reaction to the negative mainstream discourse about Islam, many students showed strong solidarity with their families by underlining that they agreed with their parents and by stressing that their commitment to certain rules was completely deliberate. They often interpreted this as being typical of being Muslim and not being German.

Constructing 'us' and 'them' in a way that reverses discrimination and exclusion is an important component of identity-building which we could observe. This was, on the one hand, done by extending the we-group to other Muslim communities, and, on the other hand, by neglecting differences within the community as being of minor importance. Alternative readings or possible identifications were ruled out by these strong constructions of collectivities.

Since apparently most teachers, students and parents whom we met in the course of our fieldwork regard German and Muslim identities as incompatible, we have to state that in many cases the interplay of school and family does not help to overcome discrimination and exclusion. As in the wider society and the public discourse, being identified by teachers as a Muslim tends to signify meanings of 'otherness' and as not being German. Those students and parents who define themselves as Muslims are convinced that Islam is not really accepted in German society, and many teachers convey the feeling that Islam does not really fit in.

Conclusion

Our research was based on a comparison of two schools which represent two ends of the educational hierarchy. The findings reflect the fact that school success in Germany very much depends on the ethnic and social background of the students' families.

In general, the educational level of the students' parents in the *Gymnasium* was higher than that of the parents of students in the *Gesamtschule*. The cultural capital of the (extended) family could thus be used in the *Gymnasium* to thoroughly support and encourage children. Many students in the *Gymnasium* had grown up with the idea of entering an academic career. Most of them had been quite successful in primary school and therefore were advised to attend a *Gymnasium* at the secondary level. In other cases the parents had the courage to oppose the teachers' advice for a *Realschule* and to send their children to a *Gymnasium* instead.

In contrast, the educational level of the students' parents in the *Gesamtschule* was rather low. Many were not even familiar with the German school system, and many could not imagine how to make an active impact on the children's school career since they lacked the necessary knowledge and networks.

Our sample was too small to draw general conclusions but the report of the Expert Council allows us to place our findings in a wider frame.

The strongly diversified educational system in Germany is highly selective and aims to form homogeneous groups of students with a similar level of performance. The related selection processes follow established normative standards which are often not appropriate for students with an immigration background who might, for instance, lack certain linguistic competences (Faas 2008). Ingrid Gogolin (1994) speaks of a prevalent 'monolingual habitus' which prevents the positive assessment of diversity.

To counter this normative bias, the Expert Council recommends that linguistic diversity should be seen as a challenge which the educational system has to accept. The 'monolingual habitus' should be overcome by programmes to better develop language competences of students who grew up in multilingual surroundings and who have learned German as a second language. It is regarded as important to have supportive structures and concepts which last throughout the years of schooling. Such an endeavour should be accompanied by personnel development. All teachers and teacher students should be trained in the teaching of linguistically and ethnically heterogeneous groups of pupils. Besides that, the percentage of teachers with a migration background should in the long run reflect the percentage of people with a migration background in the total population.

Our research shows that schools with a large number of students from migration backgrounds tend to take a position in the educational market which is lower than what should be expected from the type of school. Not surprisingly, many teachers feel frustrated by this situation and regard it as a burden to teach such a 'difficult public', which makes their work rather hard.

The almost complete absence of German classmates does in fact contribute to severe problems regarding the language competences of ethnic minority youths. Students often leave school before they reach the final grade. And yet many teachers evaluate these difficulties not as a result of segregation along ethnic and socioeconomic lines but primarily as a result of ethnic or cultural factors. In the interviews they pointed to migrant communities that were often depicted as living in 'parallel societies'. Therefore many teachers do not see their students' parents as partners in solving educational problems but in fact as the major cause of these problems.[8]

The attitudes of most teachers whom we interviewed might be interpreted as typical reflections of a vivid debate in Germany about the responsibilities of school vs. parents and about the desirable pattern of cooperation. The Expert Council suggests measures that compensate for parents' lack of resources and/or provide possibilities to better integrate parents into life at school. Schools should offer learning opportunities for parents and inform them about important characteristics of the German educational system, such as the importance of tracking after primary school, or the expectations concerning parental contributions to the learning process. In addition, the school staff should respect their mandate to support the development of the resources and abilities of each individual student regardless of their socioeconomic or cultural background. Schools have to ensure free access to education and further professional careers for everyone by countering the imbalances in the resources of their students. Furthermore, as we would suggest, schools should contribute to overcoming the negative mainstream discourse about Islam and enter into dialogues with the 'Muslim side'. Taking parents seriously by addressing them as partners in the educational process would demonstrate respect which is sorely lacking according to many of the interviewees. The professional training of future teachers should raise their awareness of discrimination and injustice, and develop their competence for 'same-ing' instead of 'othering'. Heterogeneous schools are well advised to constantly send signals which state that: 'Each of our students regardless of his/her background is one of us. We all together are forming our school.' Such an embracing attitude might be a starting point for building an identity which might make it possible to be Muslim and German at the same time.

To conclude, our findings clearly illustrate structural problems of the German school system and its often inadequate reactions to migration and integration. What we have presented is not new but emphasises once more the dilemmas which have been vivid and also well known for some time. Our observations 'in daily life' provide an insight into the reproduction of problems that have been described again and again but that still remain to be solved.

Notes

1. For a thorough analysis of institutional discrimination, see Radtke and Gomolla (2002).
2. The history of changing preferences regarding desirable patterns of interaction between parents and the school is outlined by Gomolla (2011).
3. The Expert Council was founded in 2008 by eight member foundations and is an independent academic monitoring, evaluating and advisory body. For further information, see http://www.svr-migration.de/wp-content/uploads/2010/05/flyertext_english.pdf.
4. For detailed information about the methodology of our research, please see Straßburger et al. (2010). The German institution participating in the research of the EDUMIGROM research programme was the Peace Research Institute, Frankfurt, represented by Sabine Mannitz, the leader of the German team. Interviewing, focus group discussions, and participant observation at schools and in the communities were mainly undertaken by Meryem Ucan. Analysis and discussion of the results were to a large extent a joint project. Therefore, the author wants to express her special thanks to Sabine Mannitz and Meryem Ucan, the co-authors of the German Community Study that this chapter is primarily based upon.
5. For detailed information, see the analysis of Berlin School Statistics 2007/2008 by Straßburger et al. (2010).
6. For details, see Commissioner for Integration and Migration of the Senate of Berlin (2008, pp. 45–48). Described here is the situation in 2008 and 2009 when our field research took place. However, in 2011 the Berlin school system has

been restructured to a great extent: *Hauptschule, Realschule* and *Gesamtschule* were merged to become the new *Sekundarschule.*

7. Class trips are excursions for the members of a particular grade or class and are very common in Germany. They last several days, sometimes even two weeks, and are regarded as an important pedagogical method to influence group dynamics in a positive way, to strengthen the coherence of the class community and to foster adolescents' autonomy. Since they are an integral part of the school programme, participation in class trips is compulsory. If a family's income is too low, the fee is financed by the public authorities.

8. What a partnership of parents and schools might look like is described by Gomolla who, following Jeannie Oakes and Martin Lipton (2003), distinguishes four analytical patterns: (1) to gain parents' cooperation to support the school; (2) to offer support for families as is done to a large extent in full-service schools; (3) to build bridges into communities and diverse living environments; and (4) to support the political self-organising of parents and communities for school improvement and further changes in society (2011).

13
Ethnic Identification and the Desire to Belong in the Case of Urban Roma Youth in Romania

Enikő Vincze

This chapter addresses the desires to belong of urban Roma youth in Romania. We examine how these desires are shaped by ethnic identification and, concurrently, how ethnic 'otherness' is constructed by ambivalent desires for integration and separation. On a larger scale, the study observes that, under the conditions of post-socialist transformation and of the current neoliberal regime, the case of vulnerable Roma from Romania exhibits a particular trend: their stigmatised ethnic identification becomes a cause of their advanced marginality (Wacquant 2008), and it acts as a mechanism for transforming them from citizens with universal capacities and rights into disadvantaged, racialised subjects. The aim of this contribution is to theorise on these relationships at the micro- and macrolevels on the basis of a community study conducted in Romania during the school year 2009/2010 within the framework of the EDUMIGROM research programme.[1]

After defining the conceptual framework, the second part of the study presents the social context of everyday lives of Roma youth from 'Transilvan City',[2] followed by a discussion of their ambivalent identity strategies. By addressing the relationship between ethnic identification, sociospatial segregation and racialised citizenship in the fourth part, the analysis will relate the everyday experiences of ethnic 'othering' in the context of schooling to the broader sociopolitical issues of the formation of racialised urban marginality and citizenship.

Conceptual framework

Ethnic identification is a process by which, on the one hand, people are created by institutions and discourses as subjects belonging to 'ethnic groups' and, on the other hand, one by which they identify with the positions ascribed to them. (Hall 1992, Moore 1988, 1994, Woodward 1999, McClaurin 2001). Desires of belonging and ethnic identification reciprocally shape each other. Peoples' 'choices' for integration into or separation from particular (ethnic) communities are influenced by structural and cultural forces. Ethnic differentiation is also expressed through the ways in which Roma children and their parents choose a school thought to be 'proper' for a disadvantaged ethnic Roma, or through the way in which schools select their students according to their ethnic belonging and/or socioeconomic condition. As theories of intersectionality demonstrate (Crenshaw 1989, Wing 2003, McCall 2005), ethnic identification is interwoven with other markers of differences and systems of classification: they impact on one another and together they create inequalities, and sustain power relations and social hierarchies.

Similar to Barth (1969) and Cohen (1974), we also consider that (ethnic) identities are relational, that they are always produced and used in the process of creating/maintaining/tearing down boundaries between 'us' and 'them', and that they engage both inclusion and exclusion, or sameness and difference. Identities are also situational: individual and group identities are formed by the given situations and relationships of everyday life but they also contribute to shaping daily life. They are cultural constructs (sets of meanings) through which people position themselves in relation to each other, while at the same time they are also instruments of 'othering' as well as of processes of differentiation by which meanings and social boundaries are created. People produce their identities while they react to what is happening to them in their everyday life (in terms of economic situation, production, consumption, housing, friendships, parenting, rituals, community norms and so on) and while they create themselves as similar to or different from significant 'others'. The way in which people identify themselves in their personal interactions (among others, in school) is shaped by the broader structures of power and intersecting inequalities.

Since the discussion that follows looks at the relationships between ethnicity and socioeconomic position, I also subscribe to approaches that conceptualise ethnicity as a social, cultural and political phenomenon (Verdery 1994), or as an instrument (of classification) with social, cultural and political functions. Ethnicity is both a sociocultural construct (one of the categories by which people define, explain and justify social differentiations) and a set of social relations and interactions in which communication about cultural differences is relevant for groups (Eriksen 2001). Material inequalities are not only rooted in the socioeconomic system but also in peoples' reflections about them. Even if Roma do not constitute a social class, the category of 'Gypsyness' has long been associated with 'poverty', and 'the Roma problem' has been reduced to this socioeconomic issue (neglecting the cultural dimension in the sense of both anti-Gypsy racism and ethnocultural self-identification). Distancing myself from such reductionist views, this chapter considers socioeconomic inequalities as these intersect with unequal ethnic and gender differentiations (Bradley 1996, Magyari-Vincze

2006). Due to the networks of power relations created in this way, some categories, such as impoverished ethnic Roma, or Roma women, suffer multiple disadvantages and material deprivations that are sustained to a large extent by deep-rooted cultural beliefs.

This contribution aims to describe how, from the point of view of Roma youth, the educational system (re)produces cleavages along ethnic lines. Furthermore, it follows the approach according to which the reproduction of culture through education (including distinctions and classifications) plays a key role in the reproduction of the entire social system (Bourdieu and Passeron 1990). Consequently, we stress here that the creation of ethnic cleavages, notably by the school system, is crucial to the formation of socioeconomic inequalities between the privileged/mainstream and the disadvantaged/marginal groups. Moreover, this chapter observes that, despite the fact that many schools run inclusive and multicultural educational policies, they are not able to disrupt the logic of the broader power regime of which they are a product, which is characterised by deepened socioeconomic inequalities as a result of neoliberal practices and ideologies, or of the extension of the market economy into the realm of school education, housing, healthcare and employment.

Turning now to issues of identification, it is our point of departure that adolescent identity construction is 'reproductive of prescriptive discourses of race, ethnicity, class, gender and sexuality and mirrored in the micropolitics of school' (Proweller 1999, p. 801). The case of ethnic Roma youth shows similarities with that of Afro-American adolescents for whom the insecurities and anxieties characterising the transition from childhood to adolescence (Stoughton and Sivertson 2005, p. 277) are experienced through the 'personal significance and social meaning of belonging to a particular racial group' (Tatum 1997, p. 16). Schools are not neutral spaces for performing through knowledge acquisition; rather, they are social environments in which students are challenged by both the prescriptive discourses regarding their ethnicity, gender and social status, and the desire to resist them.

Our analysis ultimately shows that the desire of Roma school children to belong to the mainstream of society proves to be unfulfilled due to the advanced urban marginality that they and their families are confronted with and which is manifested through their sociospatial segregation (Soja 2010). This process of forceful separation, which relegates them to the city's isolated peripheries, tends to make them invisible, more precisely hidden from the eyes of the mainstream, similar to the way in which homeless people are affected by anti-homelessness laws, which 'reinforce the "right" of the housed never to have to see the results of the working of society they are (at least partially) responsible for making' (Mitchell 2003). At the same time, sociospatial segregation turns the subjects living under such conditions into 'visible' actors belonging to stigmatised environments as the effects of hazardous industrial areas or municipal garbage dumps or sewage plants soil their bodies.

The broader social context of Roma youth

Romania is home to the largest number of ethnic Roma in Europe. In the 1992 census, 401,087 people (1.8 per cent) identified themselves as Roma, and by 2002 the respective number increased to 535,250 (2.5 per cent).[3] In 'Transilvan City', the ratio of the Roma population was around 0.95 per cent of a population of 250,000 in 2002 (which is below the urban average of 1.8 per cent). According to the estimates of Roma leaders, rather than 3,000 (as declared in the census), there may actually be 5,000 Roma living in the town. 'Transilvan County' is located in North-Western Romania, which is one of the areas with the highest proportion of ethnic Roma (3.5 per cent). As far as the use of the Romani language is concerned, 1.1 per cent of Romania's population declared it as their mother tongue in the 2002 census, while in the North-Western region the percentage was 1.64 (the highest in the country) and in 'Transilvan County' it was only 0.29 per cent.

'Transilvan City' is one of Romania's largest urban centres with a large Romanian majority population and a significant Hungarian minority, its history being marked by several geopolitical shifts in the Romanian-Hungarian state borders. Politically and symbolically, the city's inter-ethnic map is dominated by the Romanian-Hungarian relationship, while the 'Roma issue' only recently entered into public consciousness as a socioeconomic problem, or at least, as an exotic cultural presence during festivals. Inter-ethnic relations within the town are mostly peaceful and are characterised by separation and parallelism. Nevertheless, strong anti-Gypsy prejudices structure discriminatory attitudes towards Roma, in the case of both the majority and the ethnic Hungarian population, and occasionally the local administration fosters 'urban planning' projects that increase the severity of Roma 'ghettoisation' and thus reinforce marginalisation, further discrimination and social tension.

Today the most socially disadvantaged Roma are located in three major marginal districts of 'Transilvan City', which were the sites of our study. According to the estimate of a local Roma NGO leader, more than 2,000 out of the city's 5,000 Roma live in these neighbourhoods. The collapse of the socialist urban economic units which formerly integrated them, albeit mainly into unskilled and underappreciated jobs, relegated most of them into the most disadvantaged socioeconomic positions. Those who lost their jobs – generally due to the severe decrease in job opportunities linked to deindustrialisation – could not reintegrate into the labour market, and even failed to register as unemployed. Those who were previously able to make a decent living out of their traditional crafts cannot compete today on the capitalist market. Yet some of them, such as the Gabor or the Florist Roma, are still trying to adjust their former occupations to the market's demands. All of these changes are negatively impacting access to decent housing and are contributing to the creation of impoverished neighbourhoods where families and individuals evicted from other parts of the city or those looking 'voluntarily' for cheap informal housing congregate. Moreover, the impoverished Roma families' strategies of survival cannot support children's long-term school education, so the latter experience the effects of cumulated and structural disadvantages, or the vicious circle of poverty (enrolling into marginal schools, abandoning school at an early age, joining special schools, dropping out). Most Roma, because they did not own property in the presocialist regimes, could not benefit from the recent process of appropriation of lands, woods or buildings. Furthermore, since Romania is affected by the most recent economic crises, and since the rate of the registered unemployed has increased, the relative condition of impoverished and unregistered unemployed Roma has grown worse, while the worsening conditions have made the majority's intolerance and rejection of Roma even sharper than before.

The three compact neighbouring north-western areas of 'Transilvan City' in which the 'Roma community' is settled are marked by a mixture of premodern/rural and industrial/post-industrial elements. The hybrid nature of the area as a whole is evident when catching a glimpse of the housing conditions. However, there exist some differences between the three sites as individual houses predominate in Forest district, blocks of flats host Roma in Flower district, and improvised homes mostly distinguish the condition of Roma living in Water district. By and large the investigated territory is also characterised by a relatively diverse spectrum of occupational status (farmers, petty traders, manufacturers, industrial workers who mostly work for sanitation companies, the unemployed, day labourers some of whom work on the garbage dump, small entrepreneurs, and domestic workers are the major groupings). These diverse occupations do not simply denote differences in community traditions but more importantly reflect survival niches born during state-socialism and the post-socialist times, or demonstrate ways in which people followed diverse strategies for coping with their deplorable socioeconomic conditions.

The term 'Roma community' used in this chapter does not designate a homogeneous group of people, since the population in question is characterised by several internal differentiations generated – among others – by the distance between families living in deep poverty and those with a better socioeconomic status. The community of Water district, which is harshly separated from the outer world, lacks the elementary conditions for decent living and is close to illegality in terms of housing, labour and the possession of identity documents. For these reasons, people's lives here are characterised by strong insecurity and dependency on informal (exploitative) economies. However, since our approach was to depict schools as our points of departure, we were able to observe differences even within this neighbourhood by visiting families with a more secure economic background who therefore could afford to keep their children enrolled in school. The inhabitants of Flower and Forest districts, who live in compact groups or dispersed families, were doing slightly better. In most cases, the block apartments or the houses which they own or rent, while mostly small one-room-and-kitchen units, do have electricity, running water, gas and access to sewerage.

The severity of ghettoisation is another factor that produces and maintains differences within the observed communities. The Roma colony serves both as a source of solidarity and support and as the embodiment of deprivation or even exploitation. We learned about families with relatively better socioeconomic conditions, such as those in Flower district, whose accounts indicate that compact groups of Roma benefit from more support in their living arrangements than families who live isolated from the Roma community. Overall, however, Roma families who are dispersed across the town and are integrated into the broader urban community are usually doing better economically than those living in colonies on the town's peripheries. This is because the latter are formed and maintained by people from in and around the town who have lost their apartments and jobs and are desperately looking for cheap housing solutions and for the support that informal networks supposedly offer. While the mechanism of reciprocal assistance does indeed function in some cases, actions of solidarity are exercised under these conditions of shortages, competition for scarce resources, mutual suspicions and the inability to jointly shape the nature of cohabitation. Moreover, as illustrated by families from the waste dump of Water district, people living in encapsulated spaces become dependent and at the mercy of informal local leaders and entrepreneurs who exploit their cheap labour. The most significant difference between the Roma group from Flower district and the one from Water district lies in the degree to which the colony has become a ghetto characterised by acute social and geographical isolation from the outer world, as its inhabitants are living and working in the same space in which resources are very limited and most children lack any opportunity for schooling.

While they do not form a homogeneous population, the investigated Roma families, who all have children enrolled in the seventh or eighth grade, look like a truly functioning 'community' insofar as they share some major concerns, such as living on the margins of the town, frequent changes of homes, unemployment and day labouring in the informal economy, low levels of school education (which is the lowest in the case of the mothers in their thirties) and difficult access to quality education. To varying degrees they also share higher educational aspirations for their children and a desire for integration into majority society. Last but not least, these families, living dispersed or in compact groups, become a 'community' because they are perceived by the outer world as undifferentiated poor 'Gypsies and share experiences of unequal treatment and exclusion in different domains of life, such as the labour market, schooling, public health and housing.

The embeddedness of individuals into the larger community of the city is mediated by their belonging to restricted groups ranging from the nuclear family to the extended kinship, and to neighbourhoods, peer groups or communities of faith. The informal networks, as alternatives to the formal institutions, have the potential of supportive webs that not only function as symbolic and material resources but also counterbalance the shortcomings of unsuccessful integration. Separation from the foreign, dangerous or ignorant outer world works through the integration into the inner circles of trust, but the delimitation between these two is always relative and subject to renegotiation. 'Othering' is a complex and multilayered process. The racially stigmatised ethnic Roma groups construct and maintain distinctions among themselves: that is, how ideas about 'the Romanianised Roma', 'the Gabor Roma', 'the Pentecostal Roma' and 'the poor Roma' are used in order to create multiple hierarchies of the acceptable, the foreign and the dangerous. The emerging categories not only help inward orientation but also provide prescriptions regarding who should be accepted or, contrarily, avoided and rejected, while they also contribute to eventually maintaining a sense of superiority within the 'group' that is constructed by the mainstream population as inferior.

Strategies of ethnic identification and ambiguities of belonging

People from the Roma community of 'Transilvan City' practise a threefold identity strategy which includes the separation from other categories of Roma groups embodying negative identities, striving for integration into the majority community representing a desired life, and the maintenance of a third, hybrid but positive identity that provides people with a sense of self bridging between different lifeworlds. The latter condition and sense of inbetween-ness is, for instance, reflected in their perception of the aspired and the de facto gender orders of the ethnic minority community. For many Roma, enrolling girls in school (or at least, desiring this) on an equal footing with boys reflects both their longing for acceptance by mainstream society and their desire to distance themselves from what is thought of as 'traditional/non-modern Gypsy norms'.

Peoples' mixed identification strategies are expressed in part by their attitudes towards schooling: school embodies for them an institution leading to the desired integration, as well as one which reminds them that they remain different from the majority, at times even that they are unwanted by the mainstream. At the same time, school is defined as an institution in which some maintain their image of 'emancipated Roma' who differ from the 'traditional Gypsies' who do not want to send their children to school.

The hybridity of identity strategies and ambiguities of self-perception

The hybrid life strategies of the people whom we interviewed from Flower district, which combine the desire for integration with the will to remain separated from the outer world, shaped their attitudes towards school education. While they were aware of the necessity of schooling, they still demonstrated an oppositional position towards the system, being unsatisfied with what the school offered to them and the manner in which it treated them as Roma. The adults' attitudes had an impact on their children. The latter were ready to socialise with Romanians but mostly preferred their Roma peers when it came to more intimate relations. However, we also encountered cases of parents and children who felt uncomfortable in this neighbourhood and who were desirous of leaving it. Recognising that they were identified by the majority through their belonging to this Gypsy environment (*Cigănie*), they saw their source of troubles in their 'Gypsyness' as something negative. Predominantly, however, the sense of collectivity that these people maintained gave them the strength to transcend victimhood and pejorative identities, and to develop creative and resourceful strategies of survival and positive self-evaluation. Their voluntary ethnic differentiation (also shaped by a degree of residential segregation) was only partly based on the Romani language and their shared past, as their history was mostly about finding niches permitting personal and collective survival under the conditions of changing ethnic regimes. The 'Hungarian-ness' of those who stressed their mixed Hungarian-Gypsy origins was mentioned mostly as something exotic, as part of their childhood, but not as a fact that had any current cultural significance. At the very most it might be referred to as a generational difference between themselves and their own parents. In this context, Gypsyness was the condition shared across generations and the changing ethnopolitical regimes which demanded either Hungarianisation or Romanianisation, a challenge which both their parents and they were able to face by speaking either the Hungarian or the Romanian language.

Bianca from Water district thinks that Roma and Romanians are not different in basic features but she states that some of her 'majority colleagues are jealous of the Gypsy kids' appearance and dances at the school celebration'. The openness of Roma children towards entertaining with others is demonstrated by Cristina's words: 'I guess I have even more Romanian than Gypsy friends', and 'I also have some friends who are poorer than me.' Daniel strongly differentiates between friends and buddies: 'my friends are Roma, but my buddies could be Romanians as well'. Geanina compared her sense of Gypsyness with that of her grandfather who lives downtown: 'he is not proud of this, but I am'. Her maternal grandfather, who is an ethnic Romanian, is not too happy that his daughter married a Gypsy man and that his grandchild assumes her Roma identity as something natural. Iulia's situation is special because she has an ethnically mixed background, having a Roma father and a Hungarian mother. Sorin made some short and pragmatic remarks about his ethnicity: 'I am a Romanianised Roma. We have no traditions. Our family only speaks Romanian.' Some parents emphasised that despite their wish for integration they keep a distance from Romanians.

Mari's mother told us: 'I'm proud to be Roma... We have friends of other ethnicity. Even downtown I know people very well but they do not visit me.' Daniel's mother stated: 'I'm glad that I'm a Gypsy. But I am also glad that they say we are not Gypsies but we are Roma. In my life I have both won and lost due to my ethnicity.'

Among the Gabor Gypsy families whom we interviewed in Forest district, some saw school as an institution that attempts to integrate children into a society whose values are rejected by the family. Thus they do not consider education as something beneficial. In such cases, the attitude towards schooling has different implications for boys and girls, since girls do not go beyond the level of secondary school. In this neighbourhood, we encountered many cases of Roma girls who had abandoned school because of family traditions, such as marrying at the age of 12–13, or for 'the sake of protecting their virginity' or protecting them 'against the dangers of the outside world'.

Strategies of separation nurtured by a positive self-perception

The home environment of one of the Roma girls from the school serving Flower district was marked by the family's belonging to a community of faith and most importantly by the father's role as the Pentecostal priest of this neighbourhood. They lived in a predominantly Romanian vicinity, but their large family of 17 members constituted a small community of its own. Because of the role they attributed to religion in Roma emancipation, they exemplified the case of a self-conscious acceptance of ethnic minority affiliation while valuing social integration. They were proud of the 'Gypsies' gift for singing' that they practised during the church rituals, creating in this way a public space in which this ability was applauded. The positivity of Gypsyness was also sustained by the idea that Roma Pentecostals do not only facilitate their ethnic group's integration into the majority society but also 'show the true path of life to them'. They encourage the transgression of ethnic boundaries by creating a community of people who are ready to dissolve their personal and group individuality into the ideal embodied by the Lord Jesus. The Pentecostal community offers a supportive and protective network to its believers, one based on mutual help in dealing with problems ranging from interpersonal relations to housing or schooling. As such, they act as a group with a separate and distinct identity offered for both Roma and non-Roma.

In the case of the Gabor Gypsy families from Forest district, the model of the extended family that nurtures traditions and keeps a clear distance from the majority population shapes the identity strategies of the community. They try to keep apart not only from other ethnic groups but also from other Roma groups. For them, ethnic identity is very self-conscious; they call themselves 'Gabor Gypsy' and not 'Roma'. Their identity model built on their own particular traditions cannot accommodate outer systems of norms. Therefore school education does not occupy a prominent place in their lives. The two older sisters of Feri were not allowed to go to school after they finished the fourth or fifth grade. In contrast to the specific identity-building mechanisms of this family, the non-Gabor Roma families from the neighbourhood emphasised integration through education. In some cases, children willingly and consciously departed from the Roma identity. For example, while Mircea applied to the ninth grade through special provision for Roma pupils, his younger brother, Viorel, identified himself as Romanian but not Roma. Their father, coming from a musicians' dynasty, was bitter about this but he did not want to intervene. Hence children did not necessarily follow the identity models of their parents.

On the basis of our participant observations conducted in classrooms at the school enrolling Roma children from Flower district, we could conclude that students in the 'weaker' classes are mostly active in the sense of resisting the teacher. Their sense of inferiority within the dominant school hierarchy and the feeling that they do not really belong to this school reinforces their marginal peer-group identity. Moreover, they express their resistance to the authoritarian school order by exposing behaviours stigmatised by teachers as manifestations of their marginality. Furthermore, absenteeism, early leaving of school or the avoidance of enrolment might be forms of protest against a school system that reminds them that they do not really belong to it. The frustration and the shame felt by these students due to their socioeconomic background, combined with a generally oppositional attitude characteristic of their age, fuelled the tensions in their relationship as well as a sense of pride of belonging to a resistant peer group.

Lavinia and Stefan from the school serving Water district, as well as many of their colleagues, do not accept the prevalent hierarchy of their school. They do not want to integrate into the system, preferring to oppose it. Thus they create their own little resistance group. They smoke together during breaks and there is permanent conflict between them and their teachers, of which parents are usually unaware.

Academic success is something to be proud of in the elite classes, but it is a sign of weakness for pupils from other classes who call the 'good' students *tocilar* – a derogatory term for those who accept whatever the system dictates. From the point of view of the peer group, while in the more selective classes it is thought well of to be a (stereotypical) girl, in the other classes boys are more respected in so far as they protest against the teachers and sustain a sort of competition around who dares to bully them more. If one juxtaposes the ethnicised and gendered systems of classification and stereotypes, it might be concluded that in this regime, 'Romanians' (in the sense of those who are more teacher-friendly and successful but also obedient) are girlish (or feminised), while 'Roma' exhibit features of powerful masculinity, such as resistance and rebellion.

Negative self-perception and the strategy of assimilation

Two of the investigated families did not belong to local Roma groups through which they could have sustained their separation from the majority, since they lived in areas mostly populated by Romanians. They did not have networks of support which could have helped them to maintain the Romani language and to solve pragmatic problems of the day. Mostly they struggled with the difficulties of being in between two worlds: defining themselves as 'not traditional', or as Roma who aimed to integrate into and become accepted by the majority of society. Yet despite this desire, they remained on the margins. Because they were unable to change their situation, they were the most predestined of those observed to interiorise the negative label of Gypsyness promulgated by the majority and thus to become the most isolated. Paradoxically, however, they considered that they acted the least like 'typical' Gypsies behaving as the 'less Gypsy-like peoples'.

Aspirations towards assimilation were also expressed by Cristina's father living in Water district when he confessed that they considered themselves to be 'almost Romanians: we are not Gypsies any more'. Geanina's mother explained where they stood in terms of their ethnicity and their tendency to assimilate to the majority: 'we do not know our traditions, and actually we really do not have traditions or specific *port* (costumes, dress) like the Gabors or the tent dwellers (*Corturari*), we are Romanianised Gypsies'. At the same time, she stressed that she was proud to be Gypsy. Iulia's father spoke with nostalgia about losing his former ethnic Roma identity. He said that all Roma people are Romanianised by now because they live among Romanians and have left their original home environments.

Ethnic identification, sociospatial segregation and racialised citizenship

Ethnic Roma youths' everyday desires of belonging to or separating from the mainstream of society should be viewed on a broader sociopolitical level, since the educational system intersects with other institutional factors which affect people's social status. The larger phenomenon of sociospatial segregation exacerbates the exclusionary effects of schools and limits the impact of inclusive policies. School segregation is legitimised by residential segregation; the enrolment of Roma into special schools is 'explained' by parental choices which are actually motivated by the availability of free bussing, meals and school supplies; the separation between 'weak' and 'strong' classes or between schools serving the 'elite/downtown' and those reserved for the 'peripheral district' is sustained by arguments which call on meritocracy and performances, while the selection of students actually takes place according to their ethnosocial background. Furthermore, under the conditions of post-socialist socioeconomic transformation and the current neoliberal regime, microlevel experiences are shaped by macrolevel mechanisms, such as the increasing role played by negative ethnic identification in differentiating between the privileged/mainstream/'deserving' pupils and the disadvantaged/marginal/ 'undeserving' ones.

In the case of the Roma minority, ethnic identification tends to lead to the racialisation of citizenship, and becomes part and parcel of their marginalisation and social exclusion.[4] The mutual reinforcement between stigmatising ethnic identification and advanced marginality is very visible in the phenomenon of sociospatial segregation (Soja 2010), which in post-socialist Romania is a result of many interrelated mechanisms. These include the dispossession of former workers as a result of deindustrialisation and the precarious, insecure, underpaid and mostly informal nature of the work that is accessible to them; the scarcity of affordable public housing, and the related privatisation and marketisation of the housing sector; social polarisation between the rich and the poor that manifests itself spatially, for example, in the separation of gated communities (Hirt 2012); 'urban planning' and 'slum clearance' through administrative measures taken by local authorities as a result of which poor inner-city vicinities are demolished, with their inhabitants being forcibly evicted and moved to the city's isolated, usually environmentally hazardous, margins where they are provided with substandard housing conditions.

The socialist regime's assimilationist politics towards Roma through coercion and enforcement was replaced by the tendency during the 1990s to recognise them as an ethnocultural minority which, during the 2000s and especially since the predominance of neoliberal governance, has tended to be synonymous with outright racialisation. Assimilationism presupposed that Roma had a 'cultural problem' which was thought to be solved as they were adapting to the norms of socialist life – that is, they were becoming Romanian workers or a useful source of labour for socialist industrialisation. 'When work disappears' (Wilson 1996) the racialisation of Roma citizens, while criminalising them for their marginal status (as neoliberalism generally blames the poor for being poor), also justifies their marginalisation by pointing to their supposedly biological and/or cultural differences. Such a logic considers that they are not able to provide homes for themselves on the 'free residential market' and that they are also unable to attend prestigious and demanding schools due to 'their blood' or 'cultural traditions'. Viewed in the broader context of post-socialist transformation, the racialisation of Roma is the specific mechanism by which the new regime cuts off the universal content of rights in the case of ethnic Roma citizens, and legitimates their unjust treatment and structural discrimination in terms, for instance, of denying access to quality education.

Spatial segregation, among other processes, creates and maintains the distinction between 'deserving' and 'undeserving' citizens, between those who deserve to belong to society and those who do not, or between those who should benefit from a dignifying place in the urban landscape and those who should be grateful for having the opportunity to survive on the margins. Moreover, by sustaining that 'Gypsies are poor because they do not want to work and prefer to wait for state allowances', public authorities reinforce the common view that a 'responsible and deserving citizen should not accept assistance from the state' because if people act this way then they act like Gypsies. By evicting and relocating poor Roma to the geographical and symbolic margins of the city and by thus transforming Gypsyness into the symbol of the 'undeserving poor', the authorities are contributing to the sense of superiority among the non-Roma population. Indeed, given the Roma countermodel, even poor non-Roma people might feel that they are 'normal citizens' who are not relegated to environments which are detrimental to human dignity or, rather that they are not 'undeserving poor' like the Gypsies.

In the context of such overriding mechanisms, the identity strategies of vulnerable Roma youth observed notably in schools cannot ensure the structural transformation of their racialised sociospatial marginality, even if such strategies are fostered by their desire to belong to mainstream society. Playing a major role in the identity formation of Roma adolescents, schools have a contribution to the creation of 'Gypsy undeservingness'. Teachers from marginal schools complain about the negative consequences of enrolling Roma students, as majority parents withdraw their children from these schools. Consequently, the public opinion perceives these units as 'Gypsy schools', and the whole system identifies 'inclusive education' with 'education for disabled' or with 'education of children with special needs'. Under these conditions, some teachers conclude that Roma do not deserve to be 'helped' because they do not appreciate it, and because of their 'undeservingness' schools/teachers also have to suffer stigmatisation. Broadly speaking, public discourses on educational policies and programmes for Roma keep emphasising that the state and the schools have made huge efforts during the past 20 years to 'integrate them' and complain that, despite these endeavours, 'they' continue to abandon schooling and to perform poorly. Besides overgeneralising a negative picture, these discourses do not recognise the fact that the failures are due to the ways in which such policies were conceived and/or put into practice. At the same time, they cannot act on the broader socioeconomic factors (among them, residential segregation) that negatively affect school attendance and, further, they were not conceived as part of integrated human rights-based development programmes. And on the other hand, these policies have not paid attention to the increasing racism of the majority population and have never attempted to foster a school environment that could bring together teachers, students and their parents in order to counteract racist and classist assumptions about who deserves to belong to 'our' society. However, as school education might both facilitate social mobility and reproduce existing social hierarchies, the school environments always have the potential to challenge dominant discourses and to construct identities that empower both the majorities and the minorities to imagine and practise a more inclusive and participatory society than the one that creates schools as they are today.

Notes

1. The EDUMIGROM community study conducted in Romania used urban schools enrolling significant numbers of Roma students in areas with a relatively large Roma population as entry points to the field from where we also contacted and visited the families. Participant observations at schools (in and outside classrooms), interviews and focus groups with Roma and majority students enrolled into the seventh and the eighth grades and with teachers were complemented by observations conducted in the Roma students' home environments and by interviews and focus group discussions with parents. This methodological choice resulted, among others, in the preselection of those ethnic Roma who lived under precarious material conditions and social marginality but made efforts to ensure their children's school participation. During the research, we could identify a myriad of reasons backing up these endeavours, among them the desire to be accepted by the mainstream of society and/or by the immediate community, mingled with different degrees of longing for separation.

2. The name used to define the location of our community study is fictional, as are all the other denominations given to districts, schools and persons. In 'Transilvan City', fieldwork was conducted by a team composed of Hajnalka Harbula, Nándor L. Magyari and myself. This chapter is based in large part on two recent publications of Vincze et al. (2010) and Vincze and Habrula (2011) that first brought into discussion the relationship between desires to belong, ethnic identification, sociospatial segregation and racialised citizenship.

3. Sociologists assume that even if it shows an increase during a decade, this figure is a (definite) underestimation of Roma. Due to the stigma that Roma identity bears, there is a reluctance on the part of many Roma to identify as such in front of an official interviewer. On the basis of this fact, there are several 'unofficial' estimates of the actual number of Roma. In their survey conducted in 1998, the Institute for the Research of the Quality of Life estimated on the basis of heteroidentification that in Romania there were between 1,452,700 and 1,588,552 ethnic Roma persons, among whom 65.3 per cent identified themselves as Roma (IRQL Report 2002). According to the estimates of another researcher (Ghețău 2006), the number of Roma ranges between 1.5 and 2.0 million.

4. As defined by Wacquant, advanced marginality is the reality of 'economic penury and social destitution, ethnoracial divisions and public violence, and their accumulation in the same distressed areas', resulting from 'polarized economic growth and the fragmentation of wage labor, the casualization of employment ... mass joblessness ... of the more vulnerable segments of the working class ... and last but not least, state policies of social retrenchment and urban abandonment' (2008, pp. 232–233). On the other hand, although Romania has a different history in

terms of racial policies of that of the US or the UK, the observation according to which the inequalities persisting in housing or the racial divisions of the residential space are not only the effects of material forces like the unequal distribution of housing resources but also of the way in which they are legitimated through appeals to what is considered to be normal, rational and acceptable in a liberal democracy (Smith 1989), is relevant in this case, too.

14
Structural and Personal Forms of Discrimination in Slovak Multiethnic Schools

David Kostlán

The Roma population is steadily growing in Slovakia. This trend is a cause for worry among the Slovak majority. Roma people have poorer education than their non-Roma compatriots and most of them are unemployed. Many of them live in segregated settlements – 'behind the walls' – of the villages with no access to a water supply, electricity or gas. Such a situation is more reminiscent of the suburbs of African or Latin-American metropolises than of European standards of living. Such are the conditions of Roma families raising children – and, as many Slovaks say: 'a lot of children'. While these facts are true, they are converted into prejudiced attitudes towards the Roma community as part of the common image of the majority about how the minority lives.

The Slovak majority, the political elite and the media speak about the living conditions of the Roma ethnic minority as a 'Roma issue'. Reference to the 'Roma issue' generally implies that the Slovak state or, rather, the Slovak nation has a 'problem' with Roma people because of their different cultural norms and moral standards. Roma are viewed as 'present-oriented people' who do not save money and have no will power as necessary to what Max Weber called the 'protestant ethics' that govern modern capitalist societies.

The presumably different cultural and moral backgrounds of Roma are thought to be one of the main obstacles to the better educational attainment of Roma pupils. Such a justification of the highly unequal educational outcomes between Roma and non-Roma students sharply contradicts the views of many international and local NGOs that point to several forms of discrimination faced by Roma youth, and also to the increasing structural inequalities in the Slovak school system. These trends had been validated by the results of the PISA surveys of 2006 and 2009. These showed that Slovakia is one of the countries in which students' socioeconomic background has a major impact on their school performance (Štefančík 2010).

Discriminatory practices on the part of majority pupils (and teachers) against the ethnic minority are one of the crucial issues regarding the educational opportunities and the performance of Roma students. This chapter focuses on institutional (structural) as well as interpersonal (individual) forms of discrimination from the perspectives of the social agents involved in schooling.

In accordance with the results of earlier studies, the EDUMIGROM research in Slovakia confirmed that many Roma pupils are placed in special schools or special classes. This fact, presented by activists and NGOs as proof of the discriminatory practices of the Slovak school system, is, however, seen in a very different light by Slovak teachers. The first part of our analysis thus examines teachers' discourse on structural discrimination against Roma pupils. The second part presents Roma pupils' reflections on the interpersonal forms of discrimination. Teachers' views on segregating Roma pupils are considered in the context of their important contribution to shaping and structuring ethnic and social relations between Roma pupils and their peers from the majority. The findings of our research show that while the teachers are clearly aware of the social and cultural disadvantages of Roma pupils, they still engage in certain 'soft' discriminatory practices and strategies which are most explicit in their use of language and argumentation. These insidious forms of discrimination will be viewed through the window of Roma pupils' experiences of ethnic relations at school.

Theoretical background

Research on the sociology of education has overwhelmingly focused on class inequalities in educational attainment by providing two kinds of explanation: structural and cultural. The structural approach to educational attainment emphasises inequalities in material resources as derivatives of parental occupational status and the families' overall economic situation. The cultural approach stresses the impact of parental cultural capital and parents' knowledge and skills in helping children with schooling. In the case of Roma pupils, the EDUMIGROM research validated earlier results that had demonstrated that young people belonging to this minority group had to face both structural and cultural disadvantages. The low socioeconomic status of Roma families is exacerbated by their lack of cultural capital.

Research on the educational attainment of Roma pupils has been scarce in Slovakia. However, the available results show that Roma pupils in elementary schools suffer from higher rates of grade repetition and school absenteeism than do their majority peers and that they also attain poorer school results (UNDP 2006). These findings confirm the hypothesis that schools fail to overcome the initial dual disadvantages of Roma pupils.

According to the critical views of some scholars, the fact that schools generally experience incapability to help disadvantaged pupils to improve their educational attainment is a negative outcome of the changing educational policies in Western societies. These policies have undergone radical modifications in the past two or three decades. In the immediate past, the general tendency in parent-school relations has been a shift from the compensatory model towards the partnership model (Wilson and Tisdall 2000, p. 201). The compensatory model was based on the assumption that schools have a duty towards the disadvantaged pupils to compensate for poor parental input. Contrary to this approach, the currently prevailing partnership model puts the primary and major responsibility for children's education on the parents' shoulders. In the latter model, schools and their teachers play a role of advisory authority that can help to negotiate appropriate educational solutions with parents. Parents have been portrayed in public discourse as acting as 'consumers' with their right to choose the school. In seven out of the nine countries participating in the EDUMIGROM research, free choice of school is considered to be a formal parental right. However, the school choice has become a prerogative of the privileged because this right is not equally distributed among all parents. Much like in shopping, the better the socioeconomic conditions of families, the richer the portfolio of products that they can choose from. As a result, the right of free choice of school supports better-off families to engage in 'white flight'. This leads to an increasing disadvantage of schools located in areas dominated by low-income families and thus widens social class inequalities.

Academic research and the related scholarly debate about the links between pupils' ethnic background, their sensing of teachers' behaviour and their achievements indicate that ethnic minority pupils have more negative perceptions of the student–teacher relations than their peers from the majority and that the lower level of trust between ethnic minority pupils and their teachers contributes to their poorer educational attainment. According to den Brok and Levy (2005), 'Differences in students' perceptions that relate to variation in ethnicity can be explained in at least three different ways: through students' values and norms, through their interpretations of observed teacher behaviour, and through differential treatment by the teacher' (p. 75). Students' perceptions along the proposed three lines will be explored in the second part of this chapter on interpersonal forms of discrimination.

Knowledge and language are two types of social construct that may attract personal forms of discrimination with regard to ethnicity. Barker introduced the concept of 'new racism' as different from the racist ideologies of biological superiority so common throughout the nineteenth century. 'New racism' is connected to concepts of culture and discourse. In Barker's approach, it is the symbolic character of the cultural and discursive phenomena that is emphasised. A crucial characteristic of 'new racism' is its denial by (ethnic, national) majorities (van Dijk 1992). Such racial discourse is not about race per se but about cultural values and moral norms that the majority embraces but that others presumably do not. The particular norms and values of the dominant groups determine what is right and what is wrong. The presumed lack of 'good' and 'proper' values and norms among those considered to be 'others' is perceived as the cause of their backwardness or disadvantaged social position. Augoustinos et al. (2005) argued:

> This blend of affect and morality rests on the assumed importance of values such as individual self-reliance, obedience, discipline and hard work. Social and racial disadvantage is perceived by majority group members to be the consequence of certain groups transgressing these values rather than an outcome of structural inequities within society. (p. 317)

The analysis of racial discourse deals with the language practices through which social relations of power and dominance become (re)produced and legitimised (Augoustinos et al. 2005). Within the concept of 'new racism', critical discourse analysis of race and ethnic relations explores how knowledge about 'us' and 'them' is constructed in terms of ethnic categories, and how meanings are transformed in institutional and everyday practices within and between these categories.

Structural roots of discriminatory practices in parent-school relations

Elementary schools in Slovakia provide special programmes for children with special educational needs (SEN). The category of SEN children includes all pupils with social, mental or physical disadvantage or handicap. These children are educated either in normal classes or in special classes arranged for them. The focus group discussions carried out among teachers within the framework of the EDUMIGROM research in Slovakia reflected on whether schooling of Roma pupils from socially disadvantaged environments should be promoted in normal or special classes. Teachers considered that ethnic background did not play any role in the segregation of Roma children into special classes. For them, segregation had a positive impact since they believed that special programmes for Roma pupils would aim to reduce social inequalities. Paradoxically, some teachers justify the absence of programmes oriented towards Roma culture and language at schools by the need to avoid segregation or stress the fact that all students declare Slovak ethnicity. For instance, Denisa, the school headmaster of one of the elementary schools in our study, says: 'If we organised special activities for Roma, we would segregate them and some parents would not like it; it is not a viable way.'

The existence of special classes is justified by the prevalence of social or learning difficulties, not by race or ethnicity. However, Roma pupils constitute the majority in most of the special classes. At one of the elementary schools (A), there are two special classes: one at the first stage of elementary schooling for pupils aged 6–10 years, and another at the second stage for pupils aged 10–15 years. Thus pupils of different ages are mixed in the class which makes teaching very difficult. The school head teacher said that her intent was to close down the special class at the second stage and to offer pupils the possibility of attending a special elementary school. In her view, the special elementary school offers education of much higher quality than teaching pupils in 'collective' special classes. She describes these pupils, who are all Roma, as young persons who are qualified as having 'learning difficulties' or who are at the threshold of this category. She is convinced that the tests measuring intellectual capacities are reliable and that, apart from those 'who are in the threshold zone', these pupils should not be educated in a regular elementary school. She summarises the issue of diagnostics of Roma pupils from special classes in the following way:

> We have roughly 90 Roma kids and just 13 of them are categorised as having 'learning difficulties'. This is not so bad. And all the kids have certified diagnosis by a psychologist and by a special pedagogue from the Integration Centre for Children. It was verified. We cannot influence it. It used to happen years ago, but not now ... I do not have any reason or interest to influence it; I just wait until the results come and it is from a psychologist and then it's followed by a special pedagogical assessment. And it never happened to us that those two assessments did not fit with each other.

In the above extract, there are two issues worth underscoring. First, the head teacher argues that the diagnoses are valid and that they are not biased by any other influences because they must be proved by two independent experts – a psychologist and a special pedagogue. For her, pupils with behavioural problems do not qualify for placement in a special class. Only children having 'learning difficulties' belong there. For that reason the classmates' suspicions that bad manners are punished by sending a pupil to a special class may result from not knowing that bad manners might be a symptom of struggling with 'learning difficulties'. The second noteworthy aspect is the head teacher's satisfaction with the fact that only 13 Roma children at her school are qualified as having 'learning difficulties'. Her claim that 'this is not so bad' suggests that she is convinced that generally more Roma pupils qualify for the category of 'having learning difficulties'.

Surprisingly, we have found an utterly different situation behind organising special classes in another elementary school (B). Vlasta had been the class teacher of a special class in the school. She appreciated the fact that special classes were much smaller than standard ones and that individual work with children was thus possible. At the time of the interview, her class had ten pupils and six of them were Roma. The curriculum was almost the same as in standard classes but the pace was slower and thus there were more opportunities for one-to-one teacher–pupil interaction. Vlasta argued: 'As there are 10 of them in the class, it works; you can approach each kid, you walk around and you can help each of them. With 25 pupils, it is much harder.'

It is clear that the situation of pupils in the special classes in schools A and B differs markedly. Pupils from Vlasta's special class were not classified by expert assessment as having 'learning difficulties'. All of the pupils were of the same age and the class was ethnically mixed. Such was not the case in the two special classes in school A. Vlasta finds it more positive to educate SEN pupils in a special class. The head teacher from the former special classes (school A) would not agree because her situation is completely different. According to her, pupils having 'learning difficulties' should be taught in special schools and so she tried to send such pupils there. At the same time, she believes that those pupils who 'are in the threshold zone' should be integrated. The problem is that, on the one hand, too many integrated pupils in regular classes break the norm (three integrated pupils as a maximum are allowed to be in a standard class) and, on the other hand, their large number also creates organisational difficulties for the teacher.

Attempts to set up special classes are also motivated by the desire to keep majority pupils in a given school. In Slovakia, many schools located in rather unfavourable residential areas have to deal with the problem of 'white flight'. To keep students from the majority, schools divide the pupils at the first-grade level according to their 'readiness' to attend school, which leads to the separation of Roma pupils. The teachers refuse to categorise pupils as Roma and non-Roma, focusing rather on the social situation of the family. As one of the head teachers argued, if classes were created according to pupils' abilities, smarter students would have a chance for better education whereas slower students would be given more time to achieve basic knowledge:

> There are classrooms that are purely Roma ones... [But] I don't divide children into Roma and non-Roma, ok? But I have to defend myself against parents, you know, from taking smart children, whether these or those, away and putting them into some chosen schools... So, we divide classrooms according to the abilities of the students... When we started this for the first time, the first year, there were some negative attitudes of some parents... they rebelled against it, but later... When the first group of the children left we found out they learned much more than in a mixed group...

The negative effect of class division by ability is an increasing gap in educational attainment and motivation. The findings of our study in Slovakia demonstrated that the worst school results and a decrease in motivation for continued education often occurred in classes where, as a result of streaming students by abilities, Roma children ended up in large numbers.

One of the most successful ways of increasing the motivation for learning among disadvantaged pupils like Roma is to launch community programmes. It is documented that these are successful if working-class parents are invited into the process of school work as well as into the management of the programme. Because of the cultural gap between the school and students' home, cooperation with parents is crucial to gain their efforts to transform the school. Unfortunately, examples of this sort were not even mentioned by teachers as a good way to integrate Roma families and support their children in the educational process. Instead, Roma families were blamed for having little or no interest in school, which was interpreted as an individual and moral failure. However, as Wilson, Riddell and Tisdall (2000) argue, in many cases families from disadvantaged socioeconomic backgrounds suffer from insufficient fulfilment of basic human needs (information and training on health and hygiene, socialisation, family relationships and so on) and this state of affairs has to be altered first before starting to work on improving children's educational attainment.

The organisation of education in Slovakia expects active cooperation of the parents. If parents do not meet this expectation, it is reflected in how teachers view their children. Milan, one of the interviewed teachers, expressed this attitude by evaluating the intentions of Roma parents who do not cooperate with the school. According to his view, these parents are only interested in the material elements of schooling. He expects parents to visit the school regularly and discuss with him their child's behaviour and achievement:

> Quite large numbers of parents do not come over even once in five years. They do not come here and I cannot see a reason sometimes. I guess some of them prefer, I would say, material elements of the child's education, simply 'I take care of you at home, I give you food, clothing and what happens at school is not my business, it is a business of the teacher.' But they never realise that I should cooperate to keep an eye on the child's behaviour and learning, they will never get to know it because they will never come to me ...

A similar attitude is expressed by Andrej, the head teacher of another school. He states that the teachers are helpful to children whose parents cooperate:

> If the parent considers school as important, it is ok, he or she comes to meet me and we can come to an agreement. We can even avoid commission exams if a kid gets back into the system ... We can always make a deal in order to motivate him or her and push them a bit further, but some families never respond to an official letter and nobody shows up. So in those cases it is practically impossible to somehow solve the problem if the parent is not willing to come and listen to us about it.

In the above extract, Andrej suggests that good or bad cooperation with parents has an important influence on the school results of their child. If the child is about to fail, good communication with the parents can prevent it. Otherwise 'it is practically impossible to somehow solve the problem', which means that the child will fail and will have to repeat the grade.

As we can see from the excerpts, Slovak teachers support the partnership model of educational management that puts much of the responsibility for children's education on parents' shoulders. At the same time, teachers do not expect parents to become involved in decision-making on policies concerning the educational strategy and the routines of their school. The schools expect Roma parents to be more present and involved in schooling, but their role is reduced to individualised forms of communication with teachers. Teachers ask for parents' interest in children's school results and in learning with children at home. They do not ask for developing cooperation on the collective and institutional levels which would include their involvement in school boards. In this context, much of the pedagogical burden has to be carried by the parents, which deepens the gap between privileged and underprivileged families.

Personal forms of discrimination

Knowledge and language

It is important to note that the teachers' considerations of Roma culture and the common characteristics of Roma pupils have been elicited by the interview questions or stimulated by the stories put up for focus group discussion: it was rather exceptional that these topics came up spontaneously, if they appeared this way at all. Timotej, the head teacher of one of the elementary schools, however, was spontaneously thinking about Roma common characteristics in the context of the debate about the barriers to their schooling:

> I will be open. It is not good if we take 15 Gypsy kids out of 80 into the first class and we put them together into one class. No, it is not good. They are a nomadic nation who like to be together and here, I would say, we need to select them, not to be all together. I have experience that if they are together they start to get their way. And their way would be also some hints of bullying towards other children – towards white children – if they are together. So, really, I mean sensible work is needed and you should not give them any opportunity for racism or bullying.

Timotej's narrative is put in the context of segregating Roma pupils into classes 'for them'. He, as well as other teachers, is aware of the anti-segregation discourse that has been developed by activists, and by national and international NGOs such as Amnesty International that have been criticising the segregation practices of Roma pupils at Slovak schools (Amnesty International 2010). He refuses this practice, arguing that if Roma pupils are in dominance, they start to develop their agenda which means to bully non-Roma pupils. His argumentation is based on a mixture of negative stereotypes of the 'other' and the activist integration approach agenda. Not supporting segregation is explained by the negative effects of the Roma way of gathering. Beyond his argumentation is an image of the Roma culture and the community as a 'nomadic' nation who like to be together. This general comment on the commonly shared features of the 'Roma nation' (collectivity, nomadic character) is supported by his personal experience of its negative consequences – bullying against white pupils. His task as the school's head teacher is 'not giving them any opportunity'. We may notice that the 'Roma nation' is presented in his narrative with reference to its traditionalism or backwardness. Collectivity and nomadic character are cultural values and norms typically ascribed to premodern collectivities as tribes. Contrary to this, modern nations are territorially bounded and individualism belongs to the highly positive values that facilitate advancement and development.

Similar to other teachers (but also to Roma parents) who felt obliged to say something relevant in response to our question about the Roma identity, Andrej emphasised their sense of music. He compared Roma to Afro-Americans, especially because of their locomotive and musical skills:

> They have their ego of art, these fellow citizens. The music, they have it inborn, it is like Black Americans...I think, it is not a myth. You can see it in our school. I have not seen a programme yet, but surely, there will be a performance of brake dance or this kind of stuff. It means that if the music teacher brings Mozart or Bach CDs to Roma kids, the lesson will be problematic and distressed, and it will be very difficult to maintain some order. But if he brings guitar and plays it and sings two or three songs, then Roma kids will like the teacher and the music lesson will be a proper music lesson. This is, I guess, something they certainly have in their nature. Music, rhythm, beat...

Listening to Gypsy music, hip-hop or rap is considered to be something 'natural' for Roma children. Andrej's example, however, cannot be related only to Roma pupils. Most of the pupils regardless of their ethnicity would prefer modern pop music to classical music. The point is not the musical style that differentiates Roma children from their non-Roma peers but the outcome of disagreement with classical music; 'the lesson will be problematic, distressed and discipline not handled well'. In fact, there is no particular style of music that all Roma pupils would listen to. Some Roma pupils told us that they do not like the Gypsy music that their parents listen to. Roma boys prefer hip-hop or rap, mostly because they identify themselves with Black or Gypsy rappers. However, Roma girls do not listen to such genres much.

As shown above, teachers believe that Roma culture is different from its Slovak counterpart, and what is more, that the personal characters of Roma pupils are different from their Slovak peers because of their ethnic origin. They use categorical generalisations to demonstrate that Roma culture is based on different (premodern) values, which makes schooling of Roma pupils a demanding task.

Categorisation among Roma pupils

Teachers employed by the schools that we have visited distinguish Roma pupils almost exclusively as a category of extremely disadvantaged family backgrounds. In one of our sites, the town of Krásne, the distinction between integrated and non-integrated Roma is in use and these categories overlap with the distinction between pupils who do not represent any challenge for the educational process and those who are perceived as a difficult pedagogical problem. As a rule, non-integration is a result of insufficient cooperation on the part of Roma parents and their lack of interest in the child's work at school.

Both in the individual interviews and during the focus group discussions, the majority of the teachers were in agreement considering Roma families' limited interest in education and the poor motivation of Roma children. Izabela is a teacher assistant at a school in Krásne. She provides details of some individual cases of the first grade pupils from a socially disadvantaged environment (SDE) who are apparently neglected by their parents ('they are dirty, hungry and tired because of sleepless nights in overcrowded houses'). Many Roma pupils from SDE (the 'non-integrated' ones) lack basic skills (for example, they 'do not know the colours') and 'have problems with concentration'. She describes her own efforts (such as bringing breakfast for a child from home) and states that it is necessary to show interest in the individual children in order to make them interested in learning. In the case of small children, verbal encouragement is very effective. In the case of older pupils it does not work, however, and their interest in learning fades away. According to her experience, there are clear differences between 'integrated' and 'non-integrated' Roma pupils (Kusá et al. 2010). Integrated Roma distance themselves from non-integrated Roma in the same way as non-Roma pupils do. Izabela explains the difference between the two groups of Roma pupils in terms of cleanliness and polite behaviour. She states that the school encourages the participation of Roma pupils in the song competition and that they are successful. However, success does not stimulate them to better engage in learning. Pupils from SDEs are especially 'apathetic'. In the last grade, they sometimes make some effort as they eventually recognise the importance of having (at least) a vocational training certificate, but it is often too late (if they finish their compulsory education in the seventh or lower grade, their chances of continuing schooling are almost zero). Izabela describes the demarcation lines that prevail:

> On the ninth grade we have Roma who are actually decent, always nicely dressed; there have never been any problems with them. And they are friends with non-Roma boys and girls; they are one group, one group in the class. But they are not in one group with non-integrated Roma, never... Only integrated Roma kids are friends with their non-Roma classmates, only integrated; not the non-integrated. Even integrated Roma keep a distance from the non-integrated.

As the interview goes on, Izabela portrays the non-integrated Roma pupils as dirty, noisy and rude. Grime and smelliness are characteristics that have been generalised as 'intrinsic' features of Roma, and naming them 'dirty' and 'stinky' are the most frequent verbal abuses addressed to Roma. Many students and their parents struggle with the picture of 'the dirty and stinky Roma': they point out that they are discriminated against by the tendency to lump all Roma together. We have neither interviewed nor met children who resemble the picture of neglected Roma children provided by the pedagogues. Teacher assistants who work in the lowest grades have the most familiar experiences regarding the destitution of children, and the impact it has on their self-esteem and the contacts with their classmates.

Practices of verbal and non-verbal discrimination

We found that the main way in which Roma children become aware of their 'otherness' is by being exposed to verbal abuse and shouting. Roma pupils Dominika and Ria had experiences of verbal abuse as early as the kindergarten where non-Roma children called them 'Gypsy'. Dominika recalled: 'I did not tell anything to anybody. It was like this. It was such a peculiar feeling. Then it stopped when I grew older.'

The phrase 'dirty Gypsy' belongs to the abuses that have partly lost their ethnic association and can be addressed as an expression of antipathy to anybody. Roma pupils hear the term 'dirty Roma' also used against non-Roma persons as this has become a widespread insult. However, they do not take it as a meaningful phrase: they feel uncomfortable when they hear it. Two of our Roma interviewees characterised their feelings in the following way:

– It is rather difficult. We go along normally [with non-Roma pupils]. It is rather difficult, well, sometimes...
– When they begin to shout at you...
– For instance, you Negro, or you Gypsy, they told it to each other as a joke, they laughed, boys among themselves, but we take it in a way that it matters.

The use of the adjective 'Gypsy' as a synonym of uneducated and bad mannered is rather widespread. However, it is surprising that it is also practised among educators. Pupils are hurt by such insults. For instance, during the Roma pupils' focus group discussion at our Hrdé site and also during the personal interview with her, Paula told us that, after entering the classroom, their biology teacher often noted: 'I feel like I'm in a Gypsy village!' By this statement, the teacher points out that there is a mess in the classroom (debris and remnants of food thrown on the floor), or that it is necessary to open the window and let fresh air coming in. This upsets the Roma girls in Paula's class:

> She is always coming in and saying: 'I feel like I'm in a Gypsy village,' so what would you do? She is saying that during each lesson... Because the classroom is in shambles. But it is not only us who do it, it's also our schoolmates. Even if the classroom is ok, she says 'It stinks here like in a Gypsy village.'

Paula offers several descriptions of the teachers' comments and behaviour that suggest the second-rate status of her and her Roma classmates.

The experience of the Roma pupils in Krásne seems to be a little less harsh. Prokop, an individually integrated student mentioned an incident during which the school's deputy head teacher reminded him of his origin and excluded him from the white territory: 'She told me recently that I am Gypsy! We were talking with my friend: he was inside the school, standing near the window while I was outside. The deputy began shouting at us – go shout on a Gypsy hill!' (Kusá et al. 2010).

As mentioned previously, we have not observed the kind of untidy children described by the teachers. All of the children we saw during our field visits appeared to be well kept, and many seemed concerned about maintaining a certain personal style. A cultivated look, however, also provokes some teachers. Female teachers frequently criticise Roma girls for the excessive attention they supposedly devote to their appearance instead of learning. Ria, Dominika and Ela described their experience of criticism of this sort as expressed by a German teacher:

> She [the German teacher] is... she told us... simply....

> For instance, she told Ria: 'Ria, what can you reach with your clothing when you have empty head?' And she always held similar conversations. I did not like it.

> She has linked these two things together. I do not know why she has done it, she has linked clothing with learning.

In the excerpt above, their Roma origin was not mentioned by the teacher and not even interpreted as racism by the Roma girls. Yet clothing and pupils' look is a popular issue for teachers. Wearing items like hip-hop caps (for boys) or having make-up (for girls) is usually forbidden in schools. Moreover, an emphasis on clothing and fashion is viewed as contrary to learning by both teachers and pupils. Teachers do not appreciate the way in which pupils express their 'alternative' lifestyles by wearing particular items. This is perceived as a form of rebellion or as a symptom of a counterculture in opposition to the 'official' or normal behaviour of 'good' pupils. By contrast, pupils think this is the only way in which they can demonstrate their opinion and maintain their self-esteem.

'Softer' forms of chanting (calling 'Hey Gypsy!') are embarrassing as well. Laura takes it as very unpleasant and annoying that her schoolmates constantly make 'a case' from her ethnic origin: 'It is disgusting this shouting... For instance, if a Roma girl goes around, they start to shout at her: "Gypsy goes, look at her, Gypsy!" However, if a white girl goes around, it is normal, nobody cares.'

In addition to verbal abuse, non-verbal acts of distancing are another frequent form of 'othering'. Gazing, stepping back and pulling away, though they are not accompanied by loud shouting but only with quiet comments, are sometimes even more humiliating. It is important to note that in the following extract, Ela and Ria speak about encounters outside school:

- Well, it is true, some do not like Roma... some when they see Roma, they simply shrink back or something...
- They let you know by the way they look at you. Nothing... they don't have to tell anything. For example, when I walk around, immediately... feel that they pull away from me.

The most explicit suggestion to Roma pupils that they are different is non-Roma pupils' refusal to sit with Roma pupils at the same desk. In the classroom, children usually sit in pairs and these pairs are self-selected. A generation ago, the sitting order was seen as a pedagogical tool and excellent pupils were asked to sit with weaker pupils to 'have a positive impact on them'; self-selection of pairs was only tolerated at the second stage of elementary schooling. However, by now the free choice of seating partners has been extended also to the lowest grades. The result is an accentuated tendency towards creating ethnically homogeneous pairs. Ethnically mixed seating partners are increasingly taken as 'non-standard'.

Pupils' consideration of ethnic differences manifests itself more intensively through action than through speech. The interviewed pupils underscored ethnicity as a crucial aspect of everyday experience and encounters.

Ethnicity as a part of the daily courses of actions was most salient when ethnic and inter-ethnic friendships were discussed. While ethnicity was a pronounced aspect of the interpersonal relations, pupils could not provide reflections on their own ethnicity and they lacked the knowledge of the institutional forms of ethnic protection (for instance, how to deal with discriminatory practices on an institutional level and what their rights are). Even their feelings of being proud of their Roma origin as a reaction to the negative stereotypes that they had to face in the media and in public discourse invoked actions rather than words.

Gee (2001) explains that working-class pupils use a narrative mode that is different from that of their middle- and upper-class peers. The narrative mode of working-class pupils is more linked to social relations and inter-actions than to symbolic thoughts and reflections, which is salient for the narrative modes of middle- and upper-class pupils. Likewise, Roma pupils are unable to reflect their ethnicity in more symbolic or abstract ways. Only a few students spoke about differences between Roma and Slovak ethnic groups. One can assume that their feelings of difference arise from gen-eralising direct experiences of betrayal by a non-Roma classmate or they somehow cushion a pain (mitigate tension) arising from their rejected access to non-Roma peer groups.

Several students and parents suggest that non-Roma friends are less trust-worthy and that one cannot rely on them. Ondrej, a student from the grammar school in Krásne, thinks that his non-Roma friends would not help him if he was assaulted at the disco: 'But I know that if something happens, a non-Roma would not stand up for me, or if there is a problem with a non-Roma, he would rather back up his side, not mine.'

Many Roma students express the view that the main hindrance of friendships with non-Roma is that non-Roma are not 'accessible' and that they reject making friends with Roma. They point at this fact often indi-rectly when they speak about why they prefer to have Roma friends. For instance, Jozef, a ninth-grade student, told us: 'I understand Roma pupils better because non-Roma are ... simply, they make differences that ... you are Roma, you are Gypsy and you have no access to us.'

In the context of friendship relations, Roma have also been considered as more loyal, more sensitive and more sincere than non-Roma. Blazej, a Roma student, argues: 'I think they take everything more sensitively, possi-bly because they have grown up differently or they appreciate more what they have, possibly because they have less than them [non-Roma], and thus they value more what they have.'

These 'ethnic traits' make Roma more reliable friends than non-Roma. Some of the interviewees tried to outline the differences, but they did not manage to specify them. They at best suggested generalised views, such as 'Roma are different by heart' and 'it is much easier for me as a Roma to understand Roma than non-Roma'. The reason for lacking specifications might be that previously they have not tried to articulate the differences and to verbalise their feelings.

Conclusion

Our research revealed many forms of 'making' ethnic differences at Slovak schools. Distinctions between Slovak and Roma pupils are ever present. The teachers disagree with this view by drawing attention to structural factors that they cannot influence, such as the increasing role of parents in choosing schools or the high unemployment rate among Roma families. In fact, the teachers are aware of the increasing socioeconomic inequalities among various categories of family. According to their view, these trends make all educational processes more demanding whereby the role and influence of the school in compensating for different forms of inequality is decreasing.

The teachers are losing control of the game played between parents, schools and the community. The ethnic and socioeconomic composition of the communities plays an important role in the formation of social relations in particular neighbourhood settings. The increasing social inequalities between middle-class and working-class families, together with a neoliberal economic policy in regulating public services, have changed the functions of parental involvement in the educational system. The free will of school choice is practised among middle-class parents, and thus advantaged and disadvantaged pupils are going to be concentrated in elite and 'second-rate' quality schools, respectively. Besides the structural factors, personal forms of discrimination were revealed in the latter category of school. Here, knowledge and language practices of teachers and pupils play a crucial role in (re)producing ethnic differences. Roma pupils are seen as being different and acting differently because of their cultural norms and values which supposedly differ from the mainstream. This knowledge is transformed into language practices in schooling that have a significant impact on Roma pupils' self-identification and performance.

15
Conclusions: Ethnic Distinctions and the Making of Citizenship in Education

Julia Szalai

By putting ethnicity into focus, discussions in this book demonstrate two simultaneous trends in European education. On the one hand, it is shown from a number of perspectives that ethnicity is a powerful factor of differentiation in schooling and that it tends to shape important inequalities in knowledge, skills and the forms of economic, social and cultural participation. On the other hand, the discussions reveal great variations in the strength and forms of such differentiations across countries and communities, and even greater departures are registered in the wider ideological, political and legal contexts that host the working of ethnicity. Within these varying frameworks, remarkable further differences emerge according to whether ethnicity intersects with social class (especially with poverty), gender and the geographic aspects of living, or its impact is played out within and across a range of loosely associated social relations. The chapters show how such differences within and across countries affect inter-ethnic relations and the trends of adolescent identity formation, and how they influence young people's career perspectives within the educational system and beyond it.

Recent history has underscored the significance of the latter implications of ethnic differentiation in education with new political meanings. The rather strong manifestations of ethnicity in the urban riots of the past decade in France, Germany and the UK turned public attention and the political discourse towards issues that for long had been considered as settled in a clear and unanimous way: the departing contents of young people's citizenship rights and the role of ethnic backgrounds in differentiating between them came to the fore as important explanatory factors of widespread mobilisation and unrest. At the same time, the sharpening of racial conflicts in Central Europe and the massive flow of Roma migration towards the West have made deprivation and the vast exclusion of Europe's largest minority an important issue on the European political stage, and concluded in efforts to seek strategic responses by drawing national policies under all-European coordination. In these debates, citizenship is a key concept that implies rights and capabilities, and also the social, political and legal institutions to frame them. When looked at through this lens, new research has pointed out earlier unnoticed curtailments of rights and opportunities in various domains of everyday life, and the emerging results have informed widespread political debates around issues of social cohesion and the forms of inclusion that simultaneously observe diversity and universalism.

Despite the increased political interest, ethnic differences in education are still rarely discussed with regard to their implications on citizenship. The reasons for this are manifold. First, young people's citizenship is seen as a product of yet unfinished processes. Beyond the legal aspects that are usually set by birth, citizenship as a notion is contextualised in terms of adult life: people practise the various forms of participation as members of communities defined with economic, social, cultural and political roles where they hold responsibilities and enjoy opportunities. In most countries, entering adulthood is defined by reaching political maturity as indicated by the legally set age limit for practising the right for voting. However, the strong emphasis on voting rights, which large groups of young people are too young to share, pushes into the background other aspects of citizenship and tends to cast a shadow over those socialising processes in education by which students acquire the values, norms and behavioural patterns of how to become a citizen. Second, young people's identities are usually seen as fluid in their boundaries and content, and as too much influenced by the emerging varying frames of reference – therefore these identities are considered to be too unstable to build on them the notion of citizenship. Nevertheless, emotions, attitudes and ideas about ethnicity are part of the manner in which young people perceive and explain their belonging, and of their interpretations about group distinctions. In this sense their concepts and the ideological foundations of them can be considered as prefigurations of later mature notions of citizenship. However, amidst the traditions of education that usually acknowledge only the undivided and universal contents of citizenship, young people's 'deviating' perceptions are rarely seen as indications of evolving new concepts of citizenship with a focus on diversity, but more as failures of socialisation that schools have to correct through instruction and also through purposefully designed formative practices aiming at acculturation. Third, education itself is rarely conceptualised as a terrain of citizenship. Given the framework of compulsory schooling and the deeply ingrained values of equality attached to the notion, all that takes place within this framework is seen in its contribution to the universalist contents cementing society by providing the undivided foundations of equal citizenship on a national basis. Ethnic differentiation is considered against this latter universal context. Framed in this way, debates about citizenship in education pronounce the differences as a 'problem' and a symptom of the schools' failure to properly acculturate minority children. Hence the critics put forth clear claims: schools should respond to the 'problem' with greater efficiency, better curriculum design and efforts in the course of instruction for all students to acquire the undivided contents of nationhood and national belonging.

This concluding chapter aims to show that, despite commitments to universalism and equality, educational systems across Europe contribute in important ways to the emergence of students' departing understandings of citizenship and that ethnic distinctions in the course of schooling are a major drive behind these developments.

But before entering the discussion, some limitations of our approach need to be addressed. The first concerns the scope: what follows below looks only at certain aspects of citizenship. The macrolevel frameworks and the varying legal definitions of citizenship are not parts of the overview that follows. Likewise, the complexity of rights provided in great variations to migrants and their families in the broad areas of welfare, housing and employment remain outside the discussion. It is mainly the participatory aspects that we look at here: schools as institutions which distribute knowledge and socialise their students into the mainstream forms of expression and behaviours of representation and participation are looked at by asking whether by transmitting these cultural contents their educational process points towards universalism or whether it strengthens group-specific differences and separation. It is asked then how education is informing the frames and the contents of young people's participation in schools as the designated segments of the polity. How is the process of schooling impacting and shaping the substance of their rights and capabilities for articulating, representing and negotiating membership in the social world that surrounds them? By limiting the discussion to the dynamics of participation, it is our aim to reveal the scope of politicising the case of ethnic minorities at the level of the communities. In this way, the strengths and weaknesses of their struggles for recognition (often in combination with efforts towards changing patterns of redistribution) will be shown together with some reflections in the responses of the local majorities.

Although the departure is almost always taken from T. H. Marshall's (1950) concept of the trinity of the civic, political and social aspects of citizenship, the understandings of the concept vary greatly when applied to minorities. It can be said in broad terms that the focus of the concept is on the civic aspects with regard to indigenous minorities with a long history of extreme exclusion; while political rights for participation and representation in power are drawn to the forefront as sources of unequal citizenship of the settled new generations of one-time migrants. Finally, social rights cut across countries and communities, and are brought up most frequently as class issues informed by ethnicity in producing and reproducing poverty and social exclusion.

The civic aspects as framed in a human rights approach are important for us in understanding the case of Roma exclusion (Sobotka and Vermeersch 2012). In the European context that provides the background, the origins of the differences are identified by looking at the sharply differing states and histories of native as opposed to migrant minorities (Kymlicka 2009). By revealing the restrictions on citizens' rights in the case of native minorities, a recurrent trend is pointed out: people belonging to such minority communities are deprived on historical grounds of participating in the various fields of economic and social life from where they had been excluded simply by 'traditions' that remained in place even when the old sources of their legitimacy disappeared. Given that the traditional reasoning found its justification in claiming that these groups were 'backward' and therefore needed to be 'civilised', the curtailment of their human rights appeared for a long time as an act of goodwill on the part of those in domination – even when 'civilising' often meant in practice unfair disciplining and punishment. Nevertheless, by discovering the self-contained values and the inner rationales driving and organising the lives of native communities, and by, concurrently, revealing the momentum of subordination behind all acts of 'goodwill' of the dominant groups, the post-war era fully delegitimised such approaches and the worldview behind them. In light of the widely internalised criticism and the feeling of guilt that accompanied it, it seemed that deprivation from basic human rights in the name of 'civilising' can never return as an acceptable stand. For a long time it appeared that the problem was successfully overcome by new measures and institutions for minority protection that took a strong position in observing equal human rights in an unconditional way and for all.

Nevertheless, one is confronted with the fact that the issue is still lingering: the past two decades have brought it back by facing the exclusion of Europe's largest indigenous minority, the Roma, whose sharp deprivation from basic human rights has drawn the matters of lacking guarantees, institutions and procedures into the spotlight. Given the concentration of Roma in Central and Eastern Europe, the unmet basic rights appeared for a long time as a regional matter and as a specific malaise of post-socialist transformation. However, the scandalous deportation of Roma migrants in Italy and in France, their forced return 'home' from Sweden or Germany revealed that human rights violation in the case of this ethnic minority is an all-European phenomenon requiring the thorough rethinking of the foundations of European citizenship. In this context, education has a lot to say about how 'backwardness' is conceptualised and put into institutional relations. First, relegating Roma children into special schools set up initially for those struggling with 'learning difficulties' has severe consequences for basic human rights. Children concluding education in such schools are deprived of the opportunity to continue in the normal formations at the secondary level, and, perhaps even more importantly, from entering vocational training whereby their right for a free choice of work and living is seriously restricted. As people carrying the professionally formed stigma of 'feeble-mindedness', they may lose their basic rights to voting and representation. All of this means that not only their education but the practising of their basic civil and political rights is seriously limited, and that the restriction clearly takes place on ethnic grounds. Second, the harsh segregation of Roma children into 'Roma-only' schools and classes also has devastating implications for their citizenship. Learning and socialising only with peers from their own, severely disadvantaged community inevitably implies the acquisition of a language, form of discourse and concepts that have little or no relevance beyond the closed community. In this way, by the very processes of the in-built exclusionary trends in segregation, they become deprived of the skills, knowledge and routines of communication and dialogue that provide the foundations for being part of politics on its everyday terrains. In the longer run, such a spontaneous exclusion from the everyday domains of participation severely affects the political dimensions of citizenship and deprives Roma as 'inapt people' from the rights of equal participation and representation.

It is an important lesson of our studies about the workings of ethnicity in education that the above indicated extreme forms of human rights violation and the emptying of civic rights was not experienced among the ethnic minorities from immigrant backgrounds living in Western Europe. This is not to say that the contents and the forms of practising citizenship in their case would be equal to those of the majorities: as we will see below, important inequalities and inequities could be experienced. Nevertheless, observance of the basic civic rights and entitlements is part of the century-old legal and political structures of these societies, and provides the foundation for their democracies. While the large-scale migration of recent decades has changed many aspects of economy and society, it has never questioned the fundamental institutions safeguarding democracy. Instead, people from minority backgrounds could often draw advantages from these institutions that protected them from fundamentalist attacks and accusations of religious betrayals calling for punishment, and even excommunication. The differences experienced between the two halves of Europe call our attention to the importance of the broader institutional embedding of the contents of citizenship of minority people. One can say that the deprivations that Roma people experience are clear derivatives of the weaknesses of the new democracies in which self-assurance of the majority and the underscoring of differences in social status invoke the drawing up of lines of separation and then exclusion, while in their Western counterparts it is the opposite trend of extending basic rights that informs both the commonalities and the differences in the contents of social status and citizenship between majorities and minorities.

The differences also have implications for the effects of segregation. While residential characteristics are important in informing school segregation all across Europe, active mobilisation of the local majorities for attaining exclusion of minority children from certain schools and streams could be observed with less frequency and intensity in schools and communities in the West than in their Central European counterparts. At the same time, long-term practices and structures made the segregation of ethnic minority students as widespread in the West as outright coercion against the children of the poor and Roma did in Central Europe. Given the similarities, much of the consequences are shared: deprivation from the mainstream language and from a large part of the knowledge regarded as essential for participation, minority children's confinement to the second-order schools and streams, their devalued performance and the limitations on educational opportunities are all common features. Nevertheless, the strong observance of rights for appeal against unjust decisions, the range of scholarships and forms of welfare assistance that families can rely on, and the protective shield of NGOs working in the field together are efficient enough to reduce the negative consequences and to provide corrections at least at the individual level. These differences point towards an important conclusion. Once again, the state of democracy and its everyday working has to be emphasised in close association with the strengths and weaknesses of civil society as a major source of countervailing the exclusionary tendencies in the working of the educational institutions. These potentials do not turn inequalities around and do not change the prevailing structures of schooling, but they do help to keep the gates open for correction and provide opportunities for social mobility through alternative pathways.

These comparative observations have rather important further implications concerning the conceptualisation of segregation. As long as it is considered as an internal matter with exclusive relevance for education and the functioning of schools, segregation can hardly be reduced, even less eliminated. However, a reframing of the issue as a matter of fundamental rights that have to be reassured for the sake of maintaining the unity and universalism of citizenship pulls the problem into the political domain. In this way, interests and attitudes become rearranged while the circle of actors is enlarged. Seen within these broader implications, a new framing of the factors behind segregationist impulses emerges that provides an opportunity for schools and communities to make reforms towards re-establishing universalism that in their individual institutional efforts they prove too weak to achieve.

The picture is equally complex as far as the second, political dimension of citizenship is concerned. As is widely discussed in the literature, forms of political participation and representation are derivatives of the longer-term histories of ethnic and minority relations, and the ways by which different societies have translated these relations into legally guaranteed political rights (Kymlicka and Norman 2000, Koopmans et al. 2005, Parekh 2006, Joppke 2010). In this regard, the patterns vary according to whether post-colonial trends of emancipation were in the forefront when framing such rights or whether the expected return of economic migrants to their countries of origin made forms of representation transient and weak by defining their role more in a civil society framework than as parts of formal politics.

As said, the portraying of such macrolevel differences is beyond the scope of the current discussion. It is the local manifestations of interests and their politicisation within the set frameworks that we turn to present. While the differences in the institutional framing of minorities' political rights certainly profoundly affect the local levels, participation in local politics and political involvement in shaping local education shows variations that are sometimes surprisingly divergent from the macrolevel determinations. It turns out that on certain occasions it is the actual lack of proper representation that gives the impetus to local movements of organisation. Such a paradox might explain the speedy spreading of Muslim schools in communities with a dominance of Turks among the inhabitants. Although Turkish communities are populous in a number of countries (ranging from France to Germany and Sweden), their macrolevel political representation is generally weak. Nevertheless, strong civil political movements have accompanied the economic strengthening of these minority communities that saw it as a natural claim to have their own schools serving their own community and offering teaching into vocations for their own economy. The powerful institutionalisation of their claims through civil institutions is a direct outcome of weak political institutionalisation in society at large, while it is also an important political tool for attaining representation and claiming a share in local-level politics within the given locality.

The second example of missing macrolevel institutions of minority representation motivating local mobilisation concerns Roma organisation for giving voice to political interests in local education. While macrolevel representation is weak and rather ineffective all across Central and Eastern Europe, the politicisation of segregation as an issue of human rights violation and as a process leading to extreme exclusion has given impulse to local-level movements across the region. Roma parents have engaged in negotiating with the local authorities the redrawing of school catchment areas and in claiming admission of Roma children into the prestigious language or science streams by directly turning to the school management. While these spontaneous movements usually remained limited to the given communities and often failed to reach their initial goals, they still represent important initiatives of struggles for ethnic recognition and thus can be considered as attempts to change the political contents of Roma citizenship.

Despite such promising examples, our inquiries into the local dynamics of minority politics have shown that, without a backing of powerful macrolevel political representation and the majorities' willingness to accept a change in the ethnic landscape of power distribution, the local civil initiatives remain weak on their own to attain deep changes in education. First, since the majoritarian interests behind ethnic segregation seem to override claims for inclusion, minorities' attempts at achieving recognition through separation might even deepen the ethnic divides. Second, fundamental issues of streaming and tracking remain untouched by minority political mobilisation, as do the prevailing forms and contents of performance assessment. Hence the unbroken reproduction of the major inequalities in schooling that work to the detriment of young people from ethnic minority backgrounds continues, and is made even more apparent by the frustration over the relative weakness of their movements and claims. If one draws up a balance sheet it can be established that while issues of education induce local mobilisation among ethnic minorities, their voice hardly reaches the institutional terrains where large-scale decisions about education are made. The latter seem to be shaped by a different set of factors. Openness towards multiculturalism and the influence of politicians from minority origins prove to be the decisive factors behind educational reforms that take on board the ethnicised inequalities and inequities prevailing in the country's educational system (see Zentai, Chapter 6 in this volume).

The third vast domain regarding the contents of young people's learning of citizenship comprises the various aspects of their social rights as framed in education. Considering the special needs of ethnic minorities, three issues seem to be of particular importance here: the claims about language rights that allow for the practising and preserving of minority languages and cultures; the representation of the history of the minority community as part of shaping the collective contents of rights and their legitimation; and the freedom and constraints of incorporating and manifesting the ethnospecific aspects in identity formation as the bases of social and political participation.

Whether the practising and preserving of their own language is or is not part of the needs and claims of a minority is primarily dependent on the longer-term history of inter-ethnic relations. In general, post-colonial minorities long ago acquired the official language of their now home country: since this language was the language of schooling and administration during the colonial times, migration did not induce difficulties in this regard. For generations, this was the language that children heard and spoke at home, thus they have simply had to adjust to the literary forms, much like their working-class peers from the majority who had been socialised into dialects that the schools did not accept (Bernstein 1977).

However, for different historical reasons, language rights are not an issue for large parts of the Roma community either. Due to the historical forms of rural cohabitation and exchange, and, later, to vast processes of within-country migration, large groups of the Roma community lost their own language generations ago, and most of today's children consider the dominant language of their country to be their mother tongue.

As our studies reveal, the right to use the language of the minority is mainly an issue for economic migrants, asylum seekers and refugees, and their offspring. For these groups, the language of origin is a symbol of belonging, and keeping it alive underscores the cohesion of the community. Moreover, preserving it as the language of private life expresses the recognition of the forceful aspects of their exodus and, simultaneously, a way of distancing themselves from the dominant society of their now home country. Perhaps partly in reflection of such a distancing, people of the majority often consider the minority's presence to be transient, while the migrants themselves often hope for a return or at least for the reproduction of their distinct world amidst the new conditions. While all of these motives can be understood and accepted, language separation often becomes a source of serious disadvantages, since school children of these families tend to obtain poorer results than their native peers in all school subjects (OECD 2010). Hence schools face a serious dilemma: they either disregard the multilingual reality as an important reason for the diverging results and require a good command of the dominant language among all children, or they accept linguistic diversity whereby the unity and the cohesion of the contents of teaching might be put at risk. Under the pressure of increased politicisation of the matter, schools in Denmark and Sweden have recently started to experiment with bilingual teaching as a response to this dilemma. It is too early to tell whether these new experiments develop a satisfactory balance whereby minority languages and people's rights to practise them in all walks of life remain preserved while the negative repercussions for schooling are eliminated. At any rate, these new experiments are expressing recognition and, as such, contribute to a clear advancement in accessing minorities' social rights.

The second large area reflecting the state of minorities' social rights is the public recognition of their share in the history of society. As we know, the standard history as taught in school and as symbolised in various forms ranging from the ideological stylisation of national holidays to the rituals around certain sacred locations and objects is a history of the majority. Even if minority people have made important contributions to certain historical attainments, at best their mention is confined to outstanding individuals while their representation altogether remains on the margins. In the case of most minorities currently living in Europe, the picture is even more complex: their subordination and exploitation often provided the very foundations of the success of those in domination. Their ancestors' contributions with cheap labour, extensive services in the household, caring for children, the elderly and the ill had a substantial economic value as an organic constituent of the wealth of the (colonising) nation. Furthermore, deathly sacrifices of minority people in war also constitute part of the collective history. At the same time, elements of this history are present and living in minority families: great-grandparents, never seen but regarded as legendary figures of the family histories, may personalise heroic contributions, the lack of public recognition of whom thus becomes a painful but vivid experience. The Roma histories are perhaps even more compartmentalised by taboos and silence. We know very little about the Roma victims of the two world wars, and the extent of the recently acknowledged Roma holocaust is shamefully unknown. Likewise, while they are organic but unspoken parts of the Roma family histories, Roma participation in the revolutionary movements against the Communist rule and their sufferings during the aftermath of the events are unknown (be they the events of the 1956 revolution in Hungary, the Prague Spring in 1968 in Czechoslovakia, or the various forms of participation in oppositional activities in East Germany and so on).

Due to such deep divergences, the histories of the majority and of the minorities might easily become different in an uncompromising way. The only solution for harmonising such discrepancies is a redrafting of the historical narrative from scratch. However, this might be a grievous exercise that would require the courage to re-evaluate memories and deeply ingrained national values. It is thus understandable that so far little has been done towards such ends in European education. However, the reluctance has a high price: the taboos over the contributions of their ancestors, the missed opportunity to establish a certain harmony between official and private histories, and the subsequent marginalisation (or outright denial) of one's own ethnic group deprive minority people of an important aspect of their social rights: the right to express continuity and claim equal recognition of contributions to the public good in the course of history.

Besides the personal needs and claims, a shared and mutually inclusive historical narrative is of profound importance also for the contents and the justifications of citizenship rights. In this context it is worth recalling that it is the inclusion of the earlier excluded working class into the mainstream historical currents of British history that Marshall considers to be of outstanding importance in the evolution of the contents of citizenship through the centuries. He points out that without a reconsidering of the mainstream currents now from the perspective of the previously silenced working class, the necessary new language of citizenship and the filling of citizens' rights with the strong legitimating power of a shared history, a gradual evolution of citizenship could not have been attained. In a similar vein, we can say that engaging in the courageous process of re-evaluating and rewriting history now by including minority people's contributions is perhaps a prime precondition for creating a language and a thread of new justifications that allow for the visibility and recognition of them, which, in turn, opens the doors for revisions that make the historical contents of valuable contributions thorough constituents of citizenship. It is perhaps unnecessary to emphasise that schools as prime social institutions of acculturation bare profound responsibilities in this process by creating the space for the emerging new discourse and by shaping the forms and contents of teaching around the acknowledgement of the multiplicity of historical truths.

While claiming the right to use their own language and struggling for inclusive representations in history are important constituents of the social rights of minorities as such, they also contribute in significant ways to how identities are forged by incorporating meaningful elements of belonging. The emerging concepts of identities have immediate implications for citizenship by drawing the boundaries of togetherness and solidarity, and by designating entitlements and the social relations of shared responsibilities. In young people's perception, these relations are rarely all-inclusive: instead, in their approach to identification it is shared everyday experiences that are emphasised. Of course, ethnicity is only one of the factors shaping identities: gender, the common ways of living, desired and refused values, and the strength of cohesion within the community are all further important constituents.

Nevertheless, ethnicity stands out for two reasons. The first is its immediate appeal for expressing unity and solidarity on the macrolevel. Second, the ethnic dimension of identity formation reflects perhaps in the clearest and sharpest way desires for assimilation, integration or, contrarily, towards separation that, in turn, inform aspirations and the choice of a certain path towards adulthood. These different patterns of majority–minority relations might indicate how citizenship still remains powerful enough to maintain mutual belonging and solidarity in society at large while they also highlight the emerging trends of deconstruction and fragmentation.

While our studies confirmed that adolescent identity formation is a process in the making with a high degree of fluidity shaped by the varying frames of reference, the concurring elaborate ideas about the role of ethnicity in one's own life and in relating to the community confirmed the potency of considering ethnic identity an outstanding point of departure in shaping adolescent orientations. This makes the great variation in patterns understandable. Ethnic identifications and the narratives around them help young people to express personal experiences about togetherness and separation, and also indicate social distance. It follows that the narratives about these identities are personified and filled with chronicles about aspirations, efforts, success and failure, while they usually also bring up a picture about the personal relationships behind certain achievements or about the actors whose participation concluded in failure.

In these narratives, accounts about being discriminated against often come to the fore as important motives behind defining the contours that distinguish 'majorities' and 'minorities' from one another. However, discrimination is not perceived in a uniform way. For young people who enjoy the safe haven of their ethnic community, discrimination is seen more as the shameful behaviour of the 'other' (this time, peers or adults from the majority) than as a threat or a risk. This is clearly the case in some well-organised and resourceful Muslim communities that provide all-round protection for both their young and adult members.

Roma adolescents from the most remote villages enjoy little of such protection. A closer look makes it clear that it is not the intimacy of personal relations that differs but the availability of resources. Being poor and excluded, and belonging to a community with similar traits, evoke sharp and generalised criticism about the prevalence of prejudices and discrimination, and conclude in claims for protection from the state that should safeguard justice and render special provisions as part of the minority citizens' rights.

In other contexts, discrimination against minority people appears as a challenge. Indeed, young people in societies where equality is a highly and widely praised value see the discrimination of peers or parents from the majority as a betrayal of important shared ideals, and consider their role in responding with personal virtues of unquestionable strength and endurance. Struggles driven by strong beliefs in the 'victory' of the precious values of the ethnic community, and in personal commitment towards them, are important constituents of how ethnic minority students in the Scandinavian countries respond to discrimination, and how they position themselves in reassuring claims on equality and universalism as the foundations that bind citizenships of the majority and minorities in a common an undivided framework.

Apart from the responses to discrimination that work as magnets in drawing the borders of belonging and separation and thus imply important trends (or at least threats) of fragmentation in the content of citizenship, the collective work of building narratives around the peculiar traits and values of the ethnic community is an equally important source of identification. In these narratives of identification one's community usually appears as a stronghold of unity. Its strength and cohesion are important sources of identification, even in cases where the praised unity is actually cemented together by low social status, high rates of unemployment and poverty, and hopeless conditions of destitution and marginalisation. However, despite the widespread social ills that their members experience, such communities may demonstrate certain appealing attributes. Readiness to share the very limited resources, helping out with childcare or providing care for the ill, and lack of envy and rivalry might make these communities attractive by providing a unique cohesion and a certain degree of intimacy that young people usually highly appreciate.

It has to be noted, however, that amidst the decisive relations of poverty, ethnic background seems to lose its importance: it remains a trait that is noticed rather by the outer world than by members of the community. Instead, identification looks for different targets: amidst the generally shared destitute conditions, aspirations for expressing difference often call on the neighbourhood that symbolises uniqueness either by its specific subculture or by the physical strength and militancy that it demonstrates. While such patterns of identity formation appear everywhere where young people live in pockets of poverty in marginalised conditions, it is important to note that their prevalence is exceptionally high in post-colonial communities where social class has traditionally been a strong factor in defining commonalities and separation. E. P. Thompson's book about the rise of the English working class (1991), or Eric Hobsbawm's social history of the rise and decline of the British Empire (1999), introduce in nuanced details the century-long process towards the making of a shared working-class identity. It seems that the new generations of ethnic minorities born in the UK or France become socialised into this strong pattern of class relations that leaves only limited room for ethnicity as a secondary factor of identification.

Besides the manifold ways of expressing personified identities, usually with immediate reference to communities that one can grasp and feel in daily life, more elaborate forms of identification with the larger communities of society also appear as parts of adolescent identity formation and as pre-figurations of ideas of citizenship. The coexistence of the above mentioned personified contents with immediate reference to the ethnic community and the articulation of one's relating to the more abstract community of society held together in the framework of the nation-state appear with certain ambiguities that emerge from the difficult task of building a balance and incorporating both bondages in a harmonious way. As an outcome, two large patterns arise that are distinguishable by the ordering of priorities and their argumentation.

The first pattern is built on emphasising the dualities: while ethnic identity is often of great importance in expressing the commonalities of culture, faith, upbringing and ideas of the ethnic community, loyalty and the acknowledgement of belonging to the larger and more abstract community of the nation involves identification with an undivided nationhood and the values and culture of the national majority. This duality is phrased with great variation, but the structural pillars remain the same and represent two coexisting frameworks with equal importance: the immediate community that shapes the relationships of closeness and togetherness, and the more abstract notion of society that defines opportunities and positions, and that is the target of shaping attitudes and ideas about the longer-term future. Clearly the first pillar implies particularities and trends for defining frameworks of separation; the second pillar emphasises unity and implies the fading away of distinctions, whereby it points towards the restrengthening of the cohesive contents of citizenship. The coexistence of these two identifications is often full of controversies that derive from the difficulties of living up to both categories of identification simultaneously. More importantly, the sources of the controversies greatly differ according to the larger frameworks that the general discourses about ethnicity and the country-specific institutionalisations of ethnic differences set in education and in the various terrains of everyday life.

The contrasting examples of France and the UK can be brought up here. The French republican ideology with its colour-blind attitude to ethnicity invokes minority identifications that in all official aspects avoid reference to ethnicity while considering it as a strong cementing force in neighbourhoods. This duality finds its expression in constructing identities that look like a prism: rich manifestations of ethnicity as a culture and the embodiment of traditions in microrelations, and an equally rich demonstration of undivided French-ness when opportunities and issues of national pride are drawn into focus. The British pattern is different. Much like gender or one's place of residence, ethnicity is considered as a given that one has to live with. At the same time, togetherness as defined by ethnicity rarely becomes a source or a vehicle of collective action – if it does, then the action takes place on the basis of class identity or as an expression of the organising force of the neighbourhood. On the level of society, this implies identities that underscore the multicultural character of British-ness and claim positions on the dual grounds of social class and ethnicity.

Interestingly enough, for the most part, European minorities in their attempts to relate to the nation-state and their own community within the same framework tend to follow more the French than the British pattern. The opportunities and advantages offered by living in their now home country are strong constituents of loyalty and of expressions of 'feeling at home', while values of closeness and unquestioned solidarity are emphasised as a source of strong ties to the immediate community. This duality of belonging is perhaps sharper in the case of ethnic minorities than for youths from the majority background, but are not entirely different from theirs. By translating it into the language of citizenship, they demonstrate the unquestioned primacy of unity but claim its filling up by multicultural contents that embody the colourful values of diverse communities.

The second important pattern, though certainly less widespread, is taking ethnic identity as the sole reference, together with expressing distance from the dominant frames and values on the basis of suffered exclusion. These frustrated identities are supplied by distrust and see the national framework as an insurmountable source of hostility. Responses to such a perception are, however, manifold. A frequent way out is assimilation that is grounded in a resentful denial of ties to the ethnic community and aims at erasing all manifestations of ethnic belonging. This is a rather frequent response of adolescents from a Roma background who try to flee from the community, its depressing history and its hopeless conditions of destitution.

A diametrically conceived alternative is an accented distancing from the majority and all of its institutions. It is assumed that the community is strong enough to create its own closed world apart from society at large: with strong efforts built on solidarity, a whole 'parallel world' serving its members with education, employment and even paths for mobility can be constructed, one in which the values and traditions of the ethnic community can be practised and maintained in an undisturbed manner. The politics of enclosure requires a certain degree of well-being: the second and third generations of Muslim communities in rich countries such as Denmark or Germany are engaged in bringing the grand experiment to fruition. At any rate, these patterns of identification with a turning away from the communities and institutions of the dominant society imply rather problematic contents with regard to citizenship. While discrimination, exclusion and distrust are important elements of the claim, the strong attempts at separation dangerously break down universalism and question cross-ethnic solidarity at its foundations by denying inclusion and social cohesion beyond the boundaries of the ethnic community. With these implications, these attempts represent a threat to the ties that cement the nation-state, which is, after all, the framework of all universal rights, opportunities and institutions. At the same time, given its roots in enduring experiences of exclusion and the frustration that it has generated, paradoxically, it is a strengthening of universalism and attempts at inclusion that promise a peaceful withdrawal of the disruptive claims and practices that separatism and the politics of enclosure represent.

The reader might have noticed that schools have disappeared from the above brief account on minority identity formations and their implications on citizenship. This is not by accident. As we have seen, the frameworks of identification and their translating to prefigurations of citizenship usually involve larger units than schools. With already a good deal of knowledge to comprehend it in abstract terms and with reference to the larger-scale formations of society, young people define the yardsticks of identification in relation to their locality, their ethnic group and, frequently, their neighbourhood. Their relations at school may or may not be part of the boundary-drawing attempts. Does this imply that, for the most part, schools are irrelevant spaces from the point of view of identity formation and even more for its implications on citizenship?

One would assume the opposite. Rather, it seems that there is a tacitly shared agreement in most societies considering education to be a neutral social space with regard to citizenship. It is suggested that all that can be translated into disciplinary forms belongs to the school by teaching important contents and values in history, literature and, above all, citizenship studies – in other words, the cognitive contents are taken on board. In addition, it follows from the schools' socialising role that it responds in strong normative terms to all manifestations of inter-ethnic conflicts (from face-to-face discrimination to bullying) that occur within their walls. By framing their relating in this way, schools support certain patterns of identity formation and certain prefigurations of citizenship while unwillingly suppressing other forms. By and large, it is the broadly framed behaviours of assimilation that find their easiest way. By the joint attempts of teachers and students to erase ethnicity from the picture, the dominant contents of history and the national values that schools emphasise find their way to minority students in a seemingly unproblematic manner.

However, as we saw above, for the most part, young people strive to amalgamate two distinct aspirations: their identification with the dominant society and the simultaneous preservation of the values, norms and ties of the ethnic community. As to the latter aspiration, there is still little room for it in European schools. In this way ethnicity becomes belittled, often silenced, and the arising tensions tend to generate outright conflict. The conflict often appears as if minority children and their families were uninterested in education, and, even worse, as if they were ready to translate dissatisfaction and refusal into disruptive behaviour and the denial of the values that drive education. Such a criminalisation of ethnic 'otherness' fuels alienation and qualifies entire groups of young people as 'deviant'. By concluding in an outright refusal of education and the punishments that follow, these young people become deprived of the opportunities to return to the regular path, whereby their freedom of choice as a fundamental civic right becomes curtailed. In conclusion we can state that despite their attempts to avoid the issue, schools cannot escape their role in informing young people's identities as a core content of their citizenship. Nevertheless, it would be mistaken to claim that schools should provide the overall solution. After all, what they can and what they cannot do depends on large-scale societal processes driven by new understandings of citizenship amidst the conditions of diversity.

References

Alba, R. and R. Silberman (2009) 'The Children of Immigrants and Host-Society Educational Systems. Mexicans in the U.S. and North Africans in France', *Teachers College Record*, Vol. 111, No. 6, 1444–1475.

Alegre, M. À. and S. M. Arnett (2007) *The Effect of School Regimes on Students' Achievement. A Cross-Regional Comparison.* Paper presented at the 8th Congress of the European Sociological Association, Glasgow, 3–6 September.

Alegre, M. À. and G. Ferrer-Esteban (2010) 'How Do School Regimes Tackle Ethnic Segregation: Some Insights Supported in PISA 2006', in J. Donkers (ed.) *Quality and Inequality of Education: Cross-National Perspectives* (Berlin: Springer), pp. 137–163.

Alesina, A. and E. Glaeser (2004) *Fighting Poverty in the US and Europe. A World of Difference* (Oxford: Oxford University Press).

Alexander, C. (2009) 'Beyond Black', in L. Back and J. Solomos (eds.) *Theories of Race and Racism. A Reader,* 2nd edn (London and New York: Routledge), pp. 209–226.

Allport, G. (1954) *The Nature of Prejudice* (New York: Perseus Book Publishing).

Alsmark, G., T. Kallehave, and B. Moldenhawer (2007) 'Migration og tilhørsforhold' [Migration and belonging], in G. Alsmark, T. Kallehave, and B. Moldenhawer (eds.) *Migration och tillhörighet. Inklusions- och exklusionsprocesser i Skandinavien* (Stockholm: Makadam), pp. 7–20.

Altrichter, H., J. Bacher, M. Beham, G. Nagy, and D. Wetzelhütter (2012) 'The Effects of a Free School Choice Policy on Parents' School Choice Behaviour', *Studies in Educational Evaluation*, Vol. 37, No. 4, 230–238.

Amnesty International (2010) *Steps to End Segregation in Education* (London: Amnesty International).

Archer, L. (2003) *Race, Masculinity and Schooling. Muslim Boys and Education* (Maidenhead: Open University Press).

Archer, L. (2008) 'The Impossibility of Minority Ethnic Educational "Success"? An Examination of the Discourses of Teachers and Pupils in British Secondary Schools', *European Educational Research Journal*, Vol. 7, No. 1, 89–107.

Artiles, A. (2003) 'Special Education's Changing Identity. Paradoxes and Dilemmas in Views of Culture and Space', *Harvard Educational Review*, Vol. 73, No. 2, 2–39.

Arum, R., A. Gamoran, and Y. Shavit (2007) 'More Inclusion than Diversion. Expansion, Differentiation, and Market Structure in Higher Education', in Y. Shavit, R. Arum, and A. Gamoran (eds.) *Stratification in Higher Education. A Comparative Study* (Stanford: Stanford University Press), pp. 1–38.

Augoustinos, M., K. Tuffin, and D. Every (2005) 'New Racism, Meritocracy and Individualism. Constraining Affirmative Action in Education', *Discourse & Society*, Vol. 16, No. 3, 315–340.

Back, L. (1996) *New Ethnicities and Urban Culture. Racism and Multiculture in Young Lives* (London: Routledge).

Ball, S. J. (2003) *Class Strategies and the Education Market* (London: Routledge).

Ball, S. J. (2006) *Education Policy and Social Class. The Selected Works of Stephen J. Ball* (London: Routledge).

Ball, S. J. (2009) *The Education Debate* (Bristol: Policy Press).

Banting, K. and W. Kymlicka (2012) 'Is There Really a Backlash against Multiculturalism Policies? New Evidence from the Multiculturalism Policy Index', *Working Paper 4, The Stockholm University Linnaeus Center for Integration Studies* (Stockholm: Stockholm University).

Barth, F. (1969) *Ethnic Groups and Boundaries* (Boston: Little, Brown).

Beach, D. and J. Lunneblad (2011) 'Ethnographic Investigations of Issues of Race in Scandinavian Education Research', *Ethnography and Education*, Vol. 6, No. 1, 29–43.

Bell, M. (2003) 'The Right to Equality and Non-Discrimination', in T. Hervey and J. Kenner (eds.) *Economic and Social Rights under the EU Charter of Fundamental Rights. A Legal Perspective* (Oxford: Hart Publishing).

Bernstein, B. (1977) *Class, Codes and Control. Towards a Theory of Educational Transmission* (London: Routledge and Kegan Paul).

Berry, J. W. (1991) 'Psychology of Acculturation. Understanding Individuals Moving across Cultures', in R. W. Brislin (ed.) *Handbook of Cross-Cultural Psychology* (Boston: Allyn and Bacon), pp. 221–279.

Blatchford, P. (2005) *Improving Pupil Group Work in Classrooms*, http://www.tlrp.org/pub/documents/BlatchfordRBFinal_001.pdf (accessed 7 January 2011).

Blumer, H. (1958) 'Race Prejudice as a Sense of Group Position', *Pacific Sociological Review*, Vol. 1, No. 1, 3–7.

Bourdieu, P. (1990) *The Logic of Practice* (Cambridge: Polity Press).

Bourdieu, P. (1997) 'The Forms of Capital', in A. H. Halsey (ed.) *Education, Culture, Economy, Society* (Oxford: Oxford University Press), pp. 46–59.

Bourdieu, P. and J.-C. Passeron (1990) *Reproduction in Education, Society and Culture* (London: Sage).

Bourdieu, P. and L. Wacquant (1992) *An Invitation to Reflexive Sociology* (Cambridge: Polity Press).

Bradley, H. (1996) *Fractured Identities. Changing Patterns of Inequality* (Cambridge: Polity Press).

Brand, A. and R. Ollerearnshaw (2008) *Gangs at the Grassroots. Community Solutions to Street Violence* (London: New Local Government Network).

Breen, R. and M. Buchmann (2002) 'Institutional Variation and the Position of Young People. A Comparative Perspective', *The ANNALS of the American Academy of Political and Social Science*, Vol. 580, No. 1, 288–305.

Breen, R. and J. Jonsson (2005) 'Inequality of Opportunity in Comparative Perspective. Recent Research on Educational Attainment and Social Mobility', *Annual Review of Sociology*, Vol. 31, 223–243.

Brinbaum, Y. and H. Cebolla-Boado (2007) 'The School Careers of Ethnic Minority Youth in France. Success or Disillusion?', *Ethnicities*, Vol. 7, No. 3, 445–474.

Brubaker, R., M. Feischmidt, J. Fox, and L. Grancea (2007) *Nationalist Politics and Everyday Ethnicity in a Transylvanian Town* (Princeton: Princeton University Press).

Brunello, G. and D. Checchi (2007) 'Does School Tracking Affect Equality of Opportunity? New International Evidence', *Economic Policy*, Vol. 22, No. 52, 781–861.

Burgess, S. and E. Graves (2009) 'Test Scores, Subjective Assessment and Stereotyping of Ethnic Minorities', *CMPO Working Paper, No. 09/221* (Bristol: CMPO).

Byfield, C. (2008) *Black Boys Can Make It. How They Overcome the Obstacles to University in the UK and the USA* (Stoke-on-Trent: Trentham Press).

Carmel, E., A. Cerami, and T. Papadopoulos (2012) *Migration and Welfare in the New Europe* (Bristol: Policy Press).

Carson, M., J. Kallstenius, K. Sonmark, and B. Hobson (2011) 'Social Inclusion through Education in Sweden: Policy Recommendations', *EDUMIGROM Policy Recommendation* (Budapest: Central European University, Center for Policy Studies).

Cemlyn, S., M. Greenfields, S. Burnett, Z. Matthews, and C. Whitwell (2009) *Inequalities Experienced by Gypsy and Traveller Communities. A Review* (Manchester: Equality and Human Rights Commission).

Chambers, I. (1976) ' "A Strategy for Living": Black Music and White Subcultures', in S. Hall and T. Jefferson (eds.) *Resistance through Rituals:Youth Subcultures in Post-War Britain.* (London: Hutchinson), pp. 157–166.

Cohen, A. (1974) 'Introduction: The Lesson of Ethnicity', in A. Cohen (ed.) *Urban Ethnicity.* Vol. 3 (London: Tavistock Publications Limited), pp. ix–xxiv.

Commissioner for Integration and Migration of the Senate of Berlin (2008) *Welcome to Berlin* (Berlin: Der Beauftragte des Senats von Berlin für Integration und Migration).

Cornell, S. E. and D. Hartmann (2006) *Ethnicity and Race: Making Identities in a Changing World* (Newbury Park: Pine Forge Press).

Crenshaw, K. W. (1989) 'Toward a Race-Conscious Pedagogy in Legal Education', *National Black Law Journal*, Vol. 11, 1–14.

Crick, B. (1998) *Education for Citizenship and the Teaching of Democracy in Schools* (London: DfES).

Crossley, M. and P. Broadfoot (1992) 'Comparative and International Research in Education. Scope, Problems and Potential', *British Educational Research Journal*, Vol. 18, No. 2, 99–112.

Crul, M. and J. Doomernik (2003) 'The Turkish and Moroccan Second Generation in the Netherlands: Divergent Trends between and Polarization within the Two Groups', *International Migration Review*, Vol. 37, No. 4, 1039–1064.

Crul, M. and L. Heering (2008) 'Introduction', in M. Crul and L. Heering (eds.) *The Position of the Turkish and Moroccan Second Generation in Amsterdam and Rotterdam* (Amsterdam: Amsterdam University Press), pp. 19–25.

Crul, M. and J. Holdaway (2009) 'Children of Immigrants in Schools in New York and Amsterdam: The Factors Shaping Attainment', *Teachers College Record*, Vol. 111, No. 6, 1476–1507.

Crul, M., A. Pasztor, F. Lelie, J. J. B. Mijs, and P. Schnell (2009) *De lange route in internationaal vergelijkend perspectief. Tweede generatie Turkse jongeren in het onderwijs in Nederland, België, Duitsland, Frankrijk, Oostenrijk, Zwitserland en Zweden* [The 'Long Route' in International Comparative Perspective. Second Generation Turks in Education in the Netherlands, Belgium, Germany, France, Austria, Switzerland, and Sweden] (The Hague: Primair Onderwijs Ministerie, OCW).

Crul, M. and J. Schneider (2008) *The Second Generation in Europe. Education and the Transition to the Labour Market* (Amsterdam: TIES Publications).

Crul, M. and J. Schneider (2010) 'Comparative Integration Context Theory. Participation and Belonging in New Diverse European Cities', *Ethnic and Racial Studies*, Vol. 33, No. 7, 1249–1268.

Crul, M., P. Schnell, B. Herzog-Punzenberger, M. Wilmes, M. Slootman, and R. Aparicio-Gomez (2012) 'School Careers of Second-Generation Youth in Europe. Which Education Systems Provide the Best Chances for Success?', in M. Crul, J. Schneider, and F. Lelie (eds.) *The European Second Generation Compared. Does the Integration Context Matter?* (Amsterdam: Amsterdam University Press), pp. 101–164.

Crul, M. and H. Vermeulen (2003) 'The Second Generation in Europe', *International Migration Review*, Vol. 37, No. 4, 965–986.

Crul, M. and H. Vermeulen (2006) 'Immigration, Education, and the Turkish Second Generation in Five European Nations. A Comparative Study', in C. A. Parsons and T. M. Smeeding (eds.) *Immigration and the Transformation of Europe* (Cambridge: Cambridge University Press), pp. 235–248.

Csepeli, G. and D. Simon (2004) 'Construction of Roma Identity in Eastern and Central Europe: Perceptions and Self-identification', *Journal of Ethnic and Migration Studies*, Vol. 30, No. 1, 129–150.

den Brok, P. and J. Levy (2005) 'Teacher – Student Relationships in Multicultural Classes. Reviewing the Past, Preparing the Future', *International Journal of Educational Research*, Vol. 43, No. 1–2, 72–88.

Department for Children, School, and Families (2008) *Gangs and Group-offending. Guidance for Schools* (London: DCSF).

Diefenbach, H. (2005) 'Schulerfolg von ausländischen Kindern und Kindern mit Migrationshintergrund als Ergebnis individueller und institutioneller Faktoren', in Bundesministerium für Bildung und Forschung (ed.) *Migrationshintergrund von Kindern und Jugendlichen. Wege zur Weiterentwicklung der amtlichen Statistik* (Bonn and Berlin: Bundesministerium für Bildung und Forschung).

DiMaggio, P. (1982) 'Cultural Capital and School Success', *American Sociological Review*, Vol. 47, No. 2, 189–201.

Dobbernack, J. and T. Modood (2011) 'Tolerance and Cultural Diversity in Europe. Theoretical Perspectives and Contemporary Developments', *ACCEPT PLURALISM Working Papers, No. 3* (Florence: European University Institute).

Dronkers, J. (ed.) (2010) *Quality and Inequality of Education. Cross-National Perspectives* (New York: Springer).

Dronkers, J. and F. Fleischmann (2010) 'The Educational Attainment of Second Generation Immigrants from Different Countries of Origin in the EU Member States', in J. Dronkers (ed.) *Quality and Inequality of Education. Cross-National Perspectives* (New York: Springer).

Dupcsik, Cs. and R. Vajda (2008) 'Country Report on Ethnic Relations: Hungary', *EDUMIGROM Background Papers* (Budapest: Central European University, Center for Policy Studies).

Dustmann, C., T. Frattini, and G. Lanzara (2012) 'Educational Achievement of Second Generation Immigrants. An International Comparison', *Economic Policy*, Vol. 27, No. 69, 143–185.

Entorf, H. and M. Lauk (2008) 'Peer Effects, Social Multipliers and Migrants at School: An International Comparison', *Journal of Ethnic and Migration Studies*, Vol. 34, No. 4, 633–654.

Equality and Human Rights Commission (2010) *How Fair Is Britian? The First Triennial Review* (London: EHRC).

Erel, U. (2010) 'Migrating Cultural Capital. Bourdieu in Migration Studies', *Sociology*, Vol. 44, No. 4, 642–660.

Eriksen, T. H. (2001) 'Ethnic Identity, National Identity and Intergroup Conflict. The Significance of Personal Experiences', in R. D. Ashmore, L. Jussim, and D. Wilder (eds.) *Social Identity, Iintergroup Conflict, and Conflict Reduction* (Oxford: Oxford University Press), pp. 42–70.

ERRC (European Roma Rights Center) (2004) *Stigmata. Segregated Schooling of Roma in Central and Eastern Europe* (Budapest: ERRC).

Faas, D. (2008) 'From Foreigner Pedagogy to Intercultural Education. An Analysis of the German Response to Diversity and Its Impact on Schools and Students', *European Educational Research Journal*, Vol. 7, No. 1, 108–123.

Feischmidt, M., V. Messing, and M. Neményi (2010) 'Community Study Report: Hungary', *EDUMIGROM Community Studies* (Budapest: Central European University, Center for Policy Studies).

Felouzis, G. (2005) 'Ethnic Segregation in the Secondary School System', *Revue française de sociologie*, Vol. 46, Supplement, 3–30.

Felouzis, G., B. Fouquet, and C. Schiff (2010) 'Survey Report: France', *EDUMIGROM Survey Reports* (Budapest: Central European University, Center for Policy Studies).

Felson, R. B., A. E. Liska, S. J. South, and T. L. McNulty (1994) 'The Subculture of Violence and Delinquency. Individual vs. School Context Effects', *Social Forces*, Vol. 73, No. 1, 155–173.

Ferguson, R. F. (2005) 'Why America's Black – White School Achievement Gap Persists', in G. C. Loury, T. Modood, and S. M. Teles (eds.) *Ethnicity, Social Mobility, and Public Policy. Comparing the US and UK* (Cambridge: Cambridge University Press), pp. 309–341.

Finney, N. and L. Simpson (2009) *'Sleepwalking to Segregation'? Challenging Myths about Race and Migration* (Bristol: Policy Press).

Finney, S. (2011) *Black Aspirations. An Empirical Study of Young Black Males*, Unpublished MA thesis (Leeds: University of Leeds).

Foster, P. (1992) 'Teacher Attitudes and Afro-Caribbean Educational Attainment', *Oxford Review of Education*, Vol. 18, No. 3, 269–281.

Fox, J. and Zs. Vidra (2012) 'Roma Segregation in Educational Institutions', in M. Maussen and V. Bader (eds.) *Tolerance and Cultural Diversity in Schools. ACCEPT PLURALISM Comparative Report* (Florence: European University Institute).

Gee, J. P. (2012) *An Introduction to Discourse Analysis. Theory and Method* (Abingdon: Taylor & Francis).

Gee, J. P., A.-R. Allen, and K. Clinton (2001) 'Language, Class, and Identity. Teenagers Fashioning Themselves through Language', *Linguistics and Education*, Vol. 12, No. 2, 175–194.

Geertz, C. (1977) 'Thick Description. Towards an Interpretative Theory of Culture', in C. Geertz (ed.) *The Interpretation of Cultures* (New York: Basic Books).

Gerring, J. (2007) *Case Study Research. Principles and Practices* (Cambridge: Cambridge University Press).

Ghețău, V. (2006) 'O proiectare condiţională a populaţiei României pe principalele naţionalităţi (1992–2025)' [A Conditional Projection of Romania's Population According to Nationalities (1992–2025)], *Revista de Cercetări Sociale*, Vol. 12, No. 1, 77–106.

Gibson, M. (1993) 'The School Performance of Immigrant Minorities. A Comparative View', in E. Jacob and C. Jordan (eds.) *Minority Education. Anthropological Perspectives* (Norwood: Ablex Publishing), pp. 113–128.

Gillborn, D. (2008) *Racism and Education. Coincidence or Conspiracy?* (London: Routledge).

Gillborn, D. and G. Ladson-Billings (2010) 'Education and Critical Race Theory', in M. W. Apple, S. J. Ball, and L. A. Gandin (eds.) *The Routledge International Handbook of the Sociology of Education* (London: Routledge), pp. 37–47.

Gillborn, D. and H. S. Mirza (2000) *Educational Inequality. Mapping Race, Class and Gender* (London: OFSTED).

Gogolin, I. (1994) *Der monolinguale Habitus der multilingualen Schule* (Münster: Waxmann Verlag).

Goldthorpe, J. H. (2010) 'Class Analysis and the Reorientation of Class Theory. The Case of Persisting Differentials in Educational Attainment', *The British Journal of Sociology*, Vol. 61, No. 1, 311–335.

Gomolla, M. (2011) 'Partizipation von Eltern mit Migrationshintergrund in der Schule', in V. Fischer and M. Springer (eds.) *Handbuch Migration und Familie. Grundlagen für die Soziale Arbeit mit Familien* (Schwalbach: Wochenschauverlag), pp. 446–457.

Gordon, M. (1964) *Assimilation in American Life. The Role of Race, Religion, and National Origins* (Oxford: Oxford University Press).

Government of Sweden (2000) *Välfärd och skola* [Welfare and school], SOU Reports of the Government Commissions, No. 3 (Stockholm: Fritzes).

Graham, S. and J. Juvonen (2002) 'Ethnicity, Peer Harassement, and Adjustment in Middle School. An Exploratory Study', *The Journal of Early Adolescence*, Vol. 22, No. 2, 173–199.

Gundykunst, W. B. and Y. X. Kim (2003) *Communicating with Strangers*, 4th edn (New York: McGraw-Hill).

Hall, S. (1992) 'The Question of Cultural Identity', in S. Hall, D. Held, and T. McGrew (eds.) *Modernity and Its Futures* (Cambridge: Polity Press), pp. 273–327.

Hall, S. (2009) 'Old and New Identities, Old and New Ehtnicities', in L. Back and J. Solomos (eds.) *Theories of Race and Racism. A Reader*, 2nd edn (London: Routledge), pp. 199–209.

Hall, S. and T. Jefferson (1997): *Resistance through Rituals. Youth Subcultures in Post-War Britain* (London: Hutchinson).

Heath, A. F. and Y. Brinbaum (2007) 'Explaining Ethnic Inequalities in Educational Attainment', *Ethnicities*, Vol. 7, No. 3, 291–306.

Heath, A. F., C. Rothon, and E. Kilpi (2008) 'The Second Generation in Western Europe. Education, Unemployment, and Occupational Attainment', *Annual Review of Sociology*, Vol. 34, 211–235.

Hebdidge, D. (1974) *Aspects of Style in the Deviant Subculture of the Sixties.* (Birmingham: University of Birmingham).

Heckmann, F. and NESSE (2008) *Education and Migration. Strategies for Integrating Migrant Children in European Schools and Societies* (Brussels: European Commission, Directorate-General for Education and Culture).

Herzog-Punzenberger, B. (2003) 'Ethnic Segmentation in School and Labour Market. 40 Years Legacy of Austrian Guest Worker Policy', *International Migration Review*, Vol. 37, No. 4, 1120–1144.

Hirt, S. A. (2012) *Iron Curtains. Gates, Suburbs and Privatization of Space in the Post-Socialist City* (Oxford: Wiley-Blackwell).

Hobsbawm, E. (1999) *Industry and Empire: From 1750 to the Present Day* (London: Penguin).

Holsinger, D. B. (2009) *Inequality in Education: Comparative and Institutional Perspectives* (New York: Springer).

Home Office (2007) *Tackling Gangs Action Programme* (London: Home Office).

Honneth, A. (1995) *The Struggle for Recognition. The Moral Grammar of Social Conflicts* (Cambridge: Polity Press).

Horst, C. (2010) *Intercultural Education in Denmark. A Report to International Alliance of Leading Educational Institutes* (Aarhus: Danish School of Education, Aarhus University).

Horst, C. and T. Gitz-Johansen (2010) 'Education of Ethnic Minority Children in Denmark. Monocultural Hegemony and Counter Positions', *Intercultural Education*, Vol. 21, No. 2, 137–151.

Huttova, J., C. McDonald, and C. Harper (2008) *Making the Mark? An Overview of Current Challenges in the Education for Migrant, Minority, and Marginalised Children in Europe* (New York: OSI).

INSEE (2010) 'Trajectoire et Origines. Enquête sur la diversité des populations en France. Premiers résultats', *Document de travail 168* (Paris: NED, INSEE).

Institute for Public Policy Research (2010) *Recession Leaves Half Young Black People Unemployed* (London: IPPR).

Institute for the Research of the Quality of Life and National Agency for Roma (2002) *Indicators Regarding Roma Communities in Romania* (Bucharest: Expert Publishing House).

Jellab, A. (2008) *Sociologie du lycée professionnel. L'expérience des élèves et des enseignants dans une institution en mutation* (Toulouse: Presses Universitaires du Mirail).

Jennings, J. (2000) 'Citizenship, Republicanism and Multiculturalism in Contemporary France', *British Journal of Political Science*, Vol. 30, No. 4, 575–597.

Jensen, S. Q. (2011) 'Othering, Identity Formation and Agency', *Qualitative Studies*, Vol. 2, No. 2, 63–78.

Joppke, C. (2004) 'The Retreat of Multiculturalism in the Liberal State. Theory and Policy', *British Journal of Sociology*, Vol. 55, No. 2, 237–257.

Joppke, C. (2010) *Citizenship and Immigration* (Cambridge: Polity Press).

Joppke, C. and S. Lukes (eds.) (1999) *Multicultural Questions* (Oxford: Oxford University Press).

Jønsson, H. V. and K. Petersen (2010) 'Danmark: Den nationale velfærdsstat møder verden' [Denmark: The National Welfare State Encounters the World], in G. Brochmann and A. Hagelund (eds.) *Velferdens grenser* (Oslo: Universitetsforlaget), pp. 131–209.

Jonsson, J. O. and F. Rudolphi (2011) 'Weak Performance – Strong Determination: School Achievement and Educational Choice among Children of Immigrants in Sweden', *European Sociological Review*, Vol. 27, Issue 4, pp. 487–508.

Kahanec, M., A. Zaiceva, and K. F. Zimmermann (2010) 'Ethnic Minorities in the European Union. An Overview', in M. Kahanec and K. F. Zimmermann (eds.) *Ethnic Diversity in European Labor Markets* (Cheltenham: Edward Elgar), pp. 1–30.

Kallstenius, J. and K. Sonmark (2010) 'Community Study Report: Sweden', *EDUMIGROM Community Studies* (Budapest: Central European University, Center for Policy Studies).

Kao, G. and J. S. Thompson (2003) 'Racial and Ethnic Stratification in Educational Achievement and Attainment', *Annual Review of Sociology*, Vol. 29, 417–442.

Kasinitz, P., J. H. Mollenkopf, M. C. Waters, and J. Holdaway (2008) *Inheriting the City. The Children of Immigrants Come of Age* (New York: Russell Sage Foundation).

Kerckhoff, A. C. (2001) 'Education and Social Stratification Processes in Comparative Perspective', *Sociology of Education*, Vol. 74, 3–18.

Knowles, E. and W. Ridley (2006) *Another Spanner in the Works. Challenging Prejudice and Racism in Mainly White Schools* (Stoke-on-Trent: Trentham Press).

Kóczé, A. (2010) 'Aki érti a világ hangját, annak muszáj szólnia. Roma nők a politikai érvényesülés útján' [Those Who Hear Also the Voice of the Voiceless Must Speak. Roma Women on the Road to Influence Politics], in M. Feischmidt (ed.) *Etnicitás. Különbségteremtő társadalom* (Budapest: Gondolat), pp. 208–224.

Kohn, A. (2011) 'The Case against Grades', *Educational Leadership*, Vol. 69, No. 3, 28–33.

Konsortium, B. (2006) *Bildung in Deutschland – Ein indikatorengestützter Bericht mit einer Analyse zur Bildung und Migration* (Bielefeld: W. Bertelsmann Verlag).

Koopmans, R. (2010) 'Trade-Offs between Equality and Difference. Immigrant Integration, Multiculturalism and the Welfare State in Cross-National Perspective', *Journal of Ethnic and Migration Studies*, Vol. 36, No. 1, 1–26.

Koopmans, R., P. Statham, M. Giugni, and F. Passy (2005) *Contested Citizenship. Immigration and Cultural Diversity in Europe* (Minneapolis: University of Minnesota Press).

Kovai, C. (2012) 'A cigány-osztály és az egyenlőség uralma' ['Roma-Only' Classes and the Issue of Equality], *Beszélő Online*, http://beszelo.c3.hu/cikkek/ (accessed 30 March 2013).

Kusá, Z., D. Kostlán, and J. Rusnáková (2010) 'Community Study Report: Slovakia', *EDUMIGROM Community Studies* (Budapest: Central European University, Center for Policy Studies).

Kymlicka, W. (1995) *Multicultural Citizenship* (Oxford: Oxford University Press).

Kymlicka, W. (2009) *Multicultural Odysseyes. Navigating the New International Politics of Diversity* (Oxford: Oxford University Press).

Kymlicka, W. and W. Norman (eds.) (2000) *Citizenship in Diverse Societies* (Oxford: Oxford University Press).

Lapeyronnie, D. (2005) 'La banlieue comme théâtre colonial, ou la fracture coloniale dans les quartiers', in P. Blanchard, N. Bancel, S. Lamerie, and O. Barlet (eds.) *La fracture coloniale. La société française au prisme de l'héritage colonial* (Paris: La Découverte).

Law, I. (1997) 'Modernity, Anti-racism and Ethnic Managerialism', *Policy Studies*, Vol. 18, No. 3–4, 189–206.

Law, I. (2010) *Racism and Ethnicity. Global Debates, Dilemmas, Directions* (London: Pearson Education).

Law, I. (2011) 'Poverty and Income Maintenance', in G. Craig, K. Atkin, S. Chattoo, and R. Flynn (eds.) *Understanding 'Race' and Ethnicity* (Bristol: Policy Press), pp. 191–209.

Law, I. and S. Swann (2011) 'Social Inclusion through Education in the United Kingdom: Policy Recommendations', *EDUMIGROM Policy Recommendation* (Budapest: Central European University, Center for Policy Studies).

Law, I. and S. Swann (2011) *Ethnicity and Edication in England and Europe. Gangstas, Greeks and Gorjas* (Farnham: Ashgate).

Lundqvist, C. (2010) *Möjligheternas horisont. Etnicitet, utbildning och arbete I ungas berättelser om karriärer* [The Horizons of Opportunity. Ethnicity, Education and Work in Young People's Narratives of Careers] (Linköping: Linköping University).

Mac an Ghaill, M. (1988) *Young, Gifted and Black* (Milton Keynes: Open University Press).

MacPherson, Sir W. (1999) *The Stephen Lawrence Inquiry* (London: The Stationery Office).

Magyari-Vincze, E. (2006) *Social Exclusion at the Crossroad of Gender, Ethnicity and Class. A View through Romani Women's Reproductive Health* (Cluj: EFES).

Mannitz, S. (2004) 'Pupils' Negotiations of Cultural Differences. Discursive Assimilation and Identity Management', in W. Schiffauer, G. Baumann, R. Kastoryano, and S. Vetrovec (eds.) *Civil Enculturation. Nation-State, Schools and Ethnic Difference in Four European Countries* (Oxford: Berghahn Books), pp. 242–303.

Mannitz, S. (2011) 'Social Inclusion through Education in Germany: Policy Recommendations', *EDUMIGROM Policy Recommendation* (Budapest: Central European University, Center for Policy Studies).

Marada, R., M. Nekorjak, A. Souralová, and K. Vomastková (2010) 'Community Study Report: Czech Republic', *EDUMIGROM Community Studies* (Budapest: Central European University, Center for Policy Studies).

Marks, G. N. (2005) 'Accounting for Immigrant Non-Immigrant Differences in Reading and Mathematics in Twenty Countries', *Ethnic and Racial Studies*, Vol. 28, No. 5, 925–946.

Marshall, T. H. (1950) *Citizenship and Social Class, and Other Essays* (Cambridge: Cambridge University Press).

Mau, S. and C. Burkardt (2009) 'Migration and Welfare State Solidarity in Western Europe', *Journal of European Social Policy*, Vol. 19, No. 3, 213–229.

Maussen, M. and V. Bader (eds.) (2012) 'Comparative Tolerance and Cultural Diversity in Schools', *ACCEPT PLURALISM Working Papers No. 1* (Florence: European University Institute).

McCall, L. (2005) 'The Complexity of Intersectionality', *Signs*, Vol. 30, No. 3, 1771–1800.

McClaurin, I. (ed.) (2001) *Black Feminist Anthropology. Theory, Politics, Praxis, and Poetics* (New Brunswick: Rutgers University Press).

Migration Policy Group (2011) *The Migrant Integration Policy Index (MIPEX)* (Brussels: Migration Policy Group).

Miquel, A. and G. Ferrer-Esteban (2010) 'How Do School Regimes Tackle Ethnic Segregation. Some Insights Supported in PISA 2006', in J. Dronkers (ed.) *Quality and Inequality of Education* (New York: Springer).

Mitchell, D. (2003) *The Right to the City. Social Justice and the Fight for Public Space* (New York: Guilford Press).

Modood, T. (2005) 'The Educational Attainments of Ethnic Minorities in Britain', in G. C. Loury, T. Modood, and S. M. Teles (eds.) *Ethnicity, Social Mobility, and Public Policy* (Cambridge: Cambridge University Press), pp. 288–308.

Modood, T. (2007) *Multiculturalism. A Civic Idea* (Cambridge: Polity Press).

Modood, T. (2012) *Post-Immigration 'Difference' and Integration. The Case of Muslims in Western Europe* (London: British Academy).

Modood, T. and S. May (2001) 'Multiculturalism and Education in Britain. An Internally Contested Debate', *International Journal of Educational Research*, Vol. 35, 305–317.

Modood, T. (2010) *Still Not Easy Being British. Struggles for a Multicultural Citizenship* (Stoke-on-Trent: Trentham Press).

Moldenhawer, B. (1999) 'Turkish and Kurdish Speaking Teachers in the Danish Folkeskole. The Ambiguous Concept of Equality', *Scandinavian Journal of Educational Research*, Vol. 43, No. 4, 349–369.

Moldenhawer, B. (2005) 'Transnational Migrant Communities ad Education Strategies among Pakistani Youngsters in Denmark', *Journal of Ethnic and Migration Studies*, Vol. 31, No. 1, 51–78.

Moldenhawer, B. (2009) 'Etnicitet, uddannelse og lighed' [Ethnicity, Education and Equality], in N. Holtug and K. Lippert-Rasmussen (eds.) *Lige muligheder for alle. Social arv, kultur og retfærdighed* (Frederiksberg: Nyt fra Samfundsvidenskaberne), pp. 217–237.

Moldenhawer, B. (2011) 'Etniske fællesskaber' [Ethnic Communities], in S. Brinckmann and E. Jensen (eds.) *Fællesskaber* (Kopenhagen: Akademisk Forlag), pp. 105–129.

Moldenhawer, B., T. Kallehave, and S. Hansen (2010) 'Community Study Report: Denmark', *EDUMIGROM Community Studies* (Budapest: Central European University, Center for Policy Studies).

Moldenhawer, B. and T. Øland (2012) 'Disturbed by "the Stranger". State Crafting Remade through Educational Interventions and Moralisations', *Globalisation, Societies and Education*, Vol. 11, No. 2, 1–23.

Moldenhawer, B. and M. Padovan-Ozdemir (2011) 'Social Inclusion through Education in Denmark: Policy Recommendations', *EDUMIGROM Policy Recommendation* (Budapest: Central European University, Center for Policy Studies).

Moore, H. (1988) *Feminism and Anthropology* (Cambridge: Polity Press).

Moore, H. (1994) *A Passion for Difference. Essays in Anthropology and Gender* (Cambridge: Polity Press).

Moosa, Z. and J. Woodroffe (2010) *Poverty Pathways. Ethnic Minority Women's Livelihoods* (London: Fawcett).

Myrdal, Gunnar (1944) *An American Dilemma. The Negro Problem and Modern Democracy* (Piscataway, NJ: Transaction Publishers).

NALDIC (National Association for Language Development in the Curriculum) (2011) *National Ethnic Minority Achievement Survey* (Reading: NALDIC).

Oakes, J. and M. Lipton (2003) *Teaching to Change the World* (New York: McGraw-Hill).

OECD (2005) *School Factors Related to Quality and Equity. Results from PISA 2000* (Paris: OECD).

OECD (2006) *Where Immigrant Students Succeed. A Comparative Review of Performance and Engagement in PISA 2003* (Paris: OECD).

OECD (2007a) *Education at Glance 2007. OECD Indicators* (Paris: OECD).

OECD (2007b) *No More Failures. Ten Steps to Equity in Education* (Paris: OECD).

OECD (2010) *PISA 2009 Results. Equity in Learning Opportunities and Outcomes* (Paris: OECD).

OECD (2011) *Education at a Glance* (Paris: OECD).

OECD (2012) *Untapped skills. Realising the Potential of Immigrant Students* (Paris: OECD).

Ogbu, J. U. (1978) *Minority Education and Caste. The American System in Cross-Cultural Perspective* (New York: Academic Press).

Ogbu, J. U. (1991) 'Immigrant and Involuntary Minorities in Comparative Perspective', in M. A. Gibson and J. Ogbu (eds.) *Minority Status and Schooling: A Comparative Study of Immigrant and Involuntary Minorities* (New York: Garland), pp. 3–33.

Ogbu, J. U. (1987) 'Variability in Minority School Performance. A Problem in Search of an Explanation', *Anthropology and Education Quarterly*, Vol. 18, No. 4, 312–334.

Ogbu, J. U. and H. D. Simons (1998) 'Voluntary and Involuntary Minorities. A Cultural-Ecological Theory of School Performance with Some Implications for Education', *Anthropology & Education Quarterly*, Vol. 29, No. 2, 155–189.

Osborn, M. and P. Broadfoot (1993) 'Becoming and Being a Teacher. The Influence of the National Context', *European Journal of Education*, Vol. 28, No. 1, 105–116.

Osborne, J.W. (2001) 'Testing Stereotype Threat: Does Anxiety Explain Race and Sex Differences in Achievement?', *Contemporary Educational Psychology*, Vol. 26, No. 3, 291–310.

Parekh, B. (2006) *Rethinking Multiculturalism* (Basingstoke: Palgrave Macmillan).

Parekh, B. (2008) *A New Politics of Identity* (Basingstoke: Palgrave Macmillan).

Park, H. and G. Sandefour (2010) 'Education Gaps between Immigrant and Native Students in Europe. The Role of Grade', in J. Dronkers (ed.) *Quality and Inequality of Education* (New York: Springer), pp. 113–137.

Paterson, L. and C. Iannelli (2007) 'Social Class and Educational Attainment. A Comparative Study of England, Wales, and Scotland', *Sociology of Education*, Vol. 80, No. 4, 330–358.

Payet, J.-P. (1995) *Collèges de banlieue. Ethnographie d'un monde scolaire* (Paris: Méridiens Klienksieck).

Penn, R. and P. Lambert (2009) *Children of International Migrants in Europe. Comparative Perspectives* (Basingstoke: Palgrave Macmillan).

Perrotonm, J. (2000) 'Les dimensions ethniques de l'expérience scolaire', *L'année sociologique*, Vol. 50, No. 2, pp. 437–468.

Pfeffer, F. T. (2008) 'Persistent Inequality in Educational Attainment and Its Institutional Context', *European Sociological Review*, Vol. 24, No. 5, 543–565.

Pfeffer, F. T. (2012) 'Equality and Quality in Education', *PSC Research Report No.12–774* (Ann Arbor: University of Michigan, Population Studies Center).

Phalet, K., P. Deboosere and V. Bastiaenssen (2007) 'Old and New Inequalities in Educational Attainment. Ethnic Minorities in the Belgian Census 1991–2001', *Ethnicities*, Vol. 7, No. 4, 390–407.

Phinney, J. S. (1992) 'The Multigroup Ethnic Identity Measure. A New Scale for Use with Adolescents and Young Adults from Diverse Groups', *Journal of Adolescent Research*, Vol. 7, No. 2, 156–176.

Préteceille, E. (2012) 'Segregation, Social Mix and Public Policies in Paris', in T. Maloutas and K. Fujita (eds.) *Segregation around the World. Making Sense of Contextual Diversity* (Farnham: Ashgate), pp. 153–176.

Proweller, A. (1999) 'Shifting Identities in Private Education. Reconstructing Race at/in the Cultural Center', *Teachers College Record*, Vol. 100, No. 4, 785–805.

Prügl, E. and M. Thiel (eds.) (2009) *Diversity in the European Union* (Basingstoke: Palgrave MacMillan).

Radtke, F.-O. and M. Gomolla (2002) *Institutionelle Diskriminierung* (Opladen: VS Verlag für Sozialwissenschaften).

Raveaud M., A. van Zanten (2007) 'Choosing the Local School. Middle Class Parents' Values and Social and Ethnic Mix in London and Paris', *Journal of Educational Policy*, Vol. 22, No. 1, 107–224.

Rein, E. van (2010) *Same Work, Lower Grade. Student Ethnicity and Teachers' Subjective Assessments* (Amsterdam: VU University Amsterdam – Tinbergen Institute).

Rollock, N. and D. Gillborn (2010) *Enough Talk, Not Enough Action*, http://www.runnymedetrust.org/events-conferences/econferences/econference/enough-talking-not-enough-action.html (accessed 15 January 2013).

Roma Education Fund (2010) *Roma Inclusion in Education* (Budapest – Strasbourg: Roma Education Fund).

Runnymede Trust (2007) *Promoting Community Cohesion through Schools*, http://www.runnymedetrust.org/uploads/projects/education/EducationConference-Nov07.pdf (accessed 7 January 2011).

Sachverständigenrat deutscher Stiftungen für Integration und Migration (2010) *Einwanderungsgesellschaft 2010 – Jahresgutachten 2010 mit Integrationsbarometer*, http://www.svr-migration.de/wp-content/uploads/2010/05/einwanderungsgesellschaft_2010.pdf (accessed 9 November 2012).

Sainsbury, D. (2006) 'Immigrants' Social Rights in Comparative Perspective. Welfare Regimes, Forms in Immigration and Immigration Policy Regimes', *Journal of European Social Policy*, Vol. 16, No. 3, 229–244.

Salami, S. O. (2008) 'Gender, Identity, Status and Career Maturity of Adolescents', *Journal of Social Sciences*, Vol. 16, No. 1, 35–49.

Sanderson, S. K. and T. Vanhanen (2004) 'Reconciling the Differences between Sanderson's and Vanhanen's Results', in F. K. Salter (ed.) *Welfare, Ethnicity, and Altruism. New Findings and Evolutionary Theory* (London: Frank Cass), 119–120.

Sárközi, G. (2012) 'Államosítás elött' [Before Nationalisation Will Be Launched], http://www.millamedia.hu/2012/11/27/allamositas-elott/ (accessed 30 November 2012).

Schierup, C.-U. and A. Ålund (2011) 'From Paradoxes of Multiculturalism to Paradoxes of Liberalism', *Journal for Critical Education Policy Studies*, Vol. 9, No. 2, 125–139.

Schiff, C. (2010) 'Community Study Report: France', *EDUMIGROM Community Studies* (Budapest: Central European University, Center for Policy Studies).

Schiff, C. (2011) 'Social Inclusion in Education in France: Policy Recommendations', *EDUMIGROM Policy Recommendation* (Budapest: Central European University, Center for Policy Studies).

Schiff, C., G. Felouzis, and J. Perroton (2011) 'Combating School Segregation. The Case of France', in J. Bakker, E. Denessen, D. Peters, and G. Walraven (eds.) *International Perspectives on Countering School Segregation* (Antwerpen – Apeldoom: Garant), pp. 254–261.

Schiff, C., J. Perroton, B. Fouquet, and M. Armagnague (2008) 'Country Report on Ethnic Relations: France', *EDUMIGROM Background Papers* (Budapest: Central European University, Center for Policy Studies).

Schindler, R. B. (2007) 'Sources of Immigrants' Underacheivement: Results form PISA-Copenhagen', *Education Economics*, Vol. 15, No. 3, 293–326.

Schnell, P. (2012) *Educational Mobility of Second Generation Turks in Cross-National Perspective*. Unpublished PhD thesis (Amsterdam: University of Amsterdam).

Schnell, P., E. Keskiner, and M. Crul (2013) 'Success against the Odds: Educational Pathways of Disadvantaged Second-Generation Turks in France and the Netherlands', *Education Inquiry*, Vol. 4, No. 1, 125–147.

Schuetz, G., H. Ursprung, and L. Woessmann (2008) 'Education Policy and Equality of Opportunity', *Kyklos*, Vol. 61, No. 2, 279–308.

Shah, B., C. Dwyer, and T. Modood (2010) 'Explaining Educational Achievement and Career Aspirations among Young British Pakistanis. Mobilizing "Ethnic Capital"?', *Sociology*, Vol. 44, No. 6, 1–19.

Shain, F. (2011) *The New Folk Devils. Muslim Boys and Education in England* (Stoke-on-Trent: Trentham Press).

Simon, P. (2003) 'France and the Unknown Second Generation. Preliminary Results on Social Mobility', *International Migration Review*, Vol. 37, No. 4, 1091–1119.

Simon, P. and V. Amiraux (2006) 'There Are No Minorities Here. Cultures of Scholarship and Public Debate on Immigrants and Integration in France', *International Journal of Comparative Sociology*, Vol. 47, No. 3–4, 191–215.

Smith, S. J. (1989) *The Politics of 'Race' and Residence. Citizenship, Segregation and White Supremacy in Britain* (Cambridge: Polity Press).

Sobotka, E. and P. Vermeersch (2012) 'Governing Human Rights and Roma Inclusion. Can the EU Be a Catalyst for Local Social Change?', *Human Rights Quarterly*, Vol. 34, No. 3, 800–822.

Sockett, H. (1993) *The Moral Base for Teacher Professionalism* (New York: Teacher College Press).

Söderström, M. and R. Uusitalo (2010) 'School Choice and Segregation. Evidence from an Admission Reform', *Scandinavian Journal of Economics*, Vol. 112, No. 1, 55–76.

Soja, E. W. (2010) *Seeking Spatial Justice* (Minneapolis: University of Minnesota Press).

Somerville, W. (2007) *Immigration under New Labour* (Bristol: Policy Press).

Štefančík, R. (2010) *Politické mládežnicke organizácie na Slovensku* [Political Youth Organisations in Slovakia] (Bratislava: IUVENTA).

Stevens, P. A. J. (2007) 'Researching Race/Ethnicity and Educational Inequality in English Secondary Schools. A Critical Review of the Research Literature between 1980 and 2005', *Review of Educational Research*, Vol. 77, No. 2, 147–185.

Stoughton, E. H. and C. Sivertson (2005) 'Communicating across Cultures: Discursive Challenges and Racial Identity Formation in Narratives of Middle School Students', *Race Ethnicity and Education*, Vol. 8, No. 3, 277–295.

Straßburger, G., M. Ucan, and S. Mannitz (2010) 'Community Study Report: Germany', *EDUMIGROM Community Studies* (Budapest: Central European University, Center for Policy Studies).

Suárez-Orozco, C., M. M. Suárez-Orozco, and I. Todorova (2008) *Learning a New Land. Immigrant Students in American Society* (Cambridge, MA: Harvard University Press).

Sullivan, A. (2001) 'Cultural Capital and Educational Attainment', *Sociology*, Vol. 35, No. 4, 893–912.

Swann, S. and I. Law (2010) 'Community Study Report: United Kingdom', *EDUMIGROM Community Studies* (Budapest: Central European University, Center for Policy Studies).

Szalai, J. (2003) 'The Politics of Recognition and the "Gypsy Question". Some Current Problems in Majority – Minority Relations in Contemporary Hungary', *East-Central Europe/L'Europe du Centre-Est*, Vol. 30, Part I, 13–53.

Szalai, J. (ed.) (2010) *Being 'Visibly Different': Experiences of Second-Generation Migrant and Roma Youths at School* (Budapest: Central European University, Center for Policy Studies).

Szalai, J. (ed.) (2011) *Contested Issues of Social Inclusion through Education in Multi-Ethnic Communities across Europe* (Budapest: Central European University, Center for Policy Studies).

Szalai, J., V. Messing, and M. Neményi (2010) 'Ethnic and Social Differences in Education in a Comparative Perspective', *EDUMIGROM Comparative Papers* (Budapest: Central European University, Center for Policy Studies).

Tatum, B. D. (1997) *Why Are All the Black Kids Sitting Together in the Cafeteria and Other Conversations about Race* (New York: Basic Books).

Thompson, E. P. (1991) *The Making of the English Working Class* (London: Penguin).

Tissot, S. (2007) 'The Role of Race and Class in Urban Marginality. Discussing Loïc Wacquant's Comparison between the USA and France', *City*, Vol. 11, No. 3, 364–369.

Tomlinson, S. (2008) *Race and Education: Policy and Politics in Britain* (Maidenhead: Open University Press).

Triandaffyllidou, A. and T. Modood (2011) 'Introduction: Diversity, Integration, Secularism and Multiculturalism', in A. Triandafyllidou, T. Modood, and N. Meer (eds.) *European Multiculturalisms. Cultural, Religious and Ethnic Challenges* (Edinburgh: Edinburgh University Press), pp. 1–29.

Triandafyllidou, A. and R. Zapata-Barrero (eds.) (2012) *Addressing Tolerance and Diversity Discourses in Europe. A Comparative Overview of 16 European Countries* (Barcelona: CIDOB).

Tucci, I. (2010) 'Les descendants de migrants maghrébins en France et turcs en Allemagne: deux types de mise à distance sociale?', *Revue française de sociologie*, Vol. 51, No. 1, 3–38.

Tyler, I. (2008) ' "Chav Mum Chav Scum". Class Disgust in Contemporary Britain', *Feminist Media Studies*, Vol. 8, No. 1, 17–34.

UNDP (2006) *Správa o životniích podmienkach rómskych domácností na Slovensku* [Report on the Living Conditions of Roma Households in Slovakia] (Bratislava: UNDP).

UNDP (2012) 'Roma Education in Comparative Perspective. Findings from the UNDP/World Bank/EC Regional Roma Survey', *Roma Inclusion Working Papers* (Bratislava: UNDP).

Vallet, L.-A. and J.-P. Caille (1999) *Migration and Integration in France. Academic Careers of Immigrants' Children in Lower and Upper Secondary School*, Paper presented at the ESF Conference 'European Societies or European Society?', *Obernai*, 23–28 September.

van de Werfhorst, H. G. and J. J. B. Mijs (2010) 'Achievement Inequality and the Institutional Structure of Educational Systems. A Comparative Perspective', *Annual Review of Sociology*, Vol. 36, 407–428.

van de Werfhorst, H. G. and F. Van Tubergen (2007) 'Ethnicity, Schooling, and Merit in the Netherlands', *Ethnicities*, Vol. 7, No. 3, 416–442.

van Dijk, T. A. (1992) 'Discourse and the Denial of Racism', *Discourse & Society*, Vol. 3, No. 1, 87–118.

van Dijk, T. A. (2002) 'Discourse and Racism', in D. T. Goldberg and J. Solomos (eds.) *A Companion to Racial and Ethnic Studies* (Oxford: Blackwell), pp. 145–159.

van Zanten, A. (1997) 'Schooling Immigrants in France in the 1990s. Success or Failure of the Republican Model of Integration?', *Anthropology & Education Quarterly*, Vol. 28, No. 3, 351–374.

van Zanten, A. (2012) *L'école de la périphérie* (Paris: PUF).

Verdery, K. (1994) 'Ethnicity, Nationalism and State-Making. Ethnic Groups and Boundaries: Past and Future', in H. Vermeulen and C. Govers (eds.) *The Anthropology of Ethnicity: Beyond 'Ethnic Groups and Boundaries'* (Amsterdam: Het Spinhuis), pp. 33–59.

Verkuyten, M. (2005) 'Ethnic Group Identification and Group Evaluation among Minority and Majority Groups. Testing the Multiculturalism Hypothesis', *Journal of Personality and Social Psychology*, Vol. 88, No. 1, 121–138.

Vermeersch, P. (2005) 'Marginality, Advocacy, and the Ambiguities of Multiculturalism. Notes on Romani Activism in Central Europe', *Identities: Global Studies in Culture and Power*, Vol. 12, No. 4, 451–478.

Vertovec, S. and S. Wessendorf (2010) 'Introduction: Assessing the Backlash against Multiculturalism in Europe', in S.Vertovec and S. Wessendorf (eds.) *The Multiculturalism Backlash. European Discourses, Policies and Practices* (London: Routledge), pp. 1–31.

Vincze, E. and H. Harbula (2011) *Strategii identitare şi educaţie şcolară. Raport de cercetare despre accesul copiilor romi la şcoală* [Identity Strategies and School Education. Research Report on Roma Children's Access to School] (Cluj: EFES).

Vincze, E., H. Harbula, and N. L. Magyari (2010) 'Community Study Report: Romania', *EDUMIGROM Community Studies* (Budapest: Central European University, Centre for Policy Studies).

Wacquant, L. (2008) *Urban Outcasts. A Comparative Sociology of Advanced Marginality* (Cambridge: Polity Press).

Weekes-Bernard, D. (2007) *School Choice and Ethnic Segregation. Educational Decision-Making among Black and Minority Ethnic Parents* (London: The Runnymede Trust).

Willis P. (1977) *Learning to Labour: How Working Class Kids Get Working Class Jobs* (New York: Columbia University Press).

Wilson, A. S. and K. Tisdall (2000) 'Parent – School – Community Relationships', in I. Nicaise (ed.) *The Right to Learn. Educational Strategies for Socially Excluded Youth in Europe* (Bristol: Policy Press), pp. 199–220.

Wilson, W. J. (1996) *When Work Disappears. The World of the New Urban Poor* (New York: Vintage Books).

Wing, A. (ed.) (2003) *Critical Race Feminism. A Reader* (New York: New York University Press).

Woessmann, L. (2004) 'How Equal Are Educational Opportunities? Family Background and Student Achievement in Europe and the United States', *IZA Discussion Paper No. 1284* (Bonn: IZA).

Wood, L. A. (1994) 'An Unintended Impact of One Grading Practice', *Urban Education*, Vol. 29, No. 2, 188–201.

Woodward, K. (1999) 'Concepts of Identity and Difference', in K. Woodward (ed.) *Identity and Difference* (London: Sage), pp. 7–63.

Yosso, T. J. (2005) 'Whose Culture Has Capital? A Critical Race Theory Discussion of Community Cultural Wealth', *Race Ethnicity and Education*, Vol. 8, No. 1, 69–91.

Zhou, M. (2005) 'Ethnicity and Social Capital: Community-Based Institutions and Embedded Networks in Social Relations', in G. C. Loury, T. Modood, and S. M. Teles (eds.) *Ethnicity, Social Mobility, and Public Policy. Comparing the US and UK* (Cambridge: Cambridge University Press), pp. 131–159.

Index

absenteeism, 76, 207, 214
activist, 214, 220
adolescent, 1, 32, 67, 71, 73, 76, 78–82, 93–4, 103, 106, 112–17, 120–5, 127–9, 133–4, 197, 200, 210, 228, 238–41
Afghanistan, 63, 116
Algeria (Algerian), 54, 106, 110, 168, 169–70, 173
anthropology, 120
anti-discrimination, 31, 87, 98, 163
Arab (Arabic), 8, 17–19, 59, 78, 113–14, 125, 140, 169–70, 185–7, 190–3
assimilation, 3, 6, 11, 60, 99, 104–5, 114–16, 118, 125, 137, 139, 146, 153–4, 208, 238, 241–2
assimilationist (assimilationism), 60, 79–80, 91, 93, 98–9, 129, 167, 209
Australia, 86
Austria (Austrian), 11, 34, 36–8, 40–6, 48, 86–7, 90–2, 96–8
autostereotype, 106

baccalaureate, 77, 169, 172
backlash, 96
Bangladesh (Bangladeshi), 152, 155
Banting, Keith, 85, 98–9
Barth, Fredrik, 138, 199
Belgium (Belgian), 17–18, 86–7, 89–91, 96, 98
Berlin, 109, 125, 184–8, 196
bilingual, 7, 75
  bilingual teaching, 236
Black (Black African, Afro-American), 3, 83, 113–14, 143, 144, 147, 152–3, 155, 157, 159, 160–1, 164, 169–70, 175, 177, 200, 221–2
Black Caribbean (Afro-Caribbean, Caribbean), 6, 8, 77, 94, 106, 139, 142–3, 151–2, 157–64
Black Minority Ethnics (BMEs), 55, 61
Bordeaux, 169, 171–8, 183
Bourdieu, Pierre, 135, 136–7, 146, 200

Brevet d'Études Profesionnelles (BEP), 169
British cultural studies, 121
Brubaker, Rogers, 121, 130–1

Canada, 86–7, 99
capital, 136–7, 141, 152
  capital, cultural, 37, 69–72, 74, 82, 133, 136–9, 141, 144, 189– 90, 194, 214
  capital, economic (material), 37, 136, 141
  capital, educational, 141, 143
  capital, social, 37, 68, 92–3, 133–4, 144
  capital, symbolic, 134, 136–8, 141, 148
case study (design), 5, 37, 157–8
catchment area, 1, 21–2, 26, 234
Central Europe (Central and Eastern Europe, Central and Eastern European), 1, 3, 6, 9–10, 18, 20–3, 26–31, 53, 56–7, 63–5, 70, 80–2, 87–9, 93, 95, 99, 112, 122–6, 128–30, 132–3, 138, 228, 233–4
Certificat d'Aptitude Profesionelle (CAP), 169
child psychology, 19
China (Chinese), 151, 169
citizenship, 6, 11–12, 82, 86–90, 95–6, 98, 108, 125, 152, 198, 209, 228–30, 232–5, 237–43
  citizenship law, 97
  citizenship model, colour-blind, 27, 59, 94, 167–8
  citizenship, multicultural, 88, 90
  citizenship policy, 90, 94, 96
  citizenship, political dimension, 233
  citizenship, racialised, 198, 208–9, 211
  citizenship rights (citizens' rights), 13, 75–6, 86, 96, 228–9, 231–2, 237
  citizenship, social, 151, 230
  citizenship strategy, 98
civic integration, 96–8
class division, 218
class repetition, 71, 72, 76

class structure, 76
class (study) trip, 126, 193, 197
colonialism (colonial, colonised), 6, 89,
    152, 235
colour-blind approach, 27, 139, 146
colour-blind republican
    universalism, 167
colour-conscious approach, 95
common education (co-educate,
    co-education), 19, 42–3
communal (community) tie, 84, 107
communal resource, 111
community cohesion, 7, 129, 154,
    156, 164
community culture, 158
community programme, 219
comprehensive school (system), 18–20,
    29, 60, 65, 89, 186–7
conflict, 6–11, 28, 31, 60, 62, 78, 107,
    113, 123, 129–31, 143, 151–2, 159,
    168, 179–80, 193, 207, 228, 243
    conflict, inter-ethnic, 4, 31, 156, 242
    conflict of cultures (conflicting
        cultures), 77–8
contact hours, 36, 43
cosmopolitanism (cosmopolitan), 11,
    104–5, 114, 116, 118, 169–71
cosmopolitan localism, 169
counterculture, 120, 225
country of origin, 2, 6, 17, 109–10,
    114, 139
    country, host (host-country), 7, 35, 63,
        87, 91–2, 109–10, 114–16
cultural approach, 128, 214
cultural broker, 53–4
cultural determinism, 64
cultural habitus, 55
cultural model of schooling, 135
cultural norm, 59–60, 63, 65, 146, 160,
    182, 213, 227
cultural pluralism, 153
cultural resource, 141
cultural study, 120–1
culture, 59, 62, 70, 85–6, 104, 110, 113,
    127–8, 130, 133–46, 165–6, 191,
    200, 215
    culture, anti-school peer, 62, 146
    culture, Black, 160
    culture-blind approach, 128
    culture-conscious approach, 128

culture, dominant, 59, 146
culture, drug, 161
culture, gangsta, 158, 161, 165
culture, hybrid, 61
culture, internal, 26
culture, juvenile street, 177
culture, majority (majoritarian
    culture), 26
culture, material, 161
culture, minority, 60, 129, 154
culture, national, 97
culture of poverty, 80, 95
culture, of resistance, 132
culture, peer-group street, 179
culture, republican school, 182
culture, universal, 63
culture, working-class, 166
culture, world, 171
culture, youth (of youth), 61, 95,
    158, 166
Cyprus, 87
Czech Republic (Czech), 1, 20–1, 24–5,
    27, 31, 52, 63–4, 81, 89, 106–7, 112,
    123, 142
Czechoslovakia (former), 237

deindustrialisation, 182, 201, 209
democracy (democratic), 80, 82, 85–6,
    88, 93–8, 212, 232–3
Denmark (Danish), 1, 7, 10, 19, 21, 25,
    27, 29–30, 52–6, 62–3, 65, 75, 88–9,
    93–8, 108, 110–15, 122–4, 128,
    133–40, 143–4, 188, 236, 242
deprivation (deprived), 3, 23–4, 62, 64–5,
    71, 76, 80, 95, 98, 106, 111, 120,
    139, 142, 200, 203, 229, 231–3, 243
destitution, 106, 113, 153, 156, 211, 223,
    239, 241
    see also poverty
disadvantage, socioeconomic, 84, 112
    see also poverty
discrimination, 1, 3–6, 25, 28, 52, 66, 76,
    83, 93, 100, 107, 112, 115, 118, 125,
    127–8, 133, 135, 137–8, 140, 142–7,
    151, 153, 194, 196, 201, 213–14,
    238–9, 242
    discriminated (against), 7, 28, 73, 78,
        121, 126, 139, 192, 223, 238
    discrimination (against), 107, 125,
        181, 214, 239

discrimination, direct, 25, 93, 156, 157
discrimination, ethnic, 80, 98, 144,
    157, 182
discrimination, ethnoracial, 106
discrimination, face-to-face, 242
discrimination, indirect, 93, 157
discrimination, in-school, 181
discrimination, institutional, 64,
    196, 214
discrimination, interpersonal, 214–15
discrimination, personal, 213, 215,
    220, 227
discrimination, racial, 51, 153, 157,
    159, 163
discrimination, social, 137
discrimination, social force, of, 140
discrimination, structural, 75, 209,
    214, 227
discrimination, verbal and
    non-verbal, 223
distancing, 20, 107, 127, 199, 225,
    236, 241
diversity-blind approach, 32
diversity-conscious school, 28–30
diversity management, 85, 98

Eastern Europe (Eastern European), 78
economic crisis, 99, 182
educational attainment, 2, 5, 18, 34–5,
    39, 48–50, 70, 91, 114, 185, 213–15,
    218–19
educational career, 12, 19–20, 39, 41,
    44–5, 49, 63, 83–4, 158, 184–5, 188
educational quality (school quality), 99
educational (school) culture, 6, 146, 182
educational strategy, 12, 76, 135–9, 143,
    146–7
educational system, 7, 9–11, 18, 20, 22,
    36–7, 39, 45–7, 50, 65–6, 82–4, 88–9,
    91–3, 120, 128, 132, 137, 158, 163,
    168, 184–9, 192, 195, 200, 208,
    227–8, 230, 235
EDUMIGROM, 1–5, 10, 13, 18, 24, 26–7,
    29–31, 33, 51–2, 69, 83–4, 88–9,
    92–5, 99, 121, 135, 147, 166, 196,
    198, 211, 214–16
emotional support, 141, 189
employability, 73
England, 1, 6, 9–10, 12, 53–5, 60, 151,
    154, 157, 166

enrolment policy, 26
equality, 27, 75, 80, 82, 85–7, 91, 93–4,
    99, 120, 146, 152–7, 163, 229,
    230, 239
equal opportunity, 28, 44, 50, 89
equity, 75, 82, 94
Eritrea (Eritrean), 112–13, 144
Ethiopia (Ethiopian), 114, 116, 144
ethnic barrier, 115
ethnic boundary, 138, 169, 206
ethnic ceiling, 11, 67–9, 72–6, 78, 81–3
ethnic difference, 1, 2, 5–6, 10, 12, 27–8,
    70, 78, 104–5, 113, 118, 149, 152–3,
    158, 167, 170, 182, 225–7, 229, 241
ethnic distinction (ethnic
    differentiation), 5–6, 11, 72, 146,
    172, 228, 230
ethnic equality, 155, 157, 163
Ethnic Minority Achievement Grant
    (EMAG), 154
ethnic minority teacher, 26, 28–9, 76
ethnic polarisation, 156
ethnic protection, 226
ethnics, 55, 61
ethnolect, 76
European Union (EU), 1, 3, 9, 24, 64,
    84–6, 88, 98–100
extended family, 108–9, 114, 141,
    194, 206
extracurricular activity, 25–6, 30, 124,
    126, 178

faith (community) school, 10, 21–2, 25,
    155, 165
family, 6, 8, 12, 22, 40, 45, 49–50, 53, 60,
    70–7, 80–1, 83–7, 108–16, 125, 128,
    132, 141–3, 161, 168, 184–5,
    188–94, 197
family background (family
    characteristics), 29, 40, 45, 49, 74,
    125, 184–5, 187
family dynamics, 55
family, immigrant, 40, 49, 53, 109,
    116, 128, 168
family planning (planned type of),
    108, 110
family resources, 35, 37, 45–6, 48–9,
    141, 190, 195
family's social status (social standing),
    71, 74

family – *continued*
  family support, 48–9
  family value (expectation, hope), 108,
    111, 115
France (French), 1, 4–6, 8–10, 12, 17–18,
    21, 27–8, 51–8, 60, 62–3, 76–8,
    86–92, 94–7, 106, 108, 110–11,
    113–14, 116, 123–5, 127, 130–1,
    137, 139, 144–6, 167–71, 173–4,
    178, 181–3, 228, 231, 234, 240–1
free school choice, 22
  right of, 21–2, 200, 215
full-day schooling, 37, 49

Gabor Gipsy, 108
ghetto, 58, 80, 104–8, 111, 114, 118–19,
    127, 130, 132, 170, 177, 182–3, 203
  ghetto consciousness, 11, 104–7
  ghetto, ethnic (multiethnic, racial),
    104, 106, 132
  ghetto, quasi, 2, 9
  ghetto school, 4
  ghetto, urban ("banlieu"), 80, 111,
    113–14, 119, 145, 170, 174–5, 179
  ghetto, urban youth, 177
  ghetto youth, 146–7, 174, 177, 182–3
ghettoisation, 201, 203
grade (grading, test score, assessment,
    marking), 11, 58, 67–76, 82–3, 140,
    144–5, 166, 181
  see also performance
graduation, 26, 71, 73–4, 126, 144
grammar school (Gymnasium), 19, 25,
    124, 184, 186–7, 192, 226
  see also integrated schooling
Greece, 87, 91, 98
group membership, 87, 111, 138
Gypsy, 123, 128–30, 145, 155, 158, 164,
    203–6, 208, 210, 220–6
  anti-Gypsy, 123, 127–8, 130, 199, 201
Gypsyism, 151
Gypsyness, 199, 205–6, 208, 210
Gypsy underservingness, 210

habitus, 55, 136, 195
homework, 36–7, 45, 48, 140, 189
human rights, 80, 98, 152, 210,
    231–2, 234

Hungary (Hungarian), 1, 20–1, 25,
    28–31, 52, 56, 63, 65, 80–2, 89,
    106–8, 123–31, 140–5, 201, 205, 237

identity, 3, 4, 7, 9, 12, 21, 24, 28, 95,
    103–4, 109, 117, 125, 129, 137–43,
    158–62, 173–4, 181, 196, 202, 206
  identity-based nationalism, 98
  identity, "bourgeois", 174
  identity, class, 241
  identity, collective, 137, 141
  identity, cultural, 137, 146
  identity, emo, 160
  identity, ethnic, 4, 12, 56, 85, 103,
    105, 110, 112, 114, 117–18, 160,
    206, 238, 240–1
  identity, gendered, 165
  identity, group (group identification),
    111, 167, 194, 199
  identity, hybrid, 204
  identity model, 103, 207
  identity, outsider, 169
  identity, peer-group, 9, 207
  identity politics, 132
  identity, religious, 181
  identity, Roma, 205, 207–8,
    211, 221
  identity, shared working-class, 240
  identity, social, 159
  identity, "white", 160
identity construction (identity
    formation, identity building),
    103–5, 117, 137, 175, 178, 194, 207,
    210, 235–42
  identity formation, adolescent, 32,
    200, 228, 238, 240
  identity formation, minority, 103, 242
identity strategy, 103–6, 111, 117, 198,
    204, 206, 210
immigrant background, 53–4, 69, 91,
    93–5, 124, 127, 144, 147–8, 169,
    190, 232
individuation, 103
inequality, 84, 131, 147, 158, 227
  inequality, economic
    (socioeconomic), 91
  inequality, educational, 157–8, 227
  inequality, inter-ethnic (ethnic), 131,
    140, 163
  inequality, ethnic, 157, 163

inequality, social, 148
inequality, structural, 140
institutional dynamics, 51
institutional process, 162, 165
institutional structure (setting,
    arrangement, constellation), 35–6,
    41–5, 48–50, 71, 83, 92, 163
institutional value, 180
integrated comprehensive school
    (Gesamtschule), 186–7
integrated development programme, 210
integration approach agenda, 221
integrationiststance, 98
integration, ethnic, 206
integration in education (school,
    integrated educational system),
    56, 59, 64–5, 109, 158
integration into the labour
    market, 121
integrationist policy language, 99
integration pattern, 90
integration policy, 87, 90–1, 97–8
integration principle, 98
integration programme, 57
integration strategy, 98, 100
integrative effort, 115
non-integration/non-integrated,
    222–3
integrated schooling, 96
    see also grammar school
integration context theory, 34–7
integration (integrated), 3, 4, 6–11, 27,
    32, 37, 49, 54, 64–5, 80–1, 86–7,
    90–2, 95–8, 104, 113, 120, 128, 133,
    140–1, 153–5, 158, 170, 181, 185,
    196, 198–9, 201, 203–5, 207,
    217–18, 221–2, 224, 238
interaction (interactional), 35, 37, 45,
    50, 53, 69, 100, 117, 120–1, 129,
    156, 160, 173, 181, 185, 190–2, 196,
    199, 218, 226
intercultural competence, 53
intercultural education, 88
inter-ethnic hostility, 160, 163
inter-ethnic relation (inter-ethnic
    encounter), 2–6, 29, 73, 75, 79, 90,
    92, 107, 113, 116, 121, 124, 157,
    168, 172, 178, 201, 228, 235
intermediate school (Hauptschule), 187

intersection (intersecting; intersectional,
    intersectionality), 17, 18, 199
Iran (Iranian), 76, 116
Ireland (Irish), 87, 98, 151
Islam (Islamic), 79, 97, 110, 125–6, 128,
    193–4, 196
    see also Muslim
Islamist, 97, 154
islamophobia, 143, 151
Italy (Italian), 87, 89, 98, 231

Joppke, Christian, 85, 96–7, 234
Jordan, 188

Koopmans, Ruud, 85–7, 90–2, 234
Kymlicka, Will, 85, 87, 98–9, 231, 234

labour market, 11, 20, 25, 34–5, 39,
    72–5, 83–4, 87–8, 90–3, 121, 128,
    138–9, 144, 152, 201–3
language, 2, 6–7, 17, 22–3, 26, 40–2,
    53–4, 56, 62–3, 67, 80, 85–6, 90–1,
    97–9, 107, 113–18, 129, 133, 153,
    186–7, 195, 201, 205, 208, 214–16,
    220, 232–8
language barrier, 54, 63
language competence, 195
language disadvantage, 25
language, minority, 235–6
language, native, 56
language practice, 216, 227
language problem, 190–1
language right, 85, 235
language support, 26
Lebanon (Lebanese), 8, 79, 93, 110, 139,
    184, 186–8
legal protection, 87
linguistic disadvantage, 17
linguistic diversity, 195, 236

majority background (ethnic majority
    background; majority origin), 3, 4, 7,
    26, 54, 71–2, 145, 148, 170, 175, 241
marginalisation (social), 3, 6, 76–7, 94,
    112, 115, 121, 143–5, 147, 201, 209,
    237, 239
media, 57, 78, 85, 127, 152, 154, 170,
    213, 226
meritocratic principle, 30, 32

middle class, 2, 8, 20–3, 29, 56–7, 65–7, 70, 75–7, 94, 114–16, 133, 156, 159–60, 171–4, 185–6, 190, 227
middle class area, 178
middle class, lower, 22, 95, 104, 114, 140, 177
migrant (immigrant), 1–6, 8–9, 12, 18–20, 26–8, 32–9, 44, 49, 51–4, 56–9, 61–3, 65, 69, 76, 78, 84–91, 93–5, 97–9
migrant (immigrant), first generation, 2, 18, 35, 40, 54, 91, 109, 124, 179
migrant (immigrant), second generation, 2, 18–19, 34–50, 70, 89, 91–2, 94, 97, 109, 122, 133, 144, 173, 179, 187
migrant teacher (teacher of migration background), 28, 54, 192
migration, 40, 61, 63, 69, 78, 83–6, 88, 94, 96, 99, 103, 115–18, 151, 153, 184, 185, 188, 190, 195–6, 228, 232, 235
migration, economic ('labour'), 6, 87, 90, 137, 151
migration, post-colonial, 6, 137
Migration and Integration Policy Index (MIPEX), 86–8, 98–9
minority background (ethnic minority background; ethnic minority origin), 18–19, 29, 52, 70–4, 82, 85, 93, 123, 135, 235
minority ethnic, 92, 96, 104, 151, 153–8, 161–2
mixed school, 24, 26–8, 30, 58, 139, 142–3, 156–7
mobility, 20, 32, 89, 92, 115, 171, 178, 242
mobility, downward, 53, 57, 76, 79, 143
mobility, educational, 89, 91
mobility, ethnic, 117, 135
mobility, intergenerational, 118
mobility, social, 3, 12, 35, 64, 68, 73, 82, 92, 95, 112, 115, 120, 132, 135, 139, 143, 168, 172, 211, 233
mobility, upward, 76, 78–9, 94, 108–9, 115, 120, 124, 133, 143
Modood, Tariq, 61, 69, 86–7, 96–7, 155, 163
monolingual, 195

morals (moral), 8, 57, 60, 64, 67, 78, 80, 140, 213, 215, 219
Morocco (Moroccan), 10, 37, 110–11, 116, 169, 171, 179
multicultural citizenship, 90
multicultural curriculum, 26, 28–9
multiculturalism (multiculture), 7, 30–2, 55, 78, 84–6, 89, 94–9, 121, 129, 154–5, 157, 163, 235
multicultural pedagogy, 24
multicultural policy, 11, 12, 85, 88–90, 92, 97, 100, 154
multicultural regime (multicultural policy regime), 85–6, 88–90, 94, 96–7
multicultural strategy, 89
multicultural study, 90
multicultural teaching (intercultural teaching), 27, 58, 65, 127, 164–5, 195, 238
multicultural theory, 90
Muslim, 1, 8, 10, 21, 25, 59, 63, 78–9, 93–4, 96–7, 108, 110–11, 125–8, 140–1, 143–4, 147, 152–6, 167, 185–6, 192–4, 196, 234, 239, 242
see also Islam

national school system, 35, 52, 56
naturalisation of migrants, 98
neoliberalism (neo-liberal), 155, 209
neoliberal turn, 97
neo-Marxism (neo-Marxist), 120–1
Netherlands (the), 11, 18, 34–5, 37–49, 86–7, 89, 96–8
Network of Experts in Social Science of Education (NESSE), 20, 91
New Labour, 153–5
non-comprehensive school system, 19, 37
non-integration, 222
non-vocational higher education, 168
norm, 11, 59–60, 63, 65, 67, 79, 97, 109, 115–16, 125, 141, 146, 160, 177, 180, 182, 199, 204, 207, 209, 213, 215–16, 221, 227, 229, 243
norm, cultural, 59, 60, 63, 65, 146, 160, 182, 213, 227
norm (rule, pattern), behavioural, 104, 229

Norway (Norwegian), 17, 87, 98
nuclear family, 109, 115, 204

occupational mobility, 71
othering, 30, 72, 121, 122, 124–9, 132–3, 147, 185, 193–6, 198, 199, 204, 225
otherness (the other), 5, 11, 25–6, 69, 71–2, 84, 101, 112, 116, 131–2, 140, 144, 146, 181–2, 194, 198, 223, 243

Pakistan (Pakistani), 21, 55, 61, 63, 77–8, 94, 127, 139, 143, 152, 157–64
Pakistani student, 61, 143
Palestine (Palestinian), 110, 116
Parekh, Bhikhu, 85, 87, 96, 234
parental control and protection, 193
parental cultural capital, 70
parental educational background, 40, 41, 46–7
parental generation, 41
parental input, 215
parental intervention, 188
parental status (social class, socioeconomic status, occupational status), 35, 214
parental support (involvement), 11, 45–8, 227
parents' evening, 192–3
Paris (Parisian), 58, 110, 169–72, 174–5, 178
partnership model of educational management, 220
peer relations, 24, 31–2, 83, 124, 179
Pentecostal Roma, 204
performance, 2, 3, 5–6, 9, 11, 23–4, 27, 31, 51, 57, 62, 64–5, 67–9, 71, 87–8, 91–3, 96, 106, 112, 120, 158, 167, 170, 178, 180–8, 190–1, 195, 208, 213–14, 221, 227–35
see also grade (grading, test score, assessment, marking)
performance gap, 2, 17, 91
permeability, 36, 44–5, 48–9
PISA study (OECD PISA survey), 2, 4, 6, 18, 23, 91, 184, 213
Portugal (Portuguese), 98, 173
positive discrimination, 28, 139
post-colonial, 1, 6, 12, 76, 90, 95, 106, 122, 133, 137, 139, 148, 167, 235, 240

post-communist (post-socialist), 19, 64, 66, 86–7, 90, 93, 106, 114, 128, 198, 202, 208–9, 231
post-Marxism (post-Marxist), 121
poverty, 2, 7, 11, 29, 65, 70–4, 77, 80–2, 95, 106, 111–12, 114–15, 152–3, 156–7, 163, 170–2, 199, 202, 228, 231, 239–40
see also destitution; disadvantage, socioeconomic
power relation, 179, 199–200
pre-primary education, 43
primary school (elementary school), 19, 23, 36, 38, 41–3, 49, 51, 68, 70, 74–5, 82, 126, 128, 130, 141, 184, 187–9, 194, 195, 214, 216–17, 220, 225
principle of non-differentiation, 27–8
private school, 21, 22
public fund, 99
public school, 21, 28, 129, 167
public (social) housing, 152, 170–1, 177, 209

race (racial), 3, 5, 6, 9, 28, 51, 53, 56, 58, 61–2, 66, 85, 88, 104, 122, 130, 131, 138, 140, 143, 146–7, 151–9, 163–7, 170, 180–2, 200, 212, 215–16, 228
race (racial) equality, 75, 93, 146, 152–7, 163
racial conflict, 228
racial prejudice, 66
racism (racist), 4, 29, 51–2, 57–8, 61, 64–6, 77, 99, 118, 121, 126–8, 130–2, 135, 145–6, 151, 153–4, 156–7, 159, 163–4, 173–5, 181, 199, 210, 215, 220, 225
racism, institutional, 152
racism, majoritarian, 127
racism, new, 215–16
recognition, 7, 27, 55, 67, 75, 79, 85–6, 96, 98, 127, 140, 151–2, 155, 167, 181, 234–7
recognition struggle, 76, 82, 93, 118, 230
religious symbol, 97
religious tie, 115
remedial school, 20
republican civic integration model, 97
republican principle of equality, 145

respect, 31, 55, 59, 60, 79–80, 83, 86–7,
    105, 108, 112, 117–18, 152, 195–6
Roma culture, 65, 129, 216, 220–2
Roma teacher assistant, 28
Romania (Romanian), 1, 12, 20, 33, 52,
    56, 64–5, 80, 89, 107–9, 123, 125–6,
    128, 139, 142, 198, 201–2,
    204–9, 211

schooling, 2, 3, 5–6, 10–12, 34, 37, 41,
    43–4, 48–9, 51–2, 60, 64, 69, 70, 73,
    75–6, 79–80, 83–4, 89–96, 99, 109,
    120–1, 133, 135, 139–42, 147, 151,
    155, 157, 163, 171, 179, 181–2, 184,
    187, 195, 198, 203–6, 210, 214,
    216–17, 219, 220, 222–3, 225,
    227–8, 230, 233, 235–6
schooling, half-day, 37, 48
school qualification, 34
school system, 2, 6, 17–20, 23–5, 35–6,
    42, 52, 56, 68–9, 75, 83, 109, 133,
    137–8, 145–6
    British school system, 9, 61, 123
    Dutch school system, 45, 49
    French school system, 28, 167–8, 170,
        178, 181–2
    German school system, 60, 141,
        186–7, 194, 196
    Hungarian school system, 21, 31,
        65, 124
    Romanian school system, 200, 207
    Scandinavian school system, 7, 60
    Slovak school system, 213–14
    Turkish school system, 59
school type, 18–21, 24, 32, 192
secondary education, 19, 22, 38–42,
    44–50, 67, 89, 92–3, 154–5, 168, 172
secondary high school (Realschule), 141,
    187–8, 190, 194, 197
secondary school (schooling), 6, 8, 9, 19,
    25, 26, 36–7, 41–2, 52–3, 68, 71,
    73–5, 77, 92, 94, 157, 168, 171–2,
    178, 187–8, 206
    school, comprehensive, 18–20, 29, 60,
        65, 89, 186–7
    school (training), technical, 171–2
segregation (segregated), 1, 3, 6–11, 18,
    20–6, 30–2, 52, 64, 90–1, 94–5, 106,
    118, 125, 128, 138, 142–7, 155–6,

158, 174, 195, 208, 213, 216, 221,
    232–4
segregation, between classes, 31
segregation, educational, 12, 17, 21,
    107, 142
segregation, ethnic (ethnosocial,
    socioethnic), 2, 3, 5–6, 8–10, 12,
    17–25, 31–2, 95, 117, 141, 145,
    147, 156–8, 163, 167, 235
segregation, between schools
    (segregation within school,
    internal segregation/separation),
    4, 6
segregation, institutional, 32, 64
segregation, residential, 7, 21, 76, 78,
    94–5, 135, 144, 170, 182, 205,
    208, 210
segregation, spatial, 198, 200,
    208–9, 211
selection (preselection), 19, 20, 36–7,
    41–4, 211
selection, age, 19, 37, 42–3
selection, by ethnic background (by
    immigrant, background, minority
    background, ethnosocial
    background), 23–5, 157, 208
selection, by gender, 19, 21, 41
selection, by performance, 24, 68–9,
    195, 208
selection, by residence, 21–2, 208
selection, by (social) class, 25, 184, 208
selection, early, 3–7, 18, 43, 48
selection, first, 19, 41–4, 49
selection, late (delayed), 36–7, 44,
    49, 50
selection, negative, 181
selection, student, 1, 8, 22–3, 89
selection, teacher, 56, 65
selection, school (institutional), 11–12,
    18–19, 21–2, 68
selection, faith school, 10, 21–2, 25
selection, negative, 181
selection, private school, 21–2
selection, remedial (special) school,
    10, 20, 24–5, 202, 214, 218, 231
self-enclosure (self-enclosed), 108, 118
self-esteem, 31–2, 55, 73, 93–5, 107–8,
    113, 142–3, 223, 225
self-identification (self-identity), 5, 9, 28,
    83, 104, 139, 199, 227

self-perception, 73, 78, 204, 206, 208
self-segregation, 126, 154
self-selection (teacher, student, pupil), 21, 56, 65, 225
skin colour, 113, 128, 131
Slovakia (Slovakian), 1, 12, 33, 52, 63, 89, 122–6, 128, 131, 140, 142–3, 213–16, 218–19
see also Czech Republic
slum, 29, 104–5, 111, 113–15, 117–19, 125, 209
sociability, 95
social class, 35, 61, 69, 72, 74, 77–9, 82, 146, 169, 173–4, 199, 215, 228, 240–1
social cohesion, 154, 229, 242
social disadvantage, 78
social diversity, 29, 84–9, 95–7
social division, 144, 160
social equality, 85
social exclusion, 2, 76, 78, 95, 99, 112, 142, 154, 171, 209, 231
social integration, 85–6, 99, 111, 140, 206
social interaction, 182
socialisation, 25, 60, 65, 73, 103, 125, 219, 229
socially disadvantaged environment (SDE), 147, 216, 222
social respect, 105, 108, 117
social right, 82, 230, 235–8
social status, 1, 2, 4, 18, 22, 68–72, 79, 84, 103–8, 111, 115–18, 147, 170, 174, 200, 208, 232–3, 239
socioeconomic status, 17, 35, 143, 177, 184, 202, 214
sociology (sociological approach), 2, 120, 214
Somalia (Somali), 61, 63, 112
Spain (Spanish), 87, 91, 98
special class, 7, 31, 214–18
special educational needs, (SEN), 20, 216
stereotype (stereotypical, stereotyping), 9, 51, 57, 61, 76, 106, 113, 144, 158–66, 177, 183, 207, 221, 226
stigmatisation (stigmatised, stigmatising), 1, 7, 9, 20, 25–6, 31–2, 51, 64, 106, 111–12, 118, 127, 140, 142–3, 146, 160, 164, 172–5, 198, 200, 204, 207, 209–10

stratified school (educational) system, 18–19, 89
stream, 6, 9, 42, 168
stream, vocational, 9, 182
streaming, 20, 23, 71, 88, 158, 162, 165, 168, 218, 235
streaming, downward, 36, 49
streaming, upward, 36, 44
structural approach, 35, 214
student with learning difficulties, 24–5, 216–18, 231
subculture, 128, 168, 240
subculture, ethnic, 129
subculture, urban, 8
subculture, (urban) youth, 4, 12, 120
super-diversity, 61
suburb, 58, 145, 169, 171–2, 174, 176, 183, 213
Sweden (Swedish, Swedes), 1, 7, 11, 17, 22, 26, 30, 34–5, 37–50, 52–4, 56, 62–3, 65, 75–6, 86–95, 97–8, 110–16, 122–4, 128, 133, 138, 143–4, 154, 231, 234, 236
Switzerland (Swiss), 17–18, 86–7, 90–1

teacher-pupil relation, 51, 159
teacher self-selection, 65
teaching style, 65
technical assistance, 189
tertiary education, 36, 39–40, 42, 45–9
theory of practice, 135–6
TIES survey, 38, 40–1, 43–4
tolerance (tolerant), 21, 25, 27, 30, 32–3, 58, 78, 96, 108, 165
track, 8, 19, 29, 36, 41–5, 48–50, 73–4, 77, 79, 89
track, academic (educational, academically oriented, non-vocational), 11, 19, 38, 41–4, 49–50, 89
track, vocational, 2, 19, 36, 38, 41, 44–5, 49
tracking (specialisation), 2, 18–20, 36, 43, 48, 69, 71, 88–9, 93, 141, 180–1, 184–6, 189, 195, 235
truancy, 28, 31, 76, 132
tuition fee, 21

Turkey (Turkish), 8, 10–11, 21,
      34, 37, 40, 44–6, 49, 54, 59,
      60, 63, 65, 78–80, 109–10, 123–8,
      139, 140–1, 146, 171, 184–8,
      190–2, 234
Turkish (Turks), second-generation, 19,
      34–50, 92–3

underperformance, 152
unemployment rate, 170, 227
United Kingdom (UK), 5–6, 18, 21, 30,
      51–2, 63, 69, 76–7, 86–7, 106,
      122–4, 127–8, 133, 137, 139, 143,
      151–3, 155–7, 161, 164, 166, 212,
      228, 240–1
United States (US/USA, American), 3, 22,
      83, 116, 137, 221
university degree, 34, 70,
      140, 188
university entrance certificate, 41
urban neighbourhood, 61, 106, 111,
      172, 174

urban rioting, 171
urban school, 53, 169, 182, 211

vocational education (training), 2, 8–9,
      19, 36, 38, 41, 44–5, 49, 53–4, 57,
      60, 74, 79, 106, 145, 168, 171–3,
      175, 177, 179–80, 182, 232
vocational (training) certificate, 81,
      169, 222

Weber, Max, 213
welfare, 76, 78, 88, 135, 153, 157, 230
   welfare assistance, 233
   welfare provision, 85, 88, 94, 98
   welfare, social benefit, 190
   welfare state (regime), 7, 13, 75–6, 82,
      88, 90–1
white flight, 4, 9, 22, 23, 26–7, 30, 57,
      156, 215, 218

Yemeni, 61
Yugoslavia, former (Macedonia), 37

Printed and bound by CPI Group (UK) Ltd, Croydon, CR0 4YY